Crazy Love

ALSO BY LESLIE MORGAN STEINER

Mommy Wars: Stay-at-Home and Career Moms
Face Off on Their Choices, Their Lives, Their Families

Crazy Love

A MEMOIR

Leslie Morgan Steiner

St. Martin's Press   New York

www.stmartins.com

Library of Congress Cataloging-in-Publication Data

Steiner, Leslie Morgan.
    Crazy love : a memoir / by Leslie Morgan Steiner.
        p. cm.
    ISBN-13: 978-0-312-37745-8 (alk. paper)
    ISBN-10: 0-312-37745-2 (alk. paper)
    1. Steiner, Leslie Morgan.   2. Abused wives—United
States—Biography.   3. Abused women—United States—
Case studies.   4. Family violence—United States.
I. Title.
    HV6626.2.S737 2008
    362.82'92092—dc22
    [B]
                                                        2008034018

First Edition: April 2009

10   9   8   7   6   5   4   3   2   1

Crazy Love is a personal history. The events described in this book are real, backed up by police reports, restraining order documentation, family court, and other legal records. Many names, except for my own, as well as several geographic, chronologic, and identifying details, have been changed for the usual reasons of privacy and security. A few characters have been omitted and combined; the character of Winnie represents an amalgam of important friends.

To my husband, for understanding why I needed
to write this book

For Elin, who knew

In memory of Marilyn

For my mother, who was always there

IF YOU AND I MET AT ONE OF OUR CHILDREN'S birthday parties, in the hallway at work, or at a neighbor's barbecue, you'd never guess my secret: that as a young woman I fell in love with and married a man who beat me regularly and nearly killed me.

I don't look the part. I have an M.B.A. and an undergraduate degree from Ivy League schools. I live in a redbrick house on a tree-lined street in one of the prettiest neighborhoods in Washington, D.C. I've got fifteen years of marketing experience at Fortune 500 companies and a bestselling book about motherhood to my name. A smart, loyal husband with a sexy gap in his front teeth, a softie who puts out food for the stray kittens in our alley. Three rambunctious, well-loved children. A dog and three cats of our own. Everyone in my family is blond (the people, at least).

Ah, if only being well-educated and blond and coming from a good family were enough to defang all of life's demons.

If I were brave enough the first time I met you, I'd try to share what torture it is to fall in love with a good man who cannot leave a violent past behind. I'd tell you why I stayed for years, and how I finally confronted someone whose love I valued almost more than my own life. Then maybe the next time you came across a woman in an abusive relationship, instead of asking why anyone stays with a man who beats her, you'd have the empathy and courage to help her on her way.

We all have secrets we don't reveal the first time we cross paths with others. This is mine.

Book
One

———◆———

I MET CONOR ON THE NEW YORK CITY SUBWAY, heading downtown, twenty years ago. I was twenty-two. I remember it like yesterday.

———◆———

The window in Kathy's office was the only daylight I could see from my presswood desk in the hallway. I snuck a look. My ugly orange swivel chair squeaked.

It was a chilly, gray Monday afternoon in mid-January. The Midtown Manhattan skyscrapers were slick and dark with rain.

First thing that morning, Kathy—head of the articles department at *Seventeen* and the first boss I'd had in my life— held a meeting to dole out assignments for May. Then I interviewed a fidgety twelve-year-old Russian model who looked twenty-nine with makeup on. After that I ran out in the rain for lunch with the wacky British astrologer who wrote *Seventeen*'s monthly horoscope column.

I'd graduated from college the spring before on a day when Harvard Yard looked like the opening scene from a big-budget movie. Sun-dappled spring grass. My mom happy-drunk in a striped Vittadini wrap dress. My dad so proud I thought his face would split open, beaming as only a poor Oklahoma boy with a daughter graduating from Harvard could.

The day so lovely I wanted to hold it forever in my hands.

Working at *Seventeen* was better than eating a Baskin-Robbins sundae. We read magazines all morning and talked about sticky teenaged paradigms on the clock. In the afternoons we raided the fashion closet—a huge room where the fashion editor kept designer samples that transformed gawky teenage ostriches into goddesses. I hated the few times I'd gotten sick and had to miss a day.

Outside *Seventeen* I roamed New York City as if it were my new backyard. Dinners at the Yaffa Café and Bombay Kitchen. Hours dancing with my roommate at Danceteria or Limelight. Even the most mundane activities—folding clothes at the fluorescent-lit Laundromat across Eighth Avenue, jogging through the Meatpacking District—became adventures.

But it was tricky getting the whole work thing down. Putting on panty hose like a uniform. No runs, my frantic morning mantra. Getting on the E train instead of the express to Harlem. Figuring out how to eat when my paycheck ran out six days before the next one was due.

Everything seemed so new.

I wrote and rewrote that afternoon at my desk in the hallway as the rain poured down outside Kathy's window. Every girl in America read *Seventeen* at some age. Nearly four million girls devoured each issue; some favorites became like bibles for girls who had only a magazine to turn to for advice.

I should know.

Every day, often with little support or guidance, a teenage girl tackled staggering dilemmas. If your boyfriend offered drugs, did you do them? Did buying birth control make you a slut? Where did you get birth control at sixteen, anyway? What if your best friend drove drunk with you riding shotgun? Your stepfather came on to you? Your parents got divorced? Your mom got cancer?

My piece was slated for March, meaning I had to finish it by . . . Friday.

"Almost done?" Kathy barked as she whizzed by in her black patent-leather boots with three-inch heels. I jumped off my chair.

The story itself asked a simple enough question: Why do teenagers run away from home? But after poring over government statistics and interviewing social workers, psychiatrists, and the four runaways who would actually talk to me, I'd come to an awful understanding.

Of the estimated 1.5 million teenagers who hit the streets each year, the majority bolted because they thought any situation would be better than home.

Of those teenagers, 25 percent came from families with alcohol or drug abuse.

And 50 percent had been sexually or physically abused by someone in their household.

What kind of home was that?

The realization that broke my heart: All runaways start out fighting for a better life. The survival instinct that gave them the courage to leave bad homes made them try to turn the streets into a new home, the other runaways their families.

Within months, two-thirds were using drugs and supporting themselves through prostitution. Close to a third didn't know where they'd sleep each night. One-half tried to commit suicide. Two-thirds ended up in jail or dead from illness, drug overdoses, or beatings by pimps, johns, or other homeless people.

When I finally looked up from the computer, I was the only one left at the office, feeling like I'd been ditched by the cool girls after school in eighth grade. My watch read six P.M. It seemed like midnight as I trudged to the subway in the rain.

—◈—

Winnie took forever to unlock the three deadbolts from behind her apartment door.

We hugged; she was only five feet two inches, so the top of her head butted against my chin. As always, her hair smelled like honeysuckle.

I dropped my purse in the foyer and started unlacing my L.L. Bean duck boots, indispensable during the snowy Cambridge winters and slushy springs. Ridiculous footwear now that I lived in the fashion capital of the planet.

"How was work?" she asked. Winnie (short for Winthrop—I'm not kidding) was wearing a white cotton shirt with a high ruffled collar, threaded with a pale cream sliver of silk, tucked into a long brown suede skirt.

"Great . . . I'm writing about teen runaways."

I shook the wet boots off my stocking feet. I had a harder time shaking off the images of the fourteen-year-old girl I'd interviewed for my story. The one who slept on a subway grate and blew her hair dry in a corner of the Trailways bus terminal next to the pay phone she refused to pick up to call home.

"So how was your work, Win?"

She was a salesgirl at the Polo Mansion at Seventy-second and Madison selling outrageously priced Ralph Lauren clothes to celebrities. She had to wear all Ralph Lauren clothes. Blond Wasp perfection every day.

"Oh, God, it's a long day when you're on your feet trying to smile at all those rich assholes."

Something on the stove started hissing like an angry cat.

"Fuck!" she yelled. Even in fourth grade, she swore like a thirty-five-year-old divorcée. I followed her into the tiny kitchen.

She took the pot off the burner and turned back, smiling. Even Winnie's teeth were cute. That was one of the first things I noticed the day she showed up at elementary school. Over the years she taught me the following life essentials: how to shave my legs with Vitabath Spring Green, sleep until noon, and look up sex words in the dictionary. I loved wearing her preppy clothes, smelling like Winnie's laundry detergent even if just for a day.

The year I turned thirteen I grew four inches, began smoking pot, drinking tequila, and dating older guys. I totally outgrew Winnie's entire closet. Her Lacoste shirts wouldn't cover my belly button anymore.

When I drank, she was one of my favorite people to call late at night. "I love you, Winnie," I would slur into the phone. She was always pretty nice about those calls.

"Look!" She held out her left hand, fingers splayed, so I could get a full view of her sparkly new engagement ring.

"Congratulations, Win. I am so happy for you."

I was even happier for Rex, her fiancé. He'd get to smell her hair on their pillow every night for the rest of his life.

"I always knew he was right, even at that Trinity frat party when I first met him," Winnie said as she spooned fresh pesto into a blue enamel pasta bowl. She didn't say what I knew mattered most: Rex loved her, but not with that "My life is nothing without you" desperation that drove her crazy. A parade of high-school boyfriends had gotten Velcroed to her in exactly the same way I had as a kid. They always ended up needing her too much. I'd watched her peel them off one by one, like bubble gum stuck to her shoe.

I looked around their small apartment, filled with Winnie's Ralph Lauren fabrics and Rex's dark leather furniture. Winnie was supposed to live with me, our reunion following four years at different colleges, my chance to prove I'd become sober and responsible and likable again, right? Then at the beginning of last summer, while she waited for me to move to New York, she stayed in this apartment with Rex. Just for a few weeks, she'd said.

Audrey, the roommate I eventually found in Chelsea, was great. But here's what I wanted to ask Winnie tonight: Couldn't she postpone marriage for a few years, so that we could be roommates, to give me a chance to catch up? If I wasn't right for her as a roommate, how on earth was I going to meet a man right for me? A man like Rex who might ask me to stay for a few weeks and then ask me to stay forever.

Instead I said, "Wow, the ring is beautiful." It was.

We sat down to eat and she gave me the blow-by-blow on how Rex proposed on the beach during their New Year's trip to St. Barts.

As we stood side by side in her miniscule kitchen afterward, washing the dishes in hot, soapy water that smelled like lemons, Winnie asked how my love life was.

"Kind of anticlimactic compared to yours," I said. "All that matters to men here is how much money they make and where they live."

"Trust me, every guy who walks into the Polo Mansion tells me within thirty seconds about his address and income bracket. Please." She shook her head and laughed, crinkling the snub nose that was the envy of every girl in high school, including me. I reached into the soapy water and grabbed a bunch of silverware.

"I meet them all over the place, Win. At parties and clubs, of course. Just last week I met a guy on the bus. Someone asked me out while I was standing in line for the bathroom at Isabella's. Another guy tried to pick me up while I was jogging around the Reservoir. They're *everywhere*."

She handed me a pot to dry.

"For the first time in my life, I have this rule—one of the things I learned when I stopped drinking—" My voice cracked. I bet my face looked like a tomato. I kept talking. "—is that I will never date a man to satisfy some need of mine or someone who wants me to fill a desperate need of his."

The words sounded like cheap cardboard. But Winnie nodded, her brown eyes big and reassuring.

"I don't have sex with them, Win. We don't even kiss. We talk. For hours. In restaurants I could never afford on my salary."

She laughed.

"You know, it sounds so innocent, Les. And really fun. It's just what you need right now, right?"

She flicked soap at my face and a few suds landed on my nose.

Yep, just what I needed. But not what I wanted.

After another congratulatory hug, I headed out into the cold rainy night, exchanging Winnie's warm, bright apartment for the manicured Upper East Side streets. The heavy doors of the million-dollar brownstones, locked and festooned with polished brass knockers, seemed to declare that everyone in New York was safe at home.

Except for me.

———◆———

Sleet slapped my cheeks during the long walk to the Fifty-third Street subway. Before I ran through the turnstile to catch the train, I glimpsed myself in the token-booth window. With my wet hair hanging in dirty-blond corkscrews and wearing my old blue down coat, I looked more like a kid than a magazine editor.

The subway doors opened and I squeezed into a slippery neon-yellow subway seat. I was sandwiched between a handsome, neatly dressed older man with thick blond hair and a heavyset Latina woman with grocery bags who smelled like day-old enchiladas and cigarette smoke. At Forty-second Street, she got off along with most of the car, heaving with the effort of carrying the paper bags.

The subway felt suddenly empty—except for the blond man whose arm was now touching my elbow. I didn't slide away from him into a free seat, as every other person who'd lived in New York for five seconds would. I thought it'd be too rude.

It meant something to Conor that I did not move away from him, he told me much later.

He was wearing a dark blue cashmere coat, the navy at

his throat cutting a sharp contrast to his wheat-colored hair and shiny, fresh-scrubbed farm boy face. He wasn't as old as I thought—maybe late twenties, early thirties. He smiled.

"Hi. What's your name?" He had clean, straight teeth. I'd been in New York long enough to know that if you encouraged men on the subway, things got ugly fast. But this man felt instinctively safe, strangely familiar. How bad could he be? I told him my first name and buried my face back in *Vanity Fair*.

"Leslie, hi. My name is Conor," he said politely.

I glanced up briefly, intrigued by his persistence. I looked like a sewer rat. What could he possibly see in me?

He smiled again. "Do you work in the city?"

For a second he looked like my dad asking how I liked Harvard.

I couldn't help responding with pride.

"I work at *Seventeen*—you know, the magazine?"

"Oh, interesting . . . I work at Block Moore—you know, the investment bank?"

The only reason I'd even heard of this bank was because my freshman roommate, Lee, had several ex-boyfriends who worked there. Harvard grads who'd been captain of the football team, the hockey team, the most confident, effusive men on campus. Not boys I ever would have dated for a million reasons—mostly because in college I could barely speak to guys, much less go on dates with them. They always called after Lee dumped them, to cry on the nicey-nice roommate's shoulder and get some vicarious thrill from talking to the next best thing when Lee had gotten so sick of their pathetic late-night missives that she stopped returning their calls.

The train slowed as we entered Penn Station. I knew this man—Conor—had volunteered the name of his Wall Street firm to vouch for his credibility, proof that he wasn't a psycho subway killer. He stood and shrugged his body to straighten his expensive coat. Then he turned to me one more time, his left hand holding the silver subway pole for balance.

No wedding ring.

"I live in Jersey now, but I'm moving to a great place on East Eighty-second. My roommate and I are gonna have a party. Maybe I'll call and invite you."

"Sure," I said. The freckles across his nose made him look like a little boy, expectant, trying to seem cool and kind of arrogant. I didn't respond. I wasn't volunteering my phone number to someone I'd sat next to for six minutes on the New York subway. The doors closed behind him. I watched the back of his blond head through the cracked subway window as he walked away.

As the train pulled out, I saw a sign carved into the brick wall of the subway station, directing commuters left to Penn Station, right to Herald Square. I bet my grandfather Sammie—my mother's father—passed this same sign a hundred times on the way to his office on Thirty-fourth Street sixty years ago. After graduating from Harvard in 1929, he became a vice-president at Macy's, a marketing boy wonder who lived in Strawberry Hill, a seventy-two-room fieldstone castle overlooking the Hudson River. He ordered custom-built automobiles from England during the Depression when most men couldn't afford to feed their families. I could imagine him walking through the brick subway tunnel, wearing the black coat and hat that Winnie and I used to play with on rainy days in my grandmother's attic.

When I looked up again, the train had screeched to a stop at my station. At the exit to Twenty-third Street, I stepped over a homeless man lying on a stained cardboard box. Even passed out, he clutched an empty bottle of Jack Daniel's with his unwashed hand, fingernails black with grime. Was he somebody's grandfather, too?

The rain had let up and the temperature must have risen ten degrees since I'd left Winnie's. Eighth Avenue was slick with iridescent pools of water and the night air had a humid feel as if the fog were wisps of cotton you could reach out and touch. I walked from the subway to my apartment on West Nineteenth Street, past couples spilling out of the corner diner, taxis splashing through puddles, the shuttered Off-Track Betting window, the funky, neon-lit Man Ray sushi place.

Whenever I asked about Sammie, Mom would smile and look away. She always repeated the same words: "I loved my father so much." Despite the fact that one December when she was eight, Sammie, searching for cash for a bender, stole the money she'd stashed under the ballroom rug to buy

Christmas gifts for her older brother and younger sister. Over the years he drank up all their money, and left my grandmother Frankie to support the family teaching at a local community college. Ten years later, after Frankie finally divorced him, he would walk the eleven miles from Manhattan to Strawberry Hill to visit Mom. His money went to alcohol, not train fare.

I'm not certain whether alcoholism killed my grandfather before or after I was born. I do know that he still worked at the Macy's Herald Square headquarters when he died. He lived there, too, in the basement. He was the janitor.

So I came by my predilection for addiction honestly, I suppose. I stole a pack of Marlboros from our fireplace mantel when I was twelve, held my nose while finishing off martinis at my parents' cocktail parties, and mastered inhaling when offered my first joint the summer after eighth grade. No one taught me these things. I just *knew.*

In high school, I wore myself down to a pencil nub by being an achievement-obsessed druggie, not the easiest combination to pull off. At school I pored over *Brave New World,* Maslow's hierarchy of needs, and derivative curves. I'd duck into a utility closet during study hall to make out with my boyfriend, whose main attribute was his ability to get me drugs on a regular basis. I craved numbing out the way some teenage girls love clothes shopping or lip-synching in front of their bathroom mirror.

On weekends, my father hid at his law office downtown and my mother tossed back rum and Cokes at our home in

Bethesda on a half-acre of hundred-year-old trees. My friends and I hit the bars in Georgetown—Scandal's, Mac's, the Saloon—where the drinking age was eighteen but girls as young as fifteen had no trouble slipping in. For the nights I stayed home, I kept a stash of treasures in my bathroom closet, behind a bottle of Herbal Essences shampoo and Tickle deodorant. A fifth of Spanish tequila, a Baggie of California sensimilla, and a carved wooden pipe sat nestled against a diaphragm from Planned Parenthood (I was a very responsible teenaged drug addict). When Mom and I were home alone, she'd eventually start calling me the Washington Whore, her idea of a good way to bring up a complicated subject. Although after a while I caught on that she was venting her own frustrations and childhood fears on me, at the time her rage cut like a razor.

Let's say it was clear something was wrong.

I tried to talk to my friends and teachers about Mom's drinking before I had any idea what addiction was, before I realized it was my problem, too. My first confidant was Robert Carrola, my friend Paul's handsome, disheveled father, who also happened to be my high-school chemistry teacher. I would find Mr. Carrola in the teachers' lounge in between classes. He always listened assiduously to each sobbing chapter of my troubled relationship with my mother. He came from a large, poor, close-knit Italian family. He blamed our problems on having had too much money for too long. If only it were that simple.

Mr. Carrola's willingness to listen was one of the acts of

kindness that saved me during my adolescence—the same way I tried to save the teenage girls who read *Seventeen*.

"Mr. Carrola," I sobbed one day, snot dripping out of my nose like a shoestring. "I am not going to hope anymore that she is going to stop drinking."

I was sixteen, hurt and angry and confused about Mom, finding solace in hash under glass and Marlboros encrusted with grains of white cocaine. I was proud of my attempts to become wise and jaded. My idea was to give up on Mom.

"Nah, Leslie," he said, shaking his head. He smiled; he looked like he'd been born with that smile on his face. He gave me a Kleenex and spread my hands wide open with his warm, callused ones as if trying to open up my heart as well.

"Hope is always good." He looked me in the face grinning, full of faith in me and in life. "You know, doctors always say the liver is the only organ that can regenerate itself. But they're wrong, Leslie. The heart can, too. Promise me you'll keep hoping."

Lucky I got into Harvard before I gave up St. Pauli Girls, drugs, and being an accomplished junkie. My freshman year, a woman named Hope—corny but true—took me to my first twelve-step meeting. I stopped drinking and using drugs cold turkey, right when most Harvard freshmen were discovering the joys of substance abuse. I ate three meals a day at the Freshman Union, went to class, took a lot of naps, and in between tried—awkwardly, desperately, with help from Hope and other people I met at meetings—to focus on how I felt on the inside, not what my life looked like from the outside.

This had the bizarre effect of making me feel like I was walking around campus stark naked. Back at home in Bethesda, things weren't much better: Spending more than forty-eight hours with my parents, their tinkling glasses of rum and Coke, and the ghosts of my childhood made me flee back to Cambridge with the hair standing up on the back of my neck. I ended up spending most vacations and holidays in my empty dorm.

After four years of this drama, I got a call from *Seventeen* offering to publish a piece I'd sent in a few months before about overcoming anorexia in high school (I know, I had so many problems it's hard to keep track of them all). Soon after, *Seventeen*'s articles department hired me to start work as an editor and writer following graduation.

Hope saw me off at South Station when I moved to New York. She'd spent months insisting that I could do this, I deserved this dream-come-true job, I needed to follow where life took me. As she said good-bye, Hope put her hands on my arms. Her fingers were warm through my cotton T-shirt. She squared my shoulders and looked into my eyes as if she were adjusting a picture frame with a carpenter's level.

"You know, Leslie, you've had a tough, but good, four years here," she told me in her cigarette-rough voice. "You worked hard to get sober—at eighteen, for chrissakes. You graduated from *Harvard*. The worst is behind you. You are going to be fine."

I hugged Hope good-bye.

Five hours later, I lugged a frayed black suitcase of my

dad's past the graffiti of Penn Station. Yellow cabs were honking and swerving crazily on Eighth Avenue in the summer twilight. More people than I'd ever seen at once, even at Fourth of July fireworks on the Mall in D.C., swarmed the streets around me. Everyone looked like they were in a big hurry to get wherever they were going. Except for me.

Six months later, it was like I'd been born again. None of the scars from my seedy teenaged druggie life showed on my face. I looked like an apple-cheeked girl straight out of college with a great job, a cool apartment in Chelsea, my first American Express card. Shockingly cute New York firemen at the station near *Seventeen* whistled at me as I walked home in a miniskirt and high heels borrowed from the fashion closet. Homeless people smiled at me. I went out almost every night on the cheap since I didn't need to buy drinks.

The kind of second chance almost no one gets.

I unlocked our basement apartment door, yanked off my boots, and hung up my drenched coat on the makeshift bookshelf in the hallway. My little Siamese slunk out of the bedroom and sniffed my wet laces suspiciously, as if conducting an inspection for microscopic and totally verboten specks of dog poo. My roommate from Savannah, Georgia— the one I found to replace Winnie—got up from our lime-green beanbag chair and handed me a stack of While You Were Out messages on one of the pink pads she'd snitched from the temp job she went to between auditions. She smiled the wholesome grin that was bringing in two-thousand-dollar residual checks from a Burger King commercial. Audrey had become very skilled at answering the phone in a variety of character accents when the men I was dating called— Grace Kelly from *Rear Window*, Katharine Hepburn from *The Philadelphia Story*, Hattie McDaniel as Mammy in *Gone With the Wind*.

Oh, Hope was right. It was a fucking relief to start my life over, without drugs or alcohol just waiting to screw everything up. I was fine.

One afternoon a month or so later the chipped beige phone on my desk at *Seventeen* rang, the double ring that signaled an inside call. A woman named Lesley from the advertising department explained she had a guy on hold who must've been looking for me.

"He says he met you on the *subway*," Lesley chirped as if I were the only woman in New York who met men at places besides the library at the Princeton Club.

"The switchboard transferred him to me by mistake. I've talked to him for fifteen minutes. Fun guy. But I think he's got the wrong girl."

At least *I* meet men, I said to myself. I hung up and drummed my fingers while Snitty Face transferred the call.

"Leslie? Hi, this is . . . Conor. We met on the E train a few weeks back. . . . I've had a hell of a time tracking you down."

He paused to chuckle. His gravelly voice instantly brought back his attempt to be cool and arrogant on the subway, and the little-kid eagerness underneath. A delicious shiver went through me as I remembered how handsome he was and how he seemed so much older than he turned out to be. He'd tracked me down.

"So, my roommate and I are having that party, two weeks from Friday. I wanted to see if you'd like to make an appearance."

"Oh, I can't go that night," I explained nonchalantly. "An old client of my father's is taking my family to Vail for the weekend to thank him for some case that was just settled, that Dad worked on years ago before he became a judge."

In the moment of silence that followed, I could practically hear him raising his eyebrows. Of course I was trying to impress him: an expensive, athletic sport like skiing; a high-powered father; a weekend jaunt to Colorado.

Conor hesitated and then his voice deepened as if he'd cleared his throat.

"Well, why don't we get together some other time?"

Of course I was bluffing. What I'd said about my dad and the ski trip was true, but I'd left out a few facts. That my parents' thirty-two-year marriage was in free fall. That I'd spent most of my childhood cursing my father's devotion to his clients. That I was a lousy skier who often cried when confronted with steep moguls. That I was a drug addict, a slut, a liar.

I tried to remind myself that this guy called *me,* damn it.

"Sure." I kept my voice steady, casual. "How about a drink at P.J. Clarke's on Third?"

I was curious. One short drinks date near my office was no big investment.

"Great," he said, a little too quickly.

———❖———

United Airlines lost my luggage and skis on the flight from New York to Vail. My father, brother Hugh, and sister Sylvia had all come along for the trip. For the first time I could re-member, Mom stayed home from a family vacation, saying the autistic kids in her class would get rattled by a sub.

Mostly Hugh, Syl, and I hung out. They tried to trick me into skiing black diamonds when all I wanted were bunny slopes. My father was busy entertaining the client who'd brought us to Colorado. We saw him for maybe twenty min-utes each day. I spotted him once from the chairlift, skiing his self-taught stem christies, and thought, "Wow, that looks like my father," before I remembered that *was* my father, he was in Vail, too.

On my way back to New York Sunday night, waiting in the taxi line at La Guardia Airport wearing my black Ray-Ban sunglasses and the rumpled jeans I'd flown/skied/slept in, I met a fortyish SoHo architect who looked just like Michael Douglas. We shared a cab into Manhattan. He asked for my number.

I couldn't remember what Conor looked like except for his navy cashmere coat and thick blond hair.

P.J. Clarke's was hot and crowded with loud young bucks in suits at the bar when I walked in a few minutes late. Conor was sitting alone at a small table for two. He was wearing a Brooks Brothers wool suit. A new leather briefcase sat on the floor by his feet. His hair looked freshly trimmed, his skin shiny clean as if he'd just scruffed it with Clinique Scruffing Lotion minutes before. He stood up when he saw me and took off his coat. Underneath he had on red suspenders and a carefully pressed red pinstripe shirt stretched tight across his chest as if he were trying to show off the size of his pecs.

Okay. Whatever.

He bought me a club soda. Then, instead of talking about himself incessantly like most men in New York on first dates, Conor asked me a string of questions, almost as if he were interviewing me, to be his—his what? I barely had time to breathe in between questions.

Where did you grow up?

What does your father do?

Do you have brothers and sisters?

Where did you go to school?

What'd you do in the summertime?

What sports did you play?

When I answered, of course I left out huge blocks of truth. Amazing how easy it was to make my childhood sound normal, idyllic even. The lovely springtime in Washington, Vermont summers, Harvard, skiing, tennis, blah blah blah.

In my defense, it *was* kind of difficult to explain to a first date my brilliant alcoholic mother, Dad the workaholic, how a whiff of Hawaiian sensimilla in a Greenwich Village park still made my knees buckle, and my double-digit one-night stands with teenaged drug dealers.

I drank my club soda and plotted a quick escape.

His face stayed locked on mine the entire time. I didn't have a chance to ask him one single question. After thirty minutes I drained my drink and got up to leave. Conor stood up so fast, he practically knocked over the table.

"Well, before you go, let me give you my number," he said, sounding like a used-car salesman.

Then, of all things, he pulled a résumé out of his brief-case. I stared at it in disbelief. The gang at *Seventeen* was going to *love* this one.

Right before I burst out laughing, he caught me off guard by laughing first.

"You can check me out," he said with a crooked, sexy smile, one side of his mouth grinning more than the other, showing his clean, strong teeth. "Then next time you can decide if you want to go on a real date with me."

Shouldn't he have been nervous that I was cutting the date short?

He laughed again, throwing his head back. He suddenly looked astonishingly handsome. The overeager boy had disappeared. The loud, smoky bar vanished behind him.

Too puzzled to say anything more than "Good night," I

folded his résumé and put it in my coat pocket before turning down Third Avenue to the subway.

———◦◆◦———

When I got home, our garden apartment was cold and dark.
My Siamese was yowling her head off so loudly I could hear
her from the street. I'd gotten Criseyde the summer between
sophomore and junior year, my second year without beer and
a joint to see me through each day. I could barely carry on a
conversation with other human beings, which made roommates difficult. A cat, I could handle. Criseyde was so shy
the first time I visited the litter, I had to pull her out from behind a radiator. For the first week in my little studio apartment near the old Radcliffe dorms, she was a tiny lump
under my bedcovers. She ate by licking baby food off my finger. I was the only person she trusted. Now in Chelsea, she
went out into the backyard alone for hours, incredible bravery
given what a recluse she'd been in Cambridge.

A yellow note from Audrey stuck out from under the
brick we used as a doorstop, saying she was spending the
night at her boyfriend's.

I turned on some lights and taped Conor's cream-colored
résumé on the mirror of the massive mahogany bedroom set
Mom had given me, along with a jewelry box and a beautiful
old Hariz carpet, as part of my grandmother Frankie's estate
when she died the year I turned seventeen. I imagined what

I would have said to my grandmother if she were still alive. Like Sammie, Frankie died of alcoholism, at age seventy-six in a family where women traditionally lived alone and independently into their late nineties. She died in a hospital bed after breaking her hip in a drunken fall, killed twenty years too soon by alcohol withdrawal as much as by the infection that set into her hipbone. She was the first family member I knew who died. I was living in Madrid; the essay about that experience ended up front and center on my Harvard application. No one in my family suggested Frankie's death, or being there for Mom, might be significant enough to merit traveling across the ocean. I was too young to know better myself. I didn't come home for the funeral.

My father felt the annual real-estate taxes were prohibitive, so Mom had to sell Strawberry Hill, the childhood home Frankie had clung to after my grandfather disappeared into the streets of New York.

"You have to have something of hers," Mom had said a few months after the funeral, stroking the polished curves of the four-poster bed like you would a baby's soft head. She was as close to tears as I'd ever seen her. I went to hug her. She pulled back slightly, as if my touch would singe her skin.

"There were so many conversations I wanted to have with her," Mom said, looking down at the veins on her crossed hands. "She died too soon. You have to have this furniture to remind you of her."

Instead, Frankie's bedroom set reminded me of how my

mother found affection so unbearable. Mom always turned to alcohol, food, lavish birthday celebrations, cashmere sweaters on Christmas Day, wads of cash stuffed in my suitcase when I wasn't looking. As if words and physical contact were too powerful.

Or not powerful enough.

———❖———

"So, been out with Subway Man much?" Winnie asked over the phone a few weeks later. She'd been in Italy on her first buying trip for Ralph Lauren. "I need a full update on your love life."

I put down the query from *Seventeen*'s slush pile I'd been reading when the phone rang.

"You know, that résumé move made me laugh every time I thought of it. We've been out a few times, once a week, I guess. He's cute, Winnie, but there's something . . . nervous under the surface."

"Such as?"

"He picks restaurants so carefully. It's like he's got a *Zagat's* guide: 'New York City—How-to-Impress-Your-Date Restaurants.' We've been to every one. Touristy places that try too hard. And he always pays cash . . . crisp twenties that look like he *ironed* them."

She giggled. "What's he like? Any fun?"

"He actually is fun—amusing in an offbeat, um, loner way. He hangs on every word I say. But it's weird, Win. I can't tell you a thing about him. It's like he dropped out of the sky. He doesn't talk about family, friends. . . . All I know is he grew up in Massachusetts and graduated from college last year—which is strange because he's eight years older than we are. Lee's friends at his investment bank say he's a great guy, supersmart, the best trader on the desk, but they don't know jack shit about him either."

"I think he just got out of prison for abducting blond chicks he meets on the subways. He probably got his degree via one of those prison correspondence courses."

"Ha—very funny. At least he's not a product of Wasp in-breeding like some unmentionable recently engaged man I know."

"Touché," she snorted, trying to sound indignant, but I could hear her smiling on her end of the line.

"Anyway, I did have that architect I met at the airport wait in *Seventeen*'s lobby so Ann and Terri could walk by. They agree he looks just like Michael Douglas. He took me to lunch at Beekman Towers—you know, overlooking the U.N. in Midtown? He says he likes children but that they should be kept in a basement playroom, preferably sound-proofed. 'Why not just get goldfish, then?' I asked him."

I'd made Winnie laugh. One of my favorite things to do.

"So then I met this investment banker at some party who took me to Smith & Wollensky—ever been there? I swear my steak lunch cost more than Audrey and I spend on food in a week. During lunch he asked me to test-drive his new Ferrari in Monza next month. How's that gonna work? Oh,

Winnie, Conor bores me. I am on the verge of not seeing him again."

"Boy, have you been busy!" she exclaimed. "I better not go on any more buying trips. I'll come back and you'll be fucking married with two kids."

Then she told me all about the fabrics she saw in Italy, and how all she could think about in Milan was what kind of silk she wanted for her wedding dress.

— ❖ —

The March issue ran my runaways piece. I stopped by the newsstand at the Twenty-third and Eighth Avenue subway entrance just to stare at it in public. Perfect illustrations: shadowy silhouettes of teenage girls who should be in gym class instead of Times Square. True and gritty, not dark and glamorous like a slutty girl-band album cover.

Now I spent my days at *Seventeen* working on my first cover story. Kathy had assigned me a piece about why sex, drugs, and alcohol were actually harder on girls' bodies than boys'. Like the runaways piece, the facts told a decidedly unpretty story. As the head of the ob-gyn department at Mt. Sinai Hospital explained, women got V.D. more easily than men because of the moistness of our genital skin, alcohol hit us harder because of our lower body weights and higher percentage of body fat, and nicotine and other drugs mixed more potently with female hormones than male. Lovely.

The beauty editor stopped by my desk one afternoon to

ask if I had time to do a makeover. I thought she meant to write the copy. Then the stylist called to check dates at a local salon and I realized the makeover subject was *moi*. I felt like telling her that makeup and soft lighting couldn't compare to giving up alcohol and drugs.

I decided to deep-six Conor the next time he called. I met so many men, I was going out six nights a week. Sometimes lunch with one and dinner with another. Dating someone I wasn't completely into seemed silly.

Surprise. He didn't call. My old beige phone seemed never to ring. Did he somehow know I was bored with him? Was this a tactic to get my attention?

Then on a rare Friday night when I was too tired to go out and Audrey was snoozing at her boyfriend's, I had a dream.

Conor and I were driving in a beat-up, four-door vintage Ford, wide leather bench seats, no seat belts, cruising the empty streets of Wall Street and Lower Manhattan at dusk. The city was deserted. Conor turned the oversized, skinny steering wheel with one hand, looking like James Dean.

He kept his eyes on me as he drove, the blond hair falling over his left brow. I sat in the passenger seat mesmerized by the twists and turns the car took as if it were a Jet Ski gliding through placid water. Conor had lost all nervousness around me. We'd long ago stopped needing words to communicate. He pointed the nose of the car skyward and my stomach soared as we became airborne and flew around Manhattan's skyscrapers as if the dream were taking place inside a blue-black Batman comic strip.

After driving for what seemed like hours, Conor slowly leaned over and smiled. His blue eyes never left mine. His right hand found the space between my legs, under the cheap black fabric of my miniskirt. I orgasmed beneath his hand, a rippling shudder, my entire body imploding from the hot touch of his fingers. At the same time the car exploded into tiny colorful bits like leftover confetti.

I woke up in my bed, alone in the sunny Saturday morning quiet. I lay under the covers almost unable to move. I hadn't had sex in more than four years—and never without being drunk or stoned. I'd only had a handful of orgasms in my life. Not ever in my sleep. Was such a phenomenon possible? I'd *never* heard of it, even when Dr. Ruth Westheimer came to Harvard Law School and talked about people who had sex with dogs and the importance of finding the right dildo.

Holy shit. Maybe I would go out with Conor again.

— — ❖ — —

Seventeen shot my makeover on a Monday when the salon on Fifth Avenue was closed. The cut came first, really just a trim. Then the makeup. A muscular black man the size of a construction worker burst into the salon carrying a tiny bubble-gum pink toolbox encrusted with fake jewels. He applied six to seven layers of makeup to my face along with dabs and streaks of dark brown and black all around my eyes. I looked like a glamorous raccoon. A small crowd of tourists gathered outside the salon while we shot the photos. When I pushed open the heavy glass doors to leave, the crowd parted with a big "Ooh" as if I were a famous model. Either that or they were afraid I might grab one of their children to suck its blood.

The Friday before, Conor had finally called me at work. I could barely get the words out to tell him I was looking forward to seeing him. I agreed to a Monday night date. Tonight.

Suddenly, I felt tired of the new men in my life. Drained by the nervousness, the awkwardness, the lack of familiarity. I wanted one I could sit with in silence without twitching to think of witty stories or summoning up good night smiles so big and fake they hurt my cheeks. Someone who felt like family.

Speaking of family, I'd just gotten a huge cardboard box from my dad. Inside were five wool jackets he'd worn for the past twenty years, the way men rotate suits forever on a weekly basis, gray on Monday, navy blue on Tuesday. . . . After two decades the cuffs finally got frayed. He said he was going to throw them out. Then he thought about how I loved good fabric, how many new outfits I could buy on my puny salary, and sent the jackets to me instead of Goodwill. The suits were beautiful herringbone tweed in shades of black and blue and charcoal gray. I rolled up the sleeves and threw one on over a five-dollar T-shirt and a twenty-dollar stretchy miniskirt, and presto! I could be in *Seventeen's* LOOKS UNDER $30 fashion spread. Best of all, the castoffs still smelled a little like him, that masculine wool-aftershave-cigar-smoke combination that made me feel as close to him as I was ever going to get.

On the way back to the office I jumped every time I saw my bizarre reflection in the Fifth Avenue store windows. Up on the ninth floor at *Seventeen,* I ducked past our security guard, Stitch, a retired postman, into the ladies' room before anyone spotted me. I went through an entire roll of cheap scratchy toilet paper before my face looked passably normal. I was noncommittal when Ann and Terri asked about the makeover.

"Oh, you'll just have to see," I told them. They groaned knowingly. Not a good sign.

A few hours later, I met Conor—my palms felt ticklish just thinking about him—under the clock at Grand Central Station. He was early again. I spotted him from across the cavernous amphitheater, leaning up against the clock post, reading *The Wall Street Journal.* I came up to him and kissed him softly. He made a sound in his throat like a soft moan.

We squeezed into the crosstown shuttle and then walked down Ninth Avenue, the street crowded with New Yorkers trying to get somewhere—home, the store, their kids' school, Central Park. Everyone else seemed to be heading uptown. We were the only ones going downtown.

Once we were finally alone, side by side in a booth at the old Empire Diner near my apartment, I kept remembering the dream. Sitting next to Conor, smelling the clean scent of his soap, the wool of his suit mimicking my father's when he came through the front door every night, I couldn't stop looking at his hands. He kept them hidden—he was not a big gesturer and he never reached over to pat my thigh or arm, as so many men did way too early. But tonight I was looking for his hands and I got a thrill whenever I saw them.

Strong, quiet fingers. Round, manicured fingernails. Such elegant hands were a puzzling contrast to Conor's muscular chest and athletic waist.

I watched his hands all night long, holding his fork, picking up the check, resting easily on the table. In the dream they had gripped the steering wheel so confidently. His right hand had felt so hot beneath my skirt when he reached over.

Let's just say Conor had ceased to bore me.

He told me about work, his new roommate, the gym he'd found near his place, details about his daily life in Manhattan, the intensity of the trading desk. He was too old to be this excited. He had a few small wrinkles etched around his eyes that seemed to bespeak a wife, young kids, a mortgage. But at the same time, his face had the bright freshness of an eight-year-old boy running inside for a drink of water after baseball practice. I wanted to brush my fingers against his cheek.

I was not going to jump in bed with him tonight. I remembered all too well what it felt like to wake up next to skinny drug dealers or unshaven bartenders I could barely remember from the night before. Ugh. Dream or no dream, this time I was going to wait until I was ready.

Conor walked me home. He stopped to kiss me good night slowly, one hand on my waist, the other holding the wrought-iron security door to our basement apartment. He asked if I wanted him to come in, but backed off quickly when I shook my head and said, "Not tonight, Conor."

I think he knew I meant: *Not tonight, but soon.*

Inside my apartment, I headed for the bathroom to wash up. Pulling off my black Capri pants (yes, from the fashion closet), my fingers brushed my underwear. Soaked through. I'd totally forgotten what wet panties felt like. I'd never felt this flicker—like I was losing control and liking it. What would it feel like to make love to someone I truly cared about and trusted?

I brushed my teeth in front of the bathroom mirror I'd rescued from someone's sidewalk trash. YOU'RE GORGEOUS! spelled out in early-eighties pink, techno-square script. My mouth full of toothpaste foam, it occurred to me that maybe this was how it felt to fall in love, for real.

Monday, 5:30 P.M. I'd waited until I knew his secretary was gone so she couldn't screen his calls. Dad picked up on the first ring.

"Leslie! How's the working gal? Did you get the package I sent?"

"Yeah, Dad. I wore the gray one today. Thanks so much. You staying late tonight?"

He chuckled. "I've been here twelve hours already. I walked to work and I did not see one other person in all of downtown Washington." He pronounced "Warsh-ington" with a hint of Oklahoma twang.

My father grew up in south Oklahoma, a poor boy genius surrounded by an impoverished Baptist clan. He was the first in his family to finish high school. He was one-quarter Cherokee Indian, which explained why we all had high cheekbones, pigeon-toed feet, slightly golden skin, and nearly no body hair.

From the few stories he'd told me, his childhood was dominated—not in a good way—by his vagabond, zealously religious mother. She left her husband and moved the family as often as a dozen times a year in response to religious visions, eviction notices, and untimely visits from the police in response to late-night calls from neighbors. His older sister died from untreated leukemia, but Dad didn't talk about her much.

He graduated from a Chicago public high school and accepted a Navy R.O.T.C. scholarship at Harvard, a school neither he nor his mother had heard of before a teacher encouraged him to apply. He worked at a construction job all summer to save the train fare to Cambridge. When he left Chicago, his mother told him he was joining the devil.

He met Mom at Radcliffe. She was engaged to her brother's Kirkland House roommate, as close to incest as Wasps get. She broke it off to marry Dad under the old oak tree at Strawberry Hill. After a stint flying Navy planes to repay his college debt, Dad went to law school. My mother paid his tuition by working as a phys ed teacher in Somerville.

I don't remember my father ever making it home from his job as a Washington lawyer before seven P.M. I doubt it occurred to him that we needed time with him as much as we needed new shoes and food on the table, the very things he must have considered as precious as myrrh when he was growing up a poor white-trash nomad. He became a judge in his early fifties. I read about his opinions in *The New York Times* and *The Washington Post* more often than I actually saw him. In my lifetime, we had only had a handful of conversations about anything besides the weather, tennis, or the Redskins. I remembered every sentence verbatim.

Today was different. I was not calling to tell him about Conor. I long ago stopped telling Dad about the guys I dated. He always got them mixed up. Nothing quite compared to having my dad call my shiny new boyfriend by an ex-boyfriend's name. Dad and I never talked much about Mom's tirades, my drug usage, anorexia, or drinking. He did not seem to notice my problems, no matter how grave. It struck me as simpler and kinder to let him think I'd always been fine. Especially now that I was.

I'd called to tell him I knew he'd moved out. At my urging, he'd given Mom an ultimatum: Stop drinking or else. Last night Mom had said, "So, did your father tell you he's rented a house?"

My heart dipped when I realized what it meant. She'd

refused to quit. She'd chosen alcohol over him. He'd probably mailed me those jackets when he was clearing out the closet they'd shared for more than three decades. Their separation had been ten years in the making, I'd guess. So what if Dad was too much of an emotional coward to tell me himself, that was no surprise. He had his reasons.

I was going to make this short and sweet for his sake. And maybe for mine.

"Dad, I just have a second, but . . . Mom told me you moved out. I know this is really a hard time and you don't want to burden me. But I'm here if you need me in any way. I'm really sorry. I know you tried . . . as hard as you could."

Silence. The sound of my father shuffling yellow legal pads on his desk.

"Well, Les." He cleared his throat. "I love your mother. Thirty-two years together. But I think the marriage . . . is over. I think it was actually over quite some time ago."

No shit, Dad, I thought as I hung up the phone.

As I was walking out to the lobby, I heard Conor and Stitch laughing. I stopped for a minute to put on Dad's gray herringbone jacket.

"Yeah, I bet it's not a bad job," I heard Conor say, in his confident man-to-man voice. "Watching seventeen-year-old models after thirty years at the post office."

Stitch laughed his deep belly laugh.

"Ah, they're a good bunch here," he said. "I just try to keep the crazies away."

I'd put my sleeve on the wrong arm and had to fumble in

the hallway to get the jacket on right. When I saw Conor standing next to Stitch, chuckling deep in his throat, crooked smile on his lips, I couldn't help but smile myself.

———❖——

We headed downtown to Indochine. Conor had gotten more adept with restaurant choices. We sat at a low table in a cushioned, indigo corner. He asked if I'd like a glass of wine or a beer.

"No, thanks," I told him with a shrug. The way I always refused drinks. I didn't explain. My story would take ten years to tell. We weren't ready for that kind of drama.

"Hey, I've noticed you don't drink," he said curiously, leaning forward, smiling. His face was open, fearless: He wanted to know everything about me. "You haven't had one drink the whole time we've been dating. What's the story?"

To stall for time I studied the ornate inlaid ceiling of the restaurant.

"Well, there's just a lot of alcoholism in my mother's family, Conor. I haven't had a drink since my eighteenth birthday, the day I turned legal. Although trust me, I drank plenty before then. I don't want to turn out like some people I know who've become alcoholics."

Kind of the truth.

He pushed his glass of beer away. He gazed around at the flickering candles on every table in the restaurant. Conor smiled when he looked back at my face.

"Well, then I won't drink either."

I stared at his untouched beer glass. White foam oozed over the amber liquid, almost breathing. A few long white stripes of airy bubbles glistened along the cold, sweating glass.

I was touched. Kind of. What a lovely gesture. No alcoholic would stop drinking for someone he'd dated a half-dozen times. Break up with a girl because she *didn't* drink, sure. My sober friends would love this. Already I could hear the whole meeting laughing at how different normal drinkers were.

"No, Conor." I shook my head. "It doesn't bother me. I have friends—guys I've dated—who drink. It's been years since I've had a drink. Years since I *wanted* a drink. I have no problem going to bars. Being around alcohol doesn't make me have the slightest desire to drink again. There's no need—"

"Look, Leslie."

He stared over my head for a second, pausing as if to get the words just right. Then he looked straight at me.

"I like you. It's obvious that alcoholism disturbs you—you grew up with it and all. I know what it's like having something like that in your family. I don't want to do anything to . . . disrespect you. And I mean that in a really deep way."

He looked at me as if his blue eyes could cut through my flesh and bones to my heart. How did he know I could never trust someone who drank, ever again, because of Mom?

"Okay, it's a free country. But don't do it for me, Conor. It really doesn't mean that much."

I don't know why I lied.

After dinner, I told him I was too tired to go out to the jazz club as we'd planned. He took my hand—his smooth, warm—and started walking to my subway stop a few blocks from the restaurant. I needed to be alone, to think about Mom and Dad, apart for good. I couldn't concentrate on Conor or pretty jazz music. His vow not to drink just added to my distraction.

He walked me to the turnstile of the E train. We kissed good-bye as the station started shaking from the oncoming cars. Like all our kisses so far, this one was chaste—lips only. He squeezed both my hands long and hard as he kissed me. His hands felt like a broken-in catcher's glove. I wanted to be as close as possible to whatever it was inside Conor that made him *him* and made me feel so damn good when we were together. I was afraid to look at him. He believed in me. I couldn't handle it if something in his face destroyed the faith I felt coming through his hands like a blood transfusion.

He let me go. I pushed through the turnstile and slipped into the train just as the doors were closing. I slid into an empty subway seat and the car dissolved around me. Conor was gone.

— ⸺ ✦ ⸺ —

The next Monday, Conor and I met after work under the clock at Grand Central. That afternoon, I'd gone to La

Guardia Airport to pick up six teenage girls from around the country, finalists in *Seventeen*'s teen model contest. I'd corralled them at baggage claim like a herd of young giraffes and brought them into Manhattan in a huge black limo. The doormen at the Park Lane on Central Park South had stared as a half-dozen six-foot-tall fourteen-year-olds climbed out of the stretch. The models were now ensconced with three chaperones from the beauty department, locked in for the night. As I'd left, one started jumping on the queen-size bed, her long blond hair flying toward the ceiling.

Conor was waiting patiently, a bouquet of pale pink roses in one hand, a bulky pink bag rolled up under his other arm. He was wearing khaki pants, loafers, a blue oxford shirt, and a surprisingly preppy knit vest, the kind a twelve-year-old would wear to church. His face lit up when he saw me.

"Hi," he said, still smiling, when I came up to him. He put his arm around my shoulders. His touch warmed my bones like a mug of hot chocolate thick with milk. Conor looked like he'd just showered, his clothes fresh and perfectly pressed, as if he'd been waiting all day for this moment.

"How ya doing?" He looked at me carefully.

"Okay," I said with a tired sigh. Nannying the wanna-be models had aged me ten years.

"Here, let me have that." He took my purse/sling/backpack. "Let's take a taxi back to your place so we can drop this off."

"You know what?" I asked. "Why don't we walk? I could use the fresh air. The bag's not too heavy for you, is it?"

"Nah." He laughed. "This is nothing."

So we walked the thirty-five blocks to my apartment, across Forty-second Street and through the grit and graffiti of Hell's Kitchen, a neighborhood that was probably safe only on early Monday evenings when everyone was hungover from the weekend. I shuffled for my keys outside the basement door. Conor had never been inside.

Once I opened the door, my cat rushed toward me, spotted Conor, and skidded in a panic through the living room, heading for the few inches of safety under my bed. She moved so fast all we saw was a skinny white blur.

"What was that?" He laughed. He put down my bag and handed me the flowers. Pink, long-stemmed, lightly scented. "I hope you like these."

"Oh, God, they're beautiful. That was my Siamese, Criseyde—she's kind of shy. Do you want a glass of water?"

"No, but the flowers do. Why don't you get them some and then I have something for you."

He motioned to the bag rolled up under his arm.

I put the flowers in a vase of water and got a glass for myself from our kitchenette. Criseyde's fiery eyes stared at Conor through the crack of the door to my bedroom, like a little girl watching her parents' dinner party when she was supposed to be in bed. Conor surveyed the books lined up in makeshift brick-and-plank shelves Audrey and I had put in the living room.

"Wow," he said when he noticed I was back. "You've read all these?"

"Hey, don't be too impressed. I was an English major. They're actually just my favorites, the ones I've kept."

He raised his eyebrows. Then he turned back to the bookshelf.

"What about these old-looking ones? *Beautiful Joe? Jim Jump? Black Beauty?* These don't sound like college books." He ran his finger along the spines of the books that were my favorites as a child. Even though the jackets were tattered now, I remembered how shiny each cover looked under the Christmas tree with a gold sticker that read FROM SANTA.

"Oh, you're going to make me cry now. Each one of those books is worth about a half hour of crying. Dead dogs, dead ponies . . . you know."

"No, not really. We didn't have books in my house."

How could anyone grow up with no books? He couldn't be serious. But true or not, this was the only time he had ever mentioned his childhood.

"Okay, now sit down," he said, turning back to the room.

I sat down on the pink futon couch.

"Close your eyes."

I closed them. Giggled nervously.

"Hold out your hands."

I stretched out my hands and felt a fabric like velvet, but lighter.

"You can open your eyes now."

In my hands was a beautiful pale blue dress with a pattern of tiny white flowers.

"Oh, Conor, you didn't need to do this . . ."

"It's silk. That's why it's so soft. It reminded me of you. Something in your voice last week made me think you could use a present."

I held the dress up. It had long sleeves, a V neck, a wrap-around waist. The kind of dress I wanted to sleep in. I folded it carefully and put it back in the bag.

"Why are you frowning? Don't you like it?"

"Yes, yes. I actually love it, Conor. I just can't believe you found something that is exactly what I would have bought for myself. Thank you. It's beautiful."

He smiled slowly.

"I've always had a knack for this kind of thing. Now go try it on."

In my bathroom, I slipped off my work outfit, the usual miniskirt and wool jacket of Dad's.

I smoothed out the crumpled bag the dress came in. The store name, written in pink script lettering, looked oddly familiar. Yes—it was that store half a block from *Seventeen*. I'd stopped twice during my lunch hour, once to buy a pale fuchsia linen dress, another time when I bought the black wool number I was wearing when I met Conor that first time on the subway. What a weird coincidence.

"Hey, Conor!" I called from behind the bathroom door, where I stood naked, my nipples perking up from the chilly air, my toes curled away from the cold tiles. I heard rapid footsteps and within seconds he was standing in the hallway on the other side of the door.

"Yeah?"

"You're not going to believe this! You bought this dress at one of my favorite stores in the whole world, right near *Seventeen*."

He laughed, the lovely deep chuckle I remembered from his first phone call.

"I know. You mentioned on the phone once that you'd just gotten back from a great store nearby and that you'd eaten lunch across the street at some park with a fountain. So yesterday I cruised around the neighborhood near *Seventeen* until I found the right place."

How long did that take? How many side streets had he walked down? There were dozens of women's clothing stores in that neighborhood. Amazing how he found the right place. Amazing how special he made me feel.

"I didn't even know that store was open on Sunday."

"Actually, it wasn't. But the owner was inside taking inventory. I got him to open up for me and I told him all about you and what you like. He just got a shipment from Italy."

I pulled the blue dress over my head. It fit perfectly. There were three silk-covered buttons on the waist and a long, full skirt that made the dress look like it was made for me. The fabric was warm and soft as lingerie against my skin. I felt like Morgaine, the fairy heroine of *The Mists of Avalon*.

I smoothed my hair and came out of the bathroom. Conor was sitting on my pink futon, engrossed in John Rawls's *A Theory of Justice,* which he must have gotten from my bookshelf. Not exactly light reading.

"Oh." Conor made a sound when he noticed me standing

48

in the doorway. He put the book down but kept his thumb marking his place, as if he were afraid to let the book slip away.

"You can borrow that book, Conor. 'The veil of ignorance.' Amazing philosopher, Rawls."

"Oh, man," he said, shaking his head. "You look beautiful. Boy! Now let's get some dinner."

— ◦ —

I sat on the smooth, chilly stairs of the Metropolitan Museum of Art at Fifth Avenue and Eighty-second Street, totally dwarfed by the massive concrete columns and a giant red banner that proclaimed 5000 YEARS OF ART! I rubbed the arms of my black cashmere pullover—Mom's thirty-year-old Radcliffe sweater that I'd machine-washed instead of dry-cleaning so many times that the finely woven cashmere had become more like that soft fuzzy material little-kid pajamas are made from. Mom always said that with a good haircut and nice shoes, you could get away with anything in between. Not that she was talking to me these days. She'd refused to call me back since she'd learned I'd talked with Dad about the separation agreement they were negotiating.

I stood up and waved to Conor when his blond head emerged from the shadows across Fifth Avenue. He took the steps two at a time. His mouth was soft and warm when he kissed me.

"Oh, those lips," he said softly in his whiskey voice,

49

making my heart pitch, his eyes closed, his long lashes forming half-moon fans.

Conor carried a small bag from an expensive Upper East Side deli, filled with four-inch-thick roast beef and chicken sandwiches and oversized green apples and navel oranges so perfectly formed they looked like they'd been plucked from a Manet still life. We spread out the food in Central Park on a grassy hill slightly north of the museum, surrounded by other picnicking strangers. The sun warmed my skin as we leaned back on the new green grass.

Suddenly, as if Barbara Walters had asked a question, Conor started talking.

"My neighborhood was real working-class Irish Catholic. Although my family is all Scottish—you know, from Scotland? Everyone there calls the place 'Southie.' You probably never knew Southie existed during those four years you lived across the river in Cambridge, right?"

I tried not to show how shocked I felt. He'd once said he grew up near Boston, but he'd avoided his childhood so assiduously on our dates, Winnie had begun to make up a past for Subway Man, calling his parents Mildred and Franklin.

He looked at me challengingly. No wonder he'd been fascinated by the details of my years at Harvard. He already knew all about Harvard. I didn't say anything.

"Never met my father. He left when my mom was about five months pregnant. Punched her stomach during a fight, something about how little money they had. Never came back."

He took a bite of roast beef. No wonder he'd avoided talking about his past for so long. Imagine hitting a pregnant woman. What was it like to be the son of such a man? I sat on the sloping lawn, mesmerized by Conor's words and the way his face twisted and softened as he talked.

"After my father left, my mother moved back in with my grandparents. She was twenty-two, six months pregnant with me, working as a checkout girl at Woolworth's. We lived with my grandparents until I was four. I remember so much of those years. I know it's hard to believe, because I was so young, but it's true. It was just the two of us together all the time.

"Then, I don't know when, sometime after I turned four, my mother—we've always called her Chickie, it suits her 'cause that's how big her brain is—she married a gas station attendant she met at Woolworth's. Secretly. My grandparents couldn't believe it. They were furious. They never trusted him, he wasn't from Southie, my grandfather always said he did not believe he went by his real name."

Conor shook his head incredulously. His face was flushed, pinpricks of red flaring under his skin.

"So, they started a new family right away. Four kids in five years. My stepfather—Wade—used to feed my brother and sisters and make me sit at the table without any food. He'd say 'Conor don't git none,' and make them say it, too. He used to ask me if I was hungry, sitting there watching them eat."

Conor said this all matter-of-factly. His face had turned its normal shade again. He took a bite of an orange slice he'd carefully peeled and separated from the rest of the fruit.

It was hard for me to breathe. How could someone do that to a kid? My mom at least had waited until I was a teenager to go bat shit on me. His childhood was even more twisted than mine.

Conor took a drink of his Snapple tea. He kept talking, unable to stop, as if it were critical to tell me this story all at once.

"So . . . eventually I went to live with my grandparents. They were in their early seventies then, you know, because they'd had my ma so late. The greatest people."

A happy piece of the story. He reached into the back pocket of his jeans and took out his expensive crocodile-skin wallet. From behind several carefully folded twenties he pulled a small stack of cracked black-and-white photos with ridged white edges. His grandfather, stooped and wrinkled but with a smile that broke open his face, holding Conor on a tricycle. Conor's face, sprinkled with freckles, his blond crew cut sticking up in spikes. Conor and his tiny grandmother at the kitchen table, neither one's feet touching the floor, both drinking out of mugs that seem to dwarf them, in the tidy breakfast nook of his grandparents' South Boston walk-up apartment.

A kid-sized baseball glove lay on the table next to Conor. I could practically smell the leather. I pointed to the mitt, a question in my eyes.

"Little League. You know, in Boston, they worship the Red

Sox. I remember all my little eight-year-old friends, watching them practice for weeks with their dads in the concrete lots we used to play in. I'd hear them when I helped my grandfather water the flower beds in our yard at night. I was the only boy that didn't make the team."

Conor laughed, a handsome thirty-one-year-old man again, smiling as if recounting a treasured memory. I didn't want to insult him by feeling sorry for him, or to interrupt his story now that he was finally talking. So I glanced away and bit my lip to stop the tears coming out the corners of my eyes. When Conor wasn't looking, I wiped away the small puddles behind my sunglasses.

"So, eventually I had to choose—between going to school and taking care of my grandparents. They couldn't do anything after a while."

He was back in that time; he didn't see me anymore.

"I had to skip school to cash their pension checks, take them to doctor's appointments, fill their prescriptions at the pharmacist. They were so old. They just didn't understand I needed to be in school. So, after eighth grade was over, I decided not to go back."

When I was that age, on rainy summer days at the Vermont farmhouse my mother taught me exponential math. She drove me to the small-town library every afternoon; one summer I read forty books. She inculcated in me that A- was never an acceptable grade. By the time I graduated from high school I'd studied calculus for two years, lived in Madrid for six months to perfect my Spanish, and had been elected the first female president of my class. By day I was Mom's golden child, trying to make up for being her Washington Whore. Until the magic day when I stared in wonder at the lovely fat acceptance envelope from Harvard stuck in the brass mail slot of our Bethesda front door. There was no way she'd be ashamed of me again.

"I got so lonely," Conor went on, as if still trying to apologize after all these years. "It was strange, being a teenager and spending all my time with two people in their seventies. I starting hanging out in the afternoons—you know, while my grandparents took their naps, they loved those naps—I started hanging around a real muscle gym in the neighborhood. The owner, Jed, was a guy only a few years older. He taught me martial arts. In four years I got a black belt in karate, a black sash in kung fu. He taught me how to lift weights. I could teach you."

So that explained his muscles and the graceful, athletic way he carried himself. He reached out to touch my slim shoulders, covered by my fuzzy overwashed sweater.

"In 1978 I competed for the Mr. Massachusetts title. Next year, Jed and I started a new gym, a mix of weight training and martial arts. I slept on the gym floor at night at first. Then we started another one, pretty soon we had three. We had more money than we knew what to do with."

He peeled the white membranes off another slice of orange and placed it in his mouth. The spring breeze ruffled his hair.

"So, one August a few years after my grandparents died,

I sold the business back to Jed. Chickie and Wade laughed when I said I was going to ——— college. They'd never heard of the Ivy League. I walked into the admissions office with my grades from elementary school and my GED. At first they would only take me into the continuing ed program—you know, night school? But after one semester my professors signed a letter to recommend my unanimous acceptance into the undergrad program. I graduated magna last spring. My whole family—Chickie, Wade, my sisters and brother, even Jed—they all came to my graduation. Chickie cried when I got my diploma."

He chuckled, looking down at his gently cupped hands as if expecting to find a small bird there.

"She said, 'You're our only hope now, Conor.' Sure, she knows a meal ticket when she sees one."

He looked at the curve in the road above us. An unending stream of Rollerbladers, joggers, and young couples pushing strollers went by. His face contorted; for a minute, I glimpsed how Picasso must have seen people's faces, jigsaw puzzles of ragged pain, disappointment, and hatred. Conor took a deep breath. Gradually, the lines on his face disappeared.

"So, anyway, by graduation I'd gotten four offers from Wall Street i-banks. Took the best one. I like this education gig. In fact, I just sent off my app for Harvard Business School."

He looked at me sharply, as if checking for a hint of ridicule in my eyes.

I nodded and put my fingers over his in the cool grass.

His hand was warm. I still didn't know what to say. We'd both ended up in the same place, with good college degrees, prestigious New York employers, bright shiny futures.

Conor looked at me again. The expression on his face—like a kid at the toy store asking if he's got enough money for a stuffed animal—made me want to look away. I forced myself to look back at him.

"Hey, we've all got crazy families," I said. "That's what family is for. Right? Let's go."

We stood up, brushed the crumbs and grass off our clothes, and threw away the remains of lunch. We walked around to the museum's entrance, up the steps and through the columns. The European sculpture galleries were empty except for the security guards. We stood together for a long time in front of the Italian marble nudes, rough, indescribably innocent statues meant to grace outdoor gardens in Tuscany. I didn't want to let go of his hand. We giggled together at the garish, brightly painted German porcelain figurines with elaborate china costumes, stark white faces, and smears of red for their lips.

The temperature inside the gallery was warm, as if the heat hadn't been turned down yet for spring. After about twenty minutes Conor took off his navy sports jacket. He had on his suspenders again, vertical maroon stripes with gold clasps at pocket level. They were even more geeky as casual wear. I couldn't quite look at them.

His shirt was a white Brooks Brothers button-down cotton number, the same type he wore to work, I knew. Poking out were his surprisingly slim wrists, with a few blond hairs under the heavy cotton cuffs. Because it was Saturday he had the shirt unbuttoned at the collar, tucked into carefully ironed jeans, the seam crisp across his shins. What guy ironed his jeans? How, after everything he'd been through, could it matter to look perfect on the outside? I looked down at my wrinkled jeans that'd never once felt the heat of an iron.

The careful way he'd dressed for this casual Saturday afternoon reminded me of a young boy whose mother overdressed him to disguise humble origins. A mother whose hope was all in her son. Then it came to me: He'd dressed to look like the person he hoped to be, the Wall Street Ivy League wonder boy from an established family who'd never wear anything but preppy shirts and expensive loafers. It was like he had a page from a J. Crew catalog taped next to his mirror, and he was trying—too hard—to mimic the laughing, square-jawed models. The perfection of his execution betrayed him.

Of course what did not occur to me was what someone watching us in the sculpture galleries that day might have seen without even looking closely. Through Conor's eyes, a Waspy blond Harvard girl who knew which fork to use was even more seductive than a Brooks Brothers wardrobe.

All I could sense that day was that he trusted me, he needed me. That made me need him just as badly.

The sun faded. The afternoon cooled. We wandered the Upper East Side holding hands.

We stumbled into Café Bianco, a tiny Italian restaurant on Second Avenue. As we stepped through the heavy brass double doors, New York City slipped away. Dark-haired waiters and waitresses chattering in thick Italian accents rushed by. We sat in a quiet garden courtyard with a fountain. The few people in the restaurant seemed to be finishing up very late lunches, in that languorous New York way where you might not eat lunch until five-thirty on a Saturday afternoon. We ate our pasta puttanesca in silence, tired from the sun and the museum and the talking we'd already done.

Holding hands, we walked slowly back to Conor's apartment, a fifth-floor walk-up at Eighty-second and York not far from Rex and Winnie's. His roommate was away for the weekend, he explained as we climbed the stairs. His apartment was spotless, modern, simply furnished with a sleek black leather couch, black-and-white-flecked granite kitchen counters, gleaming white Carrara marble in the bathroom. His half-open bedroom windows, overlooking York, let in the cool night air.

Conor sat on his bed in the twilight, moving around nervously. I sat a few feet away in a chair by the windows. We talked for half an hour. Street noise, taxi horns, the occasional loud voice floated up to the fifth floor.

During a pause in our conversation, I beckoned to him with my finger. I whispered, "Come here." His eyes never left mine as he came to my chair with his hands outstretched, practically kneeling.

We took our clothes off. Quickly. The night was balmy enough that our bodies kept us warm on his queen-sized bed, carefully made up with pale peach-colored cotton sheets, crisply ironed (of course). We didn't say a word.

Later, when we came up for air, sweaty, out of breath, and refreshed all at once, our jeans and my cashmere sweater and his sport jacket and all our underwear were strewn on the floor. Conor tossed his head back on the pillow and laughed when I pointed out that we'd rocked the bed four feet away from the wall; an island in the dark room. I didn't explode from his touch, like in the dream. But I'd lost consciousness of myself in a way that was just as powerful.

The air around us was cool. I reached for my sweater and underpants. Conor had slipped under the soft sheets. I put my head on his shoulder.

"There's something else I need to tell you," he whispered. *Fuck,* I thought. Not exactly the words you want to hear ten minutes *after* having sex for the first time.

I needn't have worried.

"What I didn't tell you before is that Wade—my stepfather—he used to beat me all the time."

Oh, my God. My chest thickened. Fresh tears spit out the corners of my eyes.

"Put me in the hospital for days. Used to choke me until I passed out. Sometimes I still wake up from nightmares with his hands around my throat. Can't wear ties that are tight."

He twisted his neck against the pillow as if trying to throw off imaginary hands.

"Where was your mom?" I croaked like a tree frog, the only question I could think to ask.

"Oh, Chickie was there. Sure. He used to beat her, too."

Conor shook his head.

"In front of all of us. Smacked her, punched her, threw her down. Broke her ribs once by kicking her as she lay on the floor. I remember watching him break her nose. Blood all over the kitchen."

Conor suddenly brightened and sat up in the shadowy room. "You shoulda seen Wade the first time I came home after I got my black sash in kung fu."

I noticed with a start that he still called his mother's place "home." The edge to his voice, sharp like a paring knife, was back.

"I'd been weight lifting for about two years. Wade held up his fist to hit me 'cause of something, don't remember what, he never needed a good reason anyway. I said, real quiet, 'You better not try that with me anymore.'

"Then I pushed him, both hands on his chest, but you know, in exactly the right place, pushed him with my fingertips. He fell down, hard. I had gotten really strong, but you couldn't tell from lookin' at me."

Conor chuckled, his face blooming with joy. "Wade never came after me again."

Relief filled the dark room as he laughed. I felt like the bones in my face might crack apart. My throat ached from holding back tears. I'd have given several years of my childhood to make up for everything Conor had survived with no mother or father to protect him.

I couldn't find words to say that. Instead I put my hand on his smooth, hard bicep and brought him back down to me in his bed. His arms and chest formed a hollow around me that felt like a feathered nest in the dark. We stayed like that for a long time without talking. I didn't argue that neither of our pasts mattered now. I didn't explain that it'd been four years since I'd had sex, that in fact I'd never before had sex without being drunk or stoned. My cheeks and lips were rubbed raw from his beard stubble. My black sweater smelled like his skin; I wanted to sleep wearing it so I could smell him all night long and feel my own body under it, changed forever by the touch of his hands. I felt like Lucy in *The Lion, the Witch, and the Wardrobe.* I'd discovered an entirely new, magical world and didn't care if I never got back to the old one.

In the middle of the night, Conor walked me down to the empty street and hailed a cab. It felt too soon to spend the night, too early to wake up together with morning breath amid the harsh Sunday A.M. light. The asphalt was black beneath our feet. The taxi glowed bright yellow. The lights from the streetlamps and traffic signals shone like jewels against the shadowy apartment buildings lining York Avenue. Conor gave the driver money and my address in Chelsea and kissed me through the open taxi window, his lips soft and dry as tissue paper.

"Bye, babe," he whispered as the taxi pulled away.

"Hurry up, Sandy!"

Even though she had her back to me, Mom's words bit through the damp air like the smack of a porch door slamming shut. She yanked repeatedly on our old dog's frayed red leash when he lingered by a boxwood still wet from the afternoon rain. I'd come to Washington a few days before Easter to research Health and Human Services data on teenage girls for a big AIDS education piece *Seventeen* had planned for the fall. It was early dusk, just after six P.M. I knew Mom would be home from her job teaching autistic kids at a Montgomery County public school. I parked Dad's red Mustang a few blocks away so she wouldn't know I'd borrowed it from him earlier in the day. Both he and I had left messages on her answering machine since Dad had moved out, but she had not called us back for three weeks straight.

"Mom, hi . . ."

She whirled around, her hair a silver halo. My hands

shook a little. I tried to focus on the smell of the rain in the air, the drops on the bush nearby, shifting the negative energy of my fear outward like a yoga teacher once taught me.

"What? You're here and you didn't call me in advance?" She looked sharply at me. Then she turned toward a neighbor's grizzled old Asian gardener trimming a privet hedge in his oversized yellow boots. She brushed some water off her slacks.

"Mom, I just didn't know if you'd want to see me." I tried to put my hand on her thin forearm but she pulled away with a fierceness that took me by surprise.

"This goddamn dog. You kids made me get him and now look, I have to take care of him all by myself. Have you talked to your father?"

"Yeah, Mom, I have. You know, you could always call him yourself."

"Not that bastard. He knows where to find me."

She chuckled ruefully and looked away again.

"I'm not drinking, you know," she said, scowling. "I even went to an AA meeting. I don't know how you stand those people, their smoking and all that talk about a 'higher power.' Honestly. I've found an alcoholism therapist who's better. It was idiotic to think I needed to go to a treatment center. Who would sub for me at school? Who would take care of Sandy? Not your father."

"Well, Mom, maybe Dad leaving was a good thing if it got you to stop drinking."

She lunged toward me, jerking the dog's leash inadvertently. Sandy yipped in surprise. Her teeth were clenched and the veins on her neck stuck out like those thick rubber hoses on Bunsen burners in chemistry lab. I took a giant step backward, away from her.

"Don't think that for a minute! And he told me *you* were behind it all. That was the most humiliating thing you have ever done to me. Don't think I'm really going to quit drinking. I don't have that big a problem. I'm just stopping now to show that your father was wrong when he called me an alcoholic. You are lucky I'm even talking to you."

She was blaming *me*? Why?

She stomped ahead in her little flat leather loafers from Pappagallo. I didn't know what to do, so I followed her down the street. Alcohol had been her best friend, closer to her than any of us, for more than thirty years now. Maybe it was easier for me to get sober; I'd been only eighteen. Maybe facing what makes you drink is too much for some people. Even if Mom stopped drinking for a few months, her liver might repair itself significantly, adding years to her life. Right now I'd settle for that if it meant she'd be civil to me and return my calls.

After striding along for a block, she slowed down and let me walk next to her. Yellow daffodils were blooming everywhere, popping up in bright profusion on the neighbors' velvety green lawns. Pink and purple buds on the azalea bushes that lined the sidewalks were just beginning to open up.

She didn't yell anything else, as if she'd said all she needed to and now I could be her daughter again. She walked closer to me than she would if she were still mad. When I paused to get a pebble out of my shoe, she stopped, too, steadying me with her free arm when I lost my balance trying to slip the shoe back on.

Hope is always good, right?

When we got back to the house, I decided not to risk going inside. I tried to hug her good-bye at the top of the driveway. She let me. She smelled like lemon hand cream and Rave hair spray.

"Have a great Easter, Mom. You flying to Vermont like always?"

"Yes. My flight leaves from Dulles tomorrow afternoon. I have to get the garden plowed and make sure the house made it through the winter all right. I've got to resurrect that old place one more time."

She smiled at her Easter sardonicism and hugged me back in a sudden hard clutch. Then she pushed me away. For the first time she looked straight at me.

"Why don't you call me next time, before you come to town?"

She didn't ask where I was staying. I didn't tell her about the house Dad had rented. My guess was he'd never move back into the home he'd shared with her and us kids for so many years. I didn't tell her that Conor was taking the train down tomorrow, Good Friday, so the trading desk was shuttered, or that we were going to spend Easter with Dad. Mom didn't even know who Conor was. There was no point in telling her that I'd met the man of my dreams right when she was losing hers.

I drove back to Dad's new house. He got home from work late, nine P.M., smelling like wool and reams of legal paper and one or two cigarillos. He looked ten years younger than before he'd left Mom. When I was brushing my teeth before bed I heard him laughing into the phone in his bedroom. A deep, knowing chuckle I'd never heard before. I had no idea who he could be calling.

As I climbed under the sheets on the sofa bed in the living room of his new house, it occurred to me for the first time that my encouragement to confront Mom about her drinking had offered him an escape from the Queen of the Wasps. He took with him the social prominence he'd gained from marrying her and the impressive, lucrative career she had helped him build.

The bonus was that he got to blame his departure on me.

— —◆— — —

My rusty old key still worked. The front door I had passed through hundreds of time as a child swung open. My footsteps echoed throughout the still hallway, the silence incongruous; this place was anything but calm when we all lived here. Conor carefully wiped his feet on the dingy welcome mat and followed me inside. He didn't notice what hit me instantly—Mom's stacks of old newspapers, the stench of cat pee, mounds of clean unfolded laundry sprinkled on the gold silk Beidermeiyer couch and the wingback chairs by the fireplace.

Instead, in the foyer the first thing Conor spotted was a heavy gilt frame surrounding an old photo of my grandfather and his brothers and sisters, the Croton clan, dressed fabulously in the understated way that early-twentieth-century Wasps perfected. He didn't notice the inch of dust on the frame rim. His lips formed an O as he started to ask who those people were.

"Yip! Yack! Yap yap yap yap!" Sandy went ballistic in the kitchen where he got penned whenever Mom went away.

"That's my grandfather Sammie," I said over Sandy's machine-gun barking, pointing to the tallest man in the old sepia photo. Sammie wore his tailored suit with casual grace, as if each morning a properly bred person awakened to find oneself impeccably dressed by divine intervention. I hadn't told Conor much about my family yet. I'd brought him here on this sunny Easter morning because now I wanted him to know everything about me.

"Sammie was my grandmother's first husband. *Her* name was Frankie, well, her real name was Frances, but we always called her Frankie. She had three husbands. She died when I was in high school. Anyway, my grandfather was the only Harvard senior in the class of 1929 who owned *two* sports cars."

Standing across from me, Conor's eyes were wide and his face was so still it seemed he was not breathing. And I'd only just begun. I had to shout to be heard over the dog's incessant yapping.

"Sammie and Frankie married in August 1929. Good timing, right? It was eight weeks before Black Friday. They came home from their two-month European honeymoon to a totally penniless family. Sammie's father died a year later—financial ruin, social ruin, some strangely aggressive form of lung cancer. Sammie's mother—my great-grandmother—went crazy. Of course very quietly, genteelly. She did stuff like gave every person in the family a badminton set for Christmas, every Christmas."

We were still standing there motionless in the dark hallway. Conor seemed as mesmerized by my story as I had been by his.

"Look at them." I pointed back to the photo where my great-aunts and uncles posed with their arms looped together. "Look at those smiles. Not even the Depression and the loss of their parents can take away their belief in one another. And you know they all did fine. The girls headed to Wall Street. First they were secretaries, then they all married well; the boys headed to the military, the government, any place that would lead to respectability without the Harvard degrees they'd always thought they'd get."

Sandy had finally shut up. I could talk in a normal voice again. I took a deep breath.

"My mom barely ever talks about him," I said, pointing to Sammie. "But a few years ago at a family reunion, one of my great-aunts—my namesake, Leslie, this one right next to Sammie—told me about the last time she saw him. She and her husband were in New York City when they ran into him by chance in the revolving door at the Plaza Hotel on Fifth Avenue. Aunt Leslie wore a fur coat and pearls, ready to go to the theater for the evening."

I smoothed my hair with my hands, tightening an imaginary fur coat around my neck, and put my nose slightly in the air.

"She told me that Sammie was dressed in an old suit and grease-stained hat, the only clothes he owned. She said she had to breathe through her mouth when she hugged him. He was a bum, Conor. He was coming into the Plaza to beg. Leslie bought him dinner and cigarettes at a diner nearby, blew off the show, and listened to Sammie tell funny stories about their childhood and watched his hands shake as he tried to hold his drink. She never saw her brother again."

Conor shook his head in wonder.

"God, Leslie, now I'm really starting to understand why you don't drink."

He looked one last time at the photo, all the pride and promise in my grandfather's handsome face. Then he looked curiously into our living room, crowded with antiques from Strawberry Hill. I took his hand, flicked on the light, and led him toward the middle of the old Oriental rug Mom cut down from the Strawberry Hill ballroom to fit this smaller oval room. It was the same rug she hid her Christmas money under the year Sammie stole her stash.

"Yeah. Many, many members of my own family had alcohol and drugs ruin their lives. I could have been one of them." For unknown reasons I gestured at the Chippendale chairs lined up against one wall as if my dead alcoholic relatives were watching us. "I'm so lucky."

We walked through the formal dining room, lined with dark oil portraits of aunts and uncles, the messy sunroom. I took Conor into the kitchen, throwing the dog into another manic frenzy of barking. Sandy launched into frantic terrier sniffing of Conor's pant leg as if he were convinced a bomb lay hidden in the khaki folds and he had to find it before it detonated.

"Glass of water?" I asked once Sandy stopped yapping.

"Sure."

I handed him a Redskins glass filled with tap water.

"It's sad that your father wasn't here more. He just couldn't take it, huh?"

"I don't know. I never thought of it that way. It just always seemed like work mattered more. But at the end there he was leaving us to our own devices, to deal with Mom and her drunken rages. I guess that was a pretty sad thing to do to us kids."

What would Conor think once I dismantled the images of my idyllic childhood? Now that I'd started telling him, he had to know what my family was like behind the screen I painted when we were first dating. Would he understand why I'd created that facade?

"One afternoon in Vermont when I was eleven, Mom slammed her car door shut and said she was never coming back. I fed the other kids the only dinner I could make without turning on the stove—kielbasa and sliced cucumbers—

and sat on the front steps by myself, looking for the station wagon's headlights in the driveway. I crept inside when she pulled in at six A.M. I remember when I stopped asking friends to stay overnight. When I stopped having parties because Mom just used it as an excuse to get shit-faced and humiliate me in front of my friends. I have never heard my mother say she was sorry or that she loved me. When I left for college I knew I was not ever coming back."

Conor didn't say anything. I surveyed the kitchen counters. The beige Corian was crammed with grocery receipts and broken china that had been waiting to be glued back together for the better part of a decade. Sandy's canine heart medicine bottle sat next to Mom's allergy pills, a half-empty case of white wine, and a pile of unpaid bills.

"Anyway, that's all ancient history. But I wanted you to know it. Let me show you my room. It's here on the first floor. Everyone else slept upstairs."

I led him down a dark hallway into my old bedroom where my great-grandmother's hand-sewn quilt was still stretched tightly over my bed and my rectangular pillows were plumped up perfectly like hay bales. The room was clean and tidy like I'd left it the last time I'd stayed here. I'd mopped the floor myself every Saturday morning, a peculiar thing to do as an adolescent. Mom had hung my Harvard diploma over my desk. It was a bit crooked and Conor reached up to straighten it out.

"What was it like, Harvard?"

"Well." I rolled my eyes. "Believe it or not, I was terrified of going to college, especially to Harvard. I tell you, Conor, I prayed to the college admission gods not to let me in so that I wouldn't have to go."

He frowned at me slant-eyed and suspicious, like I'd said I was abducted by aliens as a small child. He crossed his arms over his muscular chest and looked back at the crimson-edged diploma signed by Derek Bok.

Conor was frustrated; his forehead was still creased. Had he heard what I'd just said? Had he heard anything? He walked to the bay windows that curved along one wall of my old bedroom. "What a neighborhood!" he said. "Look at all these trees! I can't see any other houses. It's like a mansion on a private estate."

So what? I felt like saying. I wanted to go from room to room with Conor and say, "Here is the butcher knife she threatened us with," "Here is the spaghetti pot she dumped on the floor in the middle of my soccer team party," "Here is the bathroom rug I used to curl up on when I was crying and no one came." By telling him I'd feel not alone anymore. Because of his childhood betrayals he'd understand mine. But he still seemed irritated. Why? Suddenly I felt we had to get out of the house before it poisoned us, too.

"You want to go for a walk? Sandy could use some exercise—the dog walker only comes once a day when Mom's gone."

I clipped on Sandy's leash—more frantic barking—and locked the front door behind us. We took a shortcut across the lawn underneath our weeping cherry tree, the branches covered with pink blossoms like a little girl's hair in bows. We retraced the steps of the walk Mom and I took three days before.

"Oh, Conor, I'm so glad you came down for the weekend. This is the best time to see D.C." I took his hand. "Isn't it gorgeous?"

The splendor of Washington in full spring bloom never failed to stun me. The flowering trees and bushes covering my neighborhood's steep hills, the cul-de-sacs, and the sloping lawns of old brick homes were so spectacular the scene looked fake. In college I'd hated the trip back to Boston after being home for Easter, abandoning these lush pastels for the drab brown of Boston's chilled version of spring. For several minutes we walked quietly, taking it all in, me thinking Conor was sharing my amazement at the show nature could put on. After a few shakes of his head, he finally spoke.

"I can't believe you grew up in a place like this," he said caustically. "Look at it! Even the fucking asphalt looks perfect. What do they do? Repave it every three months? Does everything have to be perfect here? I feel like I'm in Disneyland."

He sounded furious—at me. Like I betrayed him by growing up in such luxury. As if this type of neighborhood should not have been allowed to coexist in the same universe that let a young boy grow up fatherless among the concrete of Southie. He shook his head back and forth like we could not possibly have anything in common if this was what I took for granted every day.

"But, Conor—it's beautiful. Does a neighborhood have to be ugly in order to be real? And the whole point of my bringing you to see my house is that it never mattered how big the house was or how pretty the neighborhood because the real stuff happens behind closed doors anyway."

He turned to me quickly, holding up a finger accusatorily.

"Don't ever say we grew up the same. You don't understand. What you went without—that was just you feeling that. You had all this. Money. Parents who were educated. A fucking future. Harvard College, for God's sake! What'd you ever have to fight for? Poor baby, had to live in a messy house. Your mother drank too much. Your father worked too hard. You call those problems? You don't know anything about what it's like to fight for something you want and everyone tells you you can never have."

His nose was red; he looked close to tears. He spit out the words with such venom it was clear he was beyond such a simplistic, helpless reaction as crying. I took a step back, out of range. All I could think was: He was wrong. I did have to fight.

"Hey, I'm not the enemy here, Conor," I pleaded, putting my hands up. "I never took all this for granted." I swung my arms around the beautiful scenery. "Financial security and parents who went to fucking Harvard doesn't do much for you when all you want is for someone to say they love you, that you're good enough just like you are, parents who care enough not to get drunk or take clients out every night of your life. Maybe I was spoiled materially, but damn it, when you're a kid, love means *much* more. I'd trade that house, Harvard, vacations to Florida, all that supposed privilege— I'd trade it all to hear my parents say they loved me once, to have my mother not act like Sybil every night. But I can't hate this place just to make you feel better. I love it here—I always have."

My face felt flushed like a child with fever. Now I was the one trying not to cry. It was as if the world all around had shrunk to this globe of crackling, angry space. Even the dog was outside the perimeter of anger that fused us together and shut everything else out. I walked mechanically for a few blocks in numb silence and then turned back to Mom's. Every time we came upon another perfect tulip bed, I looked up defiantly and Conor shook his head like if there was any justice in the world, we would stumble upon a really tacky garage sale or a Budweiser can lying on a front lawn.

Then right in front of us a big silver Mercedes sedan rolled into the driveway of an elegant Tudor home so stealthily Conor and I barely had time to pause on the sidewalk before the car skimmed our toes. A man and a woman a few years older than me—probably Conor's age—stepped out, all smiles. The couple was dressed for church, the man in a navy suit with a perky white carnation in his pocket, the woman in an expensively tailored, Creamsicle-orange linen dress and matching hat that covered most of her straight blond hair, which judging by the way it brushed her shoulders, probably cost $250 a month to maintain. They helped two angelic blond children out of the cavernous backseat of the Mercedes.

I could practically smell the leather interior. The whole family smiled at us as if posing for the cover of *Town and Country*. Conor's face twisted until he looked like he was either going to scream or throw up. His arms hung by his side and he clenched and unclenched his fists.

"Hi!" I managed to say to cover up the dumb-faced way we were both staring openmouthed at this Stepford family. "Happy Easter!" The kids ran up the flagstone path to the front door, their patent leather shoes tapping out happy sounds. The man and woman laughed in unison, taking each other's hands and walking inside after them.

"Conor, come on, let's go," I said, tugging on Sandy's leash before he pooped on their lawn. Conor's ashy face looked like he'd been slapped. Now I was outside the perimeter. He was alone with whatever he felt.

He stayed quiet for the rest of the day and during the long train ride back to New York. I felt horrified at the disparity between his childhood and mine. But I didn't see how the yawning difference in our pasts made a dent in our discovery of each other. I tried to read the whole ride, sneaking looks at him over the top of the page, but he was always looking out the window, away from me.

Once we reached New York, he dropped me off at my apartment. He got back in the cab to head uptown to his place without a kiss or backward glance. Okay, he needed space right now. I didn't call him that night even though it was hard not to.

Monday. Tuesday. Wednesday.

He called me at work on Thursday afternoon once the financial markets had closed.

"Hi. It's me," he said weakly.

"Hi! You okay?"

He laughed.

"Sure. How's my little rich bitch?" He laughed, making me laugh, too. I loved the way he said "my." It made up for being called a bitch. He must have meant it as a term of endearment, right?

"Oh, God, Conor. You had me worried. Can I take you to dinner tonight for a change?" I asked hurriedly. "I can't afford those places you've been wining and dining me at. But I know a great Middle Eastern place in Alphabet City . . . best food in New York for under five bucks . . . whatya say?"

I sounded much more confident than I felt, which was more like: *please, please say yes.*

"Sounds like a plan. I'll pick ya up at work. Usual time." I heard him grinning over the phone. The Conor I knew and adored—my Conor—was back. The relief and joy I felt as I hung up the phone surprised even me.

Last night I'd stayed at Conor's, like I did all the time now. He'd given me a key.

"I want you to have this," he'd said a few weeks after our trip to D.C. He put the small piece of brass in my hand.

I was so surprised I didn't say anything. I closed my fingers around the metal, warm from his body, and slipped it into my jeans pocket. "I want you to come here whenever you want, seven days a week if that's what you feel like."

So many of my friends from college and *Seventeen* bemoaned their boyfriends' fear of commitment. They ran around New York carrying panties and a toothbrush in a bag because their boyfriends wouldn't give them half a dresser drawer at their apartments. I thought for sure our Easter trip to Washington was going to make him reconsider, at least slow down our relationship for a few weeks. But after we'd made up, Conor liked it that I spent nearly every night at his apartment, running home to get clothes, do laundry, and feed my cat once a week.

I could not stand to be apart from him.

The morning air was still cool when I kissed him good-bye at the doorway to his building. It was a sunny spring Wednesday but it was cold here under the awning in the shadow of the apartment buildings lining York Avenue. I couldn't stop kissing him. A taxi headed uptown honked at us, like it was too early in the morning to be kissing in a doorway. Conor leaned back from me and laughed.

"See ya, honey. Can't wait till tonight. It's gonna feel like forever."

He put his hands on my face and gave me one last big smooch. He turned to catch a cab down the East River Drive to Wall Street. I walked away slowly because it felt wrong to be walking away from Conor.

I headed to Winnie's apartment to pick her up. Two weeks before, Winnie had taken a job I'd helped her get in *Seventeen*'s art department. She couldn't take life at the Polo Mansion any longer. Now I got to see her every day. We often walked to and from work together; Rex's apartment on Eighty-first Street was just a few blocks from Conor's apartment at Eighty-second and York.

In front of her brownstone, Winnie stood expectantly, wearing a Ralph Lauren black linen sheath and squinting at me in the morning light.

"Oh, Winnie, I love that man!" I shouted to her when I was ten feet away. "How am I supposed to wait until the day is over?"

She shook her head and rolled her eyes and we started walking to Third Avenue.

"It's like jet fuel, being with him. It's like we're one person."

Winnie nodded and smiled mysteriously like the Cheshire Cat.

"God, I know I sound sappy and sentimental," I said, tripping over a crack in the sidewalk because I could not be bothered to look down at the ground. "But I have never felt like this, Winnie. Is this how you feel about Rex?"

"Sometimes." She laughed. "Other times, I just want to kill him."

We laughed in unison.

She was still eyeing me sideways like I was slightly crazy.

"Well, what about the future?" she asked. "Isn't he going off to Harvard Business School in the fall or something?"

"Yeah, yeah, he applied for admission this fall. But frankly it seems so far away it might be another lifetime. And in some ways that makes the present far more precious to me. Oh, Winnie, I feel like the luckiest girl in the world."

Winnie looked at me like I just might be drunk again. She puckered her lips. "Okay, Mary Poppins. Just let me know if they cart you away to the fucking loony bin. I'll bring you old issues of *Seventeen* when I visit."

I left *Seventeen* right at five-thirty. Winnie was meeting Rex at some dinner for his job, so I walked uptown to Conor's alone. I was home before six-thirty, only a few minutes before Conor got there. I was in his arms one second after he opened the door. A sigh escaped from him and I knew he'd been thinking about this minute all day, too. His cotton shirt felt soft and warm as I unbuttoned it and pulled it off him, his chest smooth and cool underneath. We made love hungrily on his bed as if it had been a year instead of twenty-four hours. *I cannot live without this feeling,* I thought as I wrapped my legs around him. As we did almost every night, after making love we lay on the bed for a long while, listening to music, holding each other but not talking, until the room darkened. Then we changed into sweats and walked the twelve blocks to his gym, Pumping Iron, holding hands with our mesh-and-leather workout gloves on.

Pumping Iron at eight P.M. on a Wednesday night was packed. Pairs of muscular men in their twenties and thirties spotted each other on the flat benches and squat racks. Despite the sprinkling of women, the gym always felt like the gritty inside of the men's locker room.

Afterward we came back to his apartment, showered, and headed out into the warm New York City night to eat dinner at Café Bianco. We sat at our favorite table, next to the fountain in the quiet outdoor garden. Christy Turlington sat at the table next to us with a bunch of supermodel friends. She was one of the most beautiful women in the world—she'd stared out of *Vogue* at me all day—but Conor didn't give her a second look as he pulled out my chair. It was eleven P.M. by the time we ordered our pasta puttanesca. We both had work the next day but I wouldn't be tired; I was never tired these days.

We sipped ice water with lemon. Conor had not had anything to drink since that night he put down his beer. I still didn't know what to say or think about it. Of course I was wary of alcoholism. Of course I preferred to be with someone who did not drink. But his decision still made me vaguely uncomfortable in a way I couldn't articulate, even to myself.

We walked home in the blue New York night with our fingers loosely interlaced. We climbed the four flights of stairs with mock groans, me in front, Conor poking my butt with his fingers to make me go faster. The truth was that the weight lifting he'd been teaching me was making me visibly stronger. The day before, I'd practically run up these stairs carrying two heavy bags of groceries. The week before, a group of models with skinny arms had asked me to try to un-stick the door to the fashion closet. I yanked on the handle and the door flew open. The girls all started clapping and I faked a goofy Arnold Schwarzenegger victory pose.

Conor made it to the top of the stairs first and he opened the door with his key. The apartment was dark and empty. His roommate Elizabeth was gone tonight as she usually was lately—she'd gotten a consulting job in Nashville during the week and the company flew her wherever she wanted on weekends.

Conor started kissing me in the foyer even before the heavy front door slammed shut and locked automatically be-hind us. His cold mouth tasted like Bianco's lemon ice water. Kissing all the way, we moved down the hallway into his room. I fell back onto his mattress. He pulled my jeans and panties off in one quick move and he spread open my legs and eased himself between my thighs. I could feel the cool Sea Island sheets under my legs, against my cheek, under my palms as I bunched the soft cotton up with my fists.

I could feel him get harder and his breath came faster as he got closer to climax. He closed his eyes; his long lashes brushed his cheeks. Then, without opening his eyes, he lifted his chest and rested his elbows easily on the bed to free his arms. His breath got shallow and rapid.

He carefully placed his hands around my neck.

He suddenly opened his cobalt eyes and looked into mine. His hands tightened around my throat. I could feel the excitement raging through his body like a freight train. I coughed; I began to choke. I tried to say, "Conor, no, stop, I can't breathe," but I couldn't make any sounds except for a croak deep in my throat. My eyes began to water. My body began to writhe involuntarily. Panic spread across my chest.

He mouthed three words slowly, under his breath, eyes unblinking. I could barely make out the words: "I . . . own . . . you." Then he shut his eyes and squeezed my neck even tighter.

Almost as if he had gone to another world, he came with a shudder deep within his body. He loosened his grip. His body crushed mine. Soon after, he rolled off and fell asleep.

Oh, my God. My throat ached. Somewhere deep in my stomach, practically as far down as where he was inside me, there was a cold, hard feeling, a kind of fear I'd never felt before, a block of ice in my womb. My lips were dry and cold. My hands shook slightly under the covers. I was going to throw up.

Oh, no, I thought, trying to banish the waves of nausea and fear. How weird. What was that? Kinky sex?

I went to the bathroom. Amid the gleaming Carrara marble I tried to reason with myself. Harmless, I guess. That's what all the sex columnists wrote, right?

Back in bed, I wrapped my arms and legs around Conor's warm body, trying to absorb the gentle rhythm of his breathing.

If I hugged him hard enough maybe the cold feeling would go away.

———❖———

A lazy Sunday afternoon, Memorial Day weekend. The city was deserted. Conor took the phone off the hook.

His bedroom felt like a tree house far above the Manhattan streets. Spring had almost become summer and the weather had gotten hot, no more cool nights now. The miles of Manhattan concrete and pavement soaked up the sun's heat all day long, then the sidewalks bounced the heat back in the late afternoon and evening. Conor and I had been lying next to each other on the bed, naked, for hours, reading and dozing. The windows were wide open and Conor's white curtains billowed in the summer breeze. I couldn't hear the usual taxi horns honking down below. The drivers had probably all decamped to Coney Island.

I rolled over onto my stomach. The bedsheets were soft and cool under my naked belly. On the floor under his windowsill I spied a torn scrap of white paper. Part of the thin envelope he'd opened a few weeks before from Harvard Business School, a brief letter that politely yet unmistakably communicated he'd been rejected. The letter invited him to apply again in the future when he had more work experience. Hadn't they read the essay describing how he'd been working since he was eleven, that he started a successful business while still a teenager? Conor had torn the letter and the envelope into small pieces and let them flutter out his bedroom window. This scrap must have blown back in.

"Rich kids half as smart as I am get in, that's why HBS does not require GMAT scores anymore," he'd said. "It's bullshit. But I have to go there. I'll apply again next year. Rat bastards."

He hadn't told anyone but me about not getting in. The guys on the trading desk would crucify him. He hadn't told his mother. He was trying not to call her as often and he told me he'd stopped sending her money. The day he got the letter was the first time I'd seen Conor angry since our trip to Washington. I had decided to hold off on telling him that Rex, who was one of those rich kids Conor thought were half as smart, got a fat envelope from HBS the same day Conor received his rejection. I hadn't known he was applying. He and Winnie were moving to Boston in the fall.

Conor rolled over and brushed my hair back from my face with his hand.

"Marry me, Leslie," he whispered. My stomach suddenly felt like a bottle with a genie coming out the top. With his blond hair, his big blue eyes, Conor looked so handsome, so hopeful—exactly like that man in the Tiffany ad proposing marriage with an eggshell-blue box hidden behind his back. Except that Conor was stark naked and he didn't have a box.

A surge of love like a current ran through me.

"Yes, Conor, of course," I whispered back. I kissed him.

What else could I say? It was like we were already married. I knew what it meant to him to have me as his girlfriend. As his wife—his *wife*—I could help him overcome the years of abuse and neglect and pain. I could help Conor better than any woman on earth. And if I could make him whole, we'd be one person. He'd be mine forever.

—————◈————

The following Thursday night, we were walking up York Avenue to the gym, wearing our leather weight belts and holding hands.

"Hey, babe, you know my sublease expires June fifteenth. Let's find a place," Conor said. "We should live together. I wouldn't live with anyone unless—I don't think it's right unless you plan to get married. But with us, there's no reason to wait. We should be together all the time. We're a family."

Oh, God. A family. The taxis and buses and other people on York Avenue faded into quiet gray.

I hadn't told anyone about him asking me to marry him. It felt too soon. But I couldn't wait to tell people. I rehearsed over and over telling Winnie that I'd caught up, I'd found someone, too, even though Conor didn't much like Winnie and I knew he'd be upset if she was the first person I told.

"Sure, of course, that sounds great, Conor," I said, smiling up to my eyelids. I broke the news to Audrey. She spent all her time at her boyfriend's, too. She said she'd probably move in with him. Our Chelsea landlord shrugged and said we'd have to fork over thirty dollars so he could place a new ad in the paper. I finally told Winnie one day over pizza at the Original Ray's across from *Seventeen*.

"So soon? You've only known him what . . . not even six months?"

"Well . . ." I pushed back my stool. It seemed to me like she'd moved in with Rex really fast as well, but the truth was they had been dating for more than three years. It only struck *me* as sudden.

"You know how I feel about him, Winnie."

"Yeah." She bit her lower lip like she wanted to say more. Then she smiled as best she could. "New York, you know. People move in together faster here. It's so damn expensive to keep two apartments when you're spending all that time together anyway."

I wished she could see, feel, how much I loved him. She'd understand then.

"Let me handle, it, honey," Conor said later that night when I showed him the apartment ads I'd circled in *The Village Voice*. He took the paper from me. "I'll get us the right place."

Sure enough, within two weeks, Conor found a small, charming sublet on Eighty-fourth and Lexington, with a balcony view of Central Park and the Metropolitan Museum of Art. It was even cuter than Rex and Winnie's place. *See, he's taking care of me already,* I wanted to say to Winnie. The lease started July 1. Filling out the sublet application, I included the trust fund Dad had created by putting a little bit of money aside for me on each birthday. It was very small money by

New York City standards, but it was more than twice what I made in a year and enough that no landlord would question my ability to contribute to our exorbitant New York City rent.

Conor also insisted on taking care of all the moving details. The day we moved, he took the day off and moved all of his furniture into the new apartment in the morning. He met me at *Seventeen* after work and we went together to my apartment in Chelsea. The Israeli movers he'd hired to move my stuff loaded it quickly into their beat-up truck.

We waved good-bye to the two men. Conor took my hand and we walked, for the last time, the four blocks up Eighth Avenue to the subway at Twenty-third Street. Only a few seconds after we got through the turnstile, the E train barreled into the station. The hot breeze whipped my hair back and blew my white sundress around like a parasol. The doors opened and we stepped into the train heading uptown, exactly the reverse of my path that night in January when I met Conor. Except now he held my hand like he would never let it go.

This time, we sat close together on the slippery yellow plastic seats. I looped my arm through his, my feet off the floor, my face buried in his warm neck, smelling his good smell. Conor gave me a well-timed shove as the train rounded a corner and I nearly slid off the seat. "Goofy!" he shouted, laughing. The other people on the train stared us down as if we were first graders misbehaving in class.

We got off at Eighty-sixth Street. Climbing up to the busy intersection at Lexington, the breeze blowing down from the street felt cool and fresh compared to the stale subway air. We walked the two blocks down Lex to our new apartment, past New Yorkers busy shopping for dinner, heading to the Reservoir for an evening jog, locking up fancy little boutiques for the night. The cement sidewalk felt like sea foam under my sandals. I put my arms around Conor, thinking: This is the happiest day of my life so far.

The small moving truck was already double-parked in front of our new building. The two movers quickly unloaded my things, mostly boxes of books and clothes, my grand-mother's dresser and four-poster bed. Conor and I cracked up every time the movers called me "Lazlee" in their thick Israeli accents. I liked it, the small thrill of being a new and different person, if only in two strangers' eyes.

Conor and I left most of the boxes to unpack later. I changed out of my work clothes and together we set up Frankie's four-poster bed, threw on some sheets, laid out two bath towels, a couple of dishes, my cat's essentials, our clothes for work the next morning. The place was so cute in its shabby-chic way I felt giddy. I put a small picture of us— the only one we had—on the mantel of the little fireplace along an exposed brick wall.

We made dinner together quickly—our first homemade meal. Hand-cut pasta, fresh pesto from Winnie's favorite Italian market, a bottle of apple cider champagne Conor bought to celebrate. The woman we were subletting from had left her wrought-iron furniture on the small balcony overlooking Eighty-fourth Street, and I set the table out there. Looking right, you could see the roof of the Metropolitan Museum of Art. I lit two candles but the soft evening breeze blew them out. Conor used a cutting board as a makeshift tray to carry out our plates, and shut the sliding glass door behind him with the back of his hand. We toasted the new apartment from the balcony, holding glasses filled with fizzing cider, eight floors above the honking taxis and the bustling New York summer twilight.

"Hey, you know who called me today?" I said casually in between sips. "That friend from college, Guy. He says the first year at HBS is not as bad as people say. He can't wait to meet you. He says if you need any help with your HBS application next year, he'd be happy to talk."

Conor's head suddenly jerked up. He put his glass down on the wrought-iron table. *Clink.*

I looked around the balcony. Conor looked so stunned I thought maybe a raccoon was hanging from the roof or he'd spotted a couple in an apartment having sex with the lights on (both of which we'd seen before). I didn't see anything unusual.

"He thinks you're a slut, Leslie," Conor said, his lips wrapped tightly against his teeth, looking down at his plate.

My head shot back in surprise as if he'd hit me.

Had I heard him right?

"He's the kind of guy who has a girl in every city waiting for him," Conor said in a low voice. "And he says he wants to meet me? To help me with my next Harvard application? What a snake."

Conor pushed his chair back so hard the table rocked and the chair legs scraped along the cement balcony. Something in him had uncoiled; the hands I loved jerked with anger as if he wanted to throw the furniture off the porch or smash it into the sliding glass door. He stormed inside and shoved the door closed behind him.

I was suddenly alone in the summer night. Our food lay uneaten on the table. In our glasses the champagne fizzed softly, sounding like bumblebees.

Sitting there, immobilized, I heard Guy's voice on the phone again. Around two P.M., he'd called from his dorm room in Boston, as he did every few months. Guy was the only undergraduate from our class of sixteen hundred students whom Harvard Business School had accepted right after graduation. We were friends who fooled around together occasionally, no fireworks but oh so nice, the only friend I'd ever had whom I did that with.

After I started seeing Conor, I stopped making out with Guy. Of course. Guy had started a serious relationship, too, with an older HBS student. He was happy that Conor and I were moving in together. I had told Conor this long ago. He hadn't shown a bit of anger or jealousy. I swear.

I sat there alone on our new balcony, my mercury rising. It was unfair of Conor to be so inexplicably possessive. Didn't he know he was ruining our first night together in our new apartment?

I pulled open the heavy sliding glass door and stepped inside. Conor sat on our lone chair in the living room, reading

The New York Times, his face cast down. He did not look up when I sat on a box next to him.

"Conor, we need to talk."

He looked up but did not put the paper down, as if my request were a casual one. Perhaps I was going to ask if he wanted some cappuccino. He raised his eyebrows and looked down again.

"I'm not a piece of property, Conor. I'm not looking for that kind of relationship. It's ridiculous that you're angry at me because one of my *friends* called me today. If you're jealous that I made out with him, or because he's at Harvard Business School and you're not, then that's your problem."

He stared at me. "Okay, if that's the way you feel, then why don't you leave now?" He looked down at the paper again.

How dare he. This was my place, too. I looked around the apartment at the packed boxes of his stuff, my stuff. The exposed brick wall and cute little fireplace with our picture on it. I couldn't figure out how or why in twenty minutes this evening had devolved from our most romantic night together to our most terrible one. I felt too angry to cry. Everything was happening too fast.

I ripped open one of my boxes labeled SHOES. I took the first pair, a set of white Tretorn sneakers. I pulled them on without socks. I was wearing pink flowered Gap shorts that looked more like men's boxers than women's clothing, and a white undershirt of Conor's. I grabbed my new keys and slammed the door of our new apartment behind me.

In the time it took to storm down to the lobby and out to the dark street my anger dissipated, smoke from a snuffed-out candle. I walked toward Central Park thinking: Was Conor scared that we were moving in together? So afraid that he'd lash out at me like this? Why hadn't I been calmer? I could have, should have, laughed it off. Told him I loved him more than any man on earth.

What was I going to do now?

As my anger cooled, the streets of our new neighborhood materialized around me. This was a nice block between Lexington and Park, quiet streets with big leafy trees, polished brownstone doors, shiny brass doorknobs and knockers. The gaslights lining the brownstone buildings flickered softly like fireflies. Across the street an older man with a potbelly walked slowly, smoking a smelly cigar, holding a fat bulldog at the end of a leash.

But this was still New York. I was a girl out alone after eleven P.M. Everyone who was coming home from work was already home. Even the doormen were all safely behind locked doors.

Wearing Conor's white undershirt, shorts that looked like boxers, and my stupid white sneakers, I started to wonder if other people might think I was homeless, a drug addict looking for a place to sleep. I had no purse, no money, no little green American Express card. A few taxis drove by. The people inside looked right through me. Conor's words about being a slut rang in my ears.

I walked for an hour slowly, aimlessly. People here were

always going somewhere, striding along purposefully. It was impossible to walk without a destination in New York City.

Where was I going?

I thought of my and Audrey's place in Chelsea. No furniture. And I'd turned the key into our landlord six hours before. Could I ring the buzzer at midnight at Winnie and Rex's happy little apartment? Winnie had just started to trust me again after years of my drinking. The thought of telling her about this fight filled me with shame.

Who could I tell that my boyfriend, my fiancé, for God's sake, whom I moved in with *today,* had kicked me out because I talked to another man on the phone? My body shook all over. My stomach felt as if it had dropped down a well.

I slowly headed back to the new apartment. I didn't know where else to go. I saw two rats, sleek as beavers, slip into a sewer at the corner of Lex and Eighty-fourth. The Korean market had moved its cut flowers and fruit inside and turned off the lights. There was no one on the street in front of our new building. I was frightened now, imagining a man with a knife jumping from the shadows, knowing no one would hear me scream. I race-walked past a narrow alley and a shuttered watch store until I got safely inside the lobby and the elevator doors closed behind me.

I turned my key quietly in our front door. I expected to find Conor waiting up, sitting in the living room staring at the front door, angry. But the kitchen and living room were empty. I peered into the bedroom. There he was, under the covers, asleep in Frankie's bed. Dried tears creased my face like Saran Wrap stretched tight. I found a black ballpoint pen and a pad of yellow legal paper, the kind Dad always had lying around. I sat on a box in the living room, writing over and over again like a child being punished in grade school, "I am not a whore." Who was I writing to? Conor? My mother? God?

I left the paper on the butcher-block kitchen pass-through, under his coffee mug, imagining Conor finding it in the morning like a suicide note. Then I washed up in our new bathroom, my toiletries in my makeup bag like I was staying in a hotel. I tiptoed into the bedroom and crawled onto the far edge of my grandmother's bed.

I couldn't sleep. I lay there alone, listening to the unfamiliar noises, the honking cars on the street below. I started to cry, quietly, with my back to Conor, hoping until my chest ached that he'd wake up and put his arms around me and tell me he was glad I'd come back safe and that it was all going to be okay, that he had no idea why he flew off the handle. That he was sorry about the fight.

Finally I fell asleep.

The next morning, I woke up before Conor, feeling hungover. I went into the kitchen and crumpled the piece of yellow paper—evidence of my insanity last night—and shoved it to the bottom of my purse, chilled that it had actually felt good to write it. I took a long, cool shower, hoping I'd feel refreshed afterward. As I was toweling off, Conor came into the bathroom.

"God, you kept me up last night," he said, shaking his head

with a pseudo-smile and a rueful look on his face. He yawned and glanced around for his shaving kit. He did not look at me; it was as if I were too insignificant for him to acknowledge with eye contact. I felt desperate to connect with him.

"Don't cry like that in our bed if you expect to stay here with me," he said.

He'd lain awake, *choosing* to let me cry myself to sleep? My stomach dipped like it does when you stare into the pool from the high dive before jumping.

I got ready for work quickly and left without eating breakfast. I spent the morning in my orange chair trying to figure out what to do. Where could I go? This was New York. I made less than twenty thousand dollars a year. I couldn't take a hotel room or find another apartment quickly. I couldn't think of any friend I could tell this whole story to and then sleep on her couch for a week or a month or however long it took to find a place to live. Would my family help? No. What could they do anyway? This was not the time to ask Mom for help; and Dad still couldn't even remember Conor's name. This was my mess.

Everything *had* to be okay with Conor. *He* was my new family, my real family. I'd never felt so good in my life as I felt with Conor. How could a relationship fall apart in twenty-four hours? Yesterday, *yesterday* we were giggling like six-year-olds on the subway.

I went over and over the previous night's conversation, excavating each syllable. I racked my brain for the few other times I'd mentioned Guy just to see if there was something legitimate that I'd missed. I hoped to find something, any-thing to validate Conor's anger. Then I could apologize and this would be over. You don't move in together for *one night* and then break up. How crazy.

As insurance, something to tell Conor if he asked, I di-aled Guy's number in Boston and asked him not to call me again.

"Leslie, okay, of course I will do anything you want. But can you tell me—is this about me, something I've done to hurt you or offend you, or is it just . . . life?"

"Oh, Guy, Conor's just jealous, I think. This is a sensitive time since we're moving in together. I'll call you again when things are better."

"All right," Guy said, kind of sadly. "I won't call. But just know I'm here if you need me. I'll be thinking about you even though I'm not calling."

Somehow I got through the afternoon and distracted my-self by doing a little work. I spent two hours in the fashion department surrounded by pretty fall cashmere sweaters. The editors didn't know me as well and wouldn't realize that something was wrong. I avoided Winnie's department scrupu-lously because she'd know in a second—God, I didn't want her to think that I'd fucked up my life again. I'd lose her, too. Crazy things like this happened when I was drinking and us-ing drugs. They were not supposed to happen now that I was sober.

I realized with a jolt that I didn't know where I was going that night when I left work.

My desk phone rang about four P.M. just after the financial markets had closed.

"Hi, hon." It was Conor. He usually called at this time but I hardly expected him to call today. He was laughing. I could hear the noise of the trading floor behind him. "You won't believe what Psycho-Seiko lost today. Those Louisiana electric numbers came out and he bet on the wrong side of the flip. Over eight hundred K washed away."

Relief flooded my body. I wanted to jump through the phone to grab hold of him. It was the old Conor, back again.

"So what time are you coming home tonight, babe?" he asked. "Babe" is what my father always called me—only me, never my sisters—when I was a little girl. The easy way Conor used the endearment almost brought tears to my eyes. Plus he said "home."

"About seven, I guess."

The fight was over. I didn't ask any questions about why.

A few weeks later, the fight had shriveled up like one of those dried mushrooms you buy from a bin in Chinatown. I was too sickened—too afraid—to mention it to anyone. Maybe Conor was right—I did get too friendly with Guy. Maybe he was slimy.

Conor hadn't said anything more about it, thank God. For weeks I assiduously avoided mentioning HBS, other men I'd dated, and random phone calls from college friends.

I unpacked my things, but the apartment didn't feel like it was mine. Sometimes it seemed like Conor's harsh words had been soaked up by the walls, like in *The Shining*. I vowed to forget the fight. I tried to love coming home to him and the place that was ours.

Except that my Siamese cat drove Conor crazy.

Conor had liked her at first. He took her for walks in Central Park on her blue velvet leash. Now his litany of complaints made her sound like the Antichrist. Unnerved that she'd been shut out of my bed, she yowled outside our door at night like a dying donkey. She licked our overnight guests as they lay in our sofa. We had to keep the sliding glass doors to the balcony closed because she fancied teetering on the railings, eight stories above Eighty-fourth Street. Her litter box smelled.

Then Conor pulled the trump card: He thought he was allergic. Did I choose my cat over my boyfriend? I started asking around to see if anyone wanted to adopt her.

My sister Sylvia agreed to take her the next time she came to visit. I tried to think of it as sending Criseyde off to boarding school, a temporary change, a place I could visit frequently. Because I couldn't imagine someone I loved asking me to make this choice. And because someone like me would never get rid of a cat for a man.

August. On the Thursday before Labor Day, Dad and Sylvia drove up from Washington in the red Mustang. They were coming to spend the night at our new apartment. Then we were all driving together to the farmhouse in Vermont for the holiday weekend. It would be Conor's first time meeting Mom, and Dad's first time visiting there since their separation.

Vermont. Summers started with sweaty, ten-hour car trips from Washington to the ramshackle summer farmhouse on Willow Street. Our green, wood-paneled station wagon was filled with suitcases, our Siamese cat, Sandy the dog, my two parakeets, a few snakes and turtles, Sylvia's smelly athletic equipment for every conceivable sport. The car did not have air-conditioning. After hours in the backseat, you had to peel your thighs off vinyl encrusted with a paste of cookie crumbs, apple juice, and sweat. One year our old Siamese stiffened in my lap as a Great Dane jumped onto the back window at a gas station, barked wildly, and pawed at the glass. She yowled and her eyes rolled back in her pretty brown head. The car filled with a sickening metallic scent as she died in my arms.

Climbing out of that hot, stuffy car into the cool, dry Vermont summer air was like emerging from hell into paradise. Then we would have long barefoot summers at the farmhouse, swimming in the cool river, playing Willow Street Wimbledon on the dirt road, having picnics on various mountaintops nearby, sleeping on the back porch with the Milky Way paving a path of stars overhead and the river gurgling nearby in the inky night. My dad stayed in Washington to work, coming up for a week in August.

One stultifying night I woke in a sleepy haze soon after Dad had arrived for his short vacation. "Get out of this house!" Mom screamed loud enough for the neighbors to hear. "My family's money paid for this all! Get the fuck out!" My father piled us, still in pajamas, into the green station wagon and drove us all the way home to Washington. Then he turned around to drive ten hours back to get my mother. We pleaded with him not to go get her.

"Teach her a lesson, Dad!" we shouted. "Don't let her treat us like this!"

"No, no, kids. It'll be better if I just go back." And he drove away.

Fifteen years later, he and Mom were still walking a rickety bridge together. Mom sounded mean and miserable, but dry. Dad and Sylvia lived in the nondescript suburban split-level filled with rented furniture. Dad took Mom out to dinner every Saturday night. Sylvia's descriptions of their encounters did not sound encouraging.

"Dad kind of slinks in from their dates," she said. "He sits out on the back porch smoking his little cigarillos for at least an hour. All I can see from my bedroom window is the orange tip glowing in the dark."

Mom as usual was spending the whole summer at the farmhouse, alone for the first time. She acted like nothing significant—such as Dad leaving her—had changed. It was like pretending she didn't have a boil under her armpit. She was too proud to imagine any man would quit *her*.

Conor and I and Dad and Syl walked in the swelter of
the New York City summer night to El Pollo, blessedly air-
conditioned. El Pollo served three things: salad, Peruvian
chicken, and Peruvian-style curly fries the same color and
curliness as Sylvia's long blond hair. Conor told dumb jokes
throughout dinner. It felt like we were double-dating.

We emerged from the restaurant around nine. The night
was still so hot our shoes sank into the soft tar on the streets.
On the way back to our apartment, Sylvia leaned into an un-
covered manhole on Eighty-sixth Street, and shouted "Hello"
to hear the long booming echo. A homeless man, probably
sleeping inside the manhole to escape the heat, answered
back in a deep, scratchy, drunken baritone. Sylvia screamed
and nearly jumped into the oncoming traffic as the three of
us bent over laughing.

The next day, Friday, we left New York before eight A.M.
Most people were asleep or at least still inside their refriger-
ated apartments. Already the streets were hot and damp with
Manhattan dew—the runoff from doormen hosing down the
sidewalks in front of their buildings. There was no traffic. We
sped up the Major Deegan Expressway, past the exit to Strawberry Hill. No one lived in seventy-two-room houses anymore,
and it was empty now, six years after Frankie's funeral, while
the developer who bought it grappled with what he could turn
the place into.

Sylvia piped up, leaning her head into the front seat to
make sure Conor, sitting in the passenger seat next to my
dad, heard her.

"You told him about Strawberry Hill?"

I turned to her in the backseat next to me. I shook my head and rolled my eyes. I snuck my hand under her seat belt and pinched her skinny little butt.

"Of course I've told him about Strawberry Hill. And Gasparilla. And Vermont. And how you are such a great soccer star. All the family highlights."

The car whizzed past the exit for the Mass Pike, the exit I took for four years driving back to Harvard from visits to my family in Washington and my interview trips to *Seventeen*. The same one Conor took to get to his mother's home in Southie. The same exit Winnie and Rex would take in a few days when they moved to Harvard's b-school dorms. When I finally broke the news to Conor about Rex getting in, he looked as if I'd helped Rex steal Conor's spot just by knowing them. I guessed we wouldn't be visiting Winnie and Rex in Boston anytime soon.

Dad steered the car left to follow the big green signs that read VERMONT. My brother had flown in the day before from Minnesota, where he'd spent the last year at Macalester College. Hugh had stayed in St. Paul for the summer to avoid hand-to-hand combat with Mom following Dad's departure. Smart. He'd agreed to fly in for Labor Day weekend because he knew how much having the family together at the farmhouse meant to her.

Once we crossed the Vermont state line, the temperature dropped ten degrees. Gone were the office buildings and McDonald's restaurants we'd been flying past. The highway narrowed to a two-lane road cut out of jagged rock walls. Thick oaks, interspersed with pines, filled the median so we could not see or hear traffic going back to Boston. We passed a yellow MOOSE CROSSING diamond. After about twenty minutes, Sylvia spotted the blue-green outline of the mountains. At a toll booth Dad rolled down the white vinyl top. The mountain breeze smelled of pine needles, freshwater lakes, and worms.

The Mustang's wheels crunched onto the gravel driveway just before noon. Up at the top of a small grassy hill, the rambling yellow house and barn sat behind a dozen massive blue spruce trees. My mother had planted the trees too close to the house, so now, fifteen years later, their branches scraped the shingle walls and their roots crumpled the foundation a bit more each summer. We got out and brushed the wrinkles out of our clothes. I looked to Conor: Would he think I was crazy to love this old ramshackle place, or would he see its magic, too?

I heard the screen door slam and then Mom emerged from behind the trees that framed the front porch, a smile on her face, a glass of suspicious brown liquid in her hand, wearing her favorite old cutoff flowered jeans and a white T-shirt from some tennis tournament she'd won. I hugged her—filling my lungs with a mix of the industrial-strength SPF-45 sunscreen and the bug spray she wore all summer. I tried not to sniff for liquor on her breath. I didn't want to know if she'd started drinking again.

Conor shook her hand.

"It's nice to meet you, Ann. I've heard such wonderful things about you from Leslie."

"Yes, of course. Glad you could make it." She barely glanced at Conor, looking over his shoulder to Dad, the real prize, who stood awkwardly behind us, as if he wanted to be mistaken for a spruce tree. I could tell he was not sure whether to hug her or just get back in the car and drive off before she fixed him in her sights. She said, too cheerfully, "Hello, Stan!" He nodded nervously, like a fly caught in a spiderweb who was thinking, *So far, so good.* Sylvia—who could sniff out family strife like a canary in a coal mine— had quietly slipped out back to check out the river.

Conor got our bags out of the Mustang's tiny trunk. I led him through a break in the sweet-smelling trees along a small dirt path to the side entrance of the horse stables we called the sleeping porch. Dad had converted the stalls into a large bedroom. The horses' names were still etched into the planks of wood over the beds, and the swinging door to the barn had gnaw marks where the horses cribbed the wood in boredom during the long Vermont winters. Years ago Dad had cut holes into the barn to make windows along each wall. Through the largest one I could see Sylvia out in the back pasture, standing quietly by the river, surrounded by orange tiger lilies.

A few minutes later, she pried open the back door to the sleeping porch. "Hallo!" she called in a fake British accent as she came in. She flopped on the bed in the middle stall.

"Oh, don't worry, you lovebirds," she said. "I'm not sleeping out here. I'll take over the loft. Come on, Conor, I'll show it to you."

We followed her through the crooked passageway to the wooden ladder at the bottom of the loft, a cavern with a peaked roof overlooking the summer kitchen. She scrambled up the ladder and disappeared through the rabbit-hole entrance my dad cut when the loft was where we kids slept. I showed Conor the farmhouse kitchen, complete with the original oak cabinetry and cast-iron sink, and took him up the steep, narrow staircase to the two tiny upstairs bedrooms. We trooped carefully back down the steep stairs and I pointed out the L-shaped indoor bathroom and the little door to the outdoor shower. Dad's suitcase was on the linen shelf outside the bathroom; he was probably unsure where he was supposed to sleep that night. I skipped my parents' bedroom, perpetually darkened by the enormous blue trees, dusty and messy due to my mother's typical "I have better things to do than make the bed" housekeeping.

After lunch, Conor and I swam across the cold river, carrying our shoes above our shoulders. We went for a long hike through the nearby Sand Piles, indigenous hills of white sand owned by a local construction company. As little kids we had played there for hours. When we grew too old for hide-and-seek and king-of-the-mountain, we rode ponies and bikes along the trails. Conor and I held hands as we walked on a sandy path to the neighboring farmer's grass airstrip. It was still common to hear a propeller plane land there every week or so. We picked two dozen ears from the corn rows that lined the half-mile airstrip. In the hot after-noon sun I shucked one ear and we ate the sweet kernels raw off the cob.

That night, we all ate dinner by candlelight in the cool summer kitchen. Delicious white corn, fresh bread from a nearby bakery, salad from Mom's garden, steak grilled on our little barbecue that sat at the edge of the homemade beach out back.

I pointed to the rafters above that led to Sylvia's loft.

"See these rafters, Conor? One time our old cat—Powder—fell off one, got the wind knocked out of her when she landed twelve feet below on the wooden floor. She woke up with Sandy sniffing her—Sandy must have thought Pow-der was dead. Then Powder sank her claws into Sandy's nose until blood spurted all over the room."

Holding his fork carefully in midair, Conor nodded and smiled and everyone else laughed at the story they'd heard a dozen times before. I kept going. "Once Hugh, when he was ten, walked the length of the summer kitchen, rafter by rafter. Right, Hugh?"

My brother nodded, his mouth full of corn.

"Sylvia—she was about seven—saw him do it."

Conor looked around as if visiting Madame Tussaud's Wax Museum. He had no way of knowing whether the mis-matched antiques, three dozen old tennis racquets hanging on the walls, yellow oil bills from the 1920s stuck on a nail, constituted normal décor for a vacation home or an insane asylum.

"What a delicious dinner, Ann," he said nervously, looking for approbation.

"Mmm," she said, sipping the one glass of wine she allowed herself with dinner.

"Glad you like it, Conor," Dad filled in.

Later that night, hours after we'd fallen asleep with our arms wrapped around each other under a thick quilt in the double bed on the open-air sleeping porch, he woke me up excitedly.

"Leslie, Leslie—you've got to see this!"

I groggily climbed out of bed and followed him to the back porch, wondering what he'd seen. A deer? A skunk? A bear? I stepped onto the cold wooden planks.

"Brr," I said, rubbing my arms.

"I came out here to take a leak," he explained. "Then I looked up." He took my hand and leaned back to look up at the sky.

"Have you ever seen anything like that in your life? What is going on? Some meteorological phenomenon? I had to wake you up. Should we get everyone else?"

The Milky Way was so thick with stars it looked like you could walk across it. He craned his neck back while he spoke, afraid the magical night sky would disappear if he looked away.

"You know what, Conor?" I said, leaning into him. "The sky looks like this every night here. We're in the mountains, one hundred miles from any large city with lights. Sometimes it's even brighter in the winter."

"No way." He looked at me in astonishment. "I never could have imagined the sky could look so . . . big."

I stayed with him for ten minutes, gazing at the sky. The moon and stars shone so brightly we could count the vivid orange tiger lilies lining the riverbed. He stayed outside once I headed back in. When he finally climbed into bed, his icy feet woke me up as they searched out my warm ones at the bottom of our bed. We made love sleepily until the bedsheets were hot from our bodies moving together like one.

———❖———

In the morning Mom made blueberry pancakes and then we climbed Little Sugarloaf together, an easy hike up a small mountain overlooking the pristine glacial lake below. At the top, we sat on smooth granite boulders the size of dump trucks and listened to the echo of swimmers splashing a half mile below on the beach. As kids, we'd always pestered Dad to lead a sleep-out on the top of Sugarloaf, but every time we attempted it, someone—eventually followed by everyone—chickened out as darkness fell, and Dad would lead us down the mountain in the early night, every twig snap surely the approach of a mountain lion. Today, we munched wild berries in the sunshine and slapped at the mosquitoes.

That afternoon, back at the farmhouse, I left Conor in the summer kitchen while I put on cutoff shorts, a tank top, and old black rubber riding boots to help Mom in the

garden. I pulled my hair off my face in a ponytail and covered all exposed skin in her special combination of sunscreen and bug spray. Despite the physical discomfort, this
was one of the best places in the world to talk with her. A
strange privacy existed, as if the garden were surrounded by
twelve-foot-high invisible walls. In between spitting out
gnats and digging our fingers deep into the soil to pluck out
the long roots of the weeds, she told me how mad she was at
Dad (she had made him sleep on the living-room couch the
previous night) and she related a few funny stories about
some gay friends she met at the one AA meeting she went
to. I listened and asked a few questions, eager to show I was
interested, glad she was confiding in me. I wasn't about to
contest her version of Dad's betrayal or her opinion that she
was not really an alcoholic.

After a long, hot two hours of weeding, I quit. I took off
my boots and sat on the sandy riverbank, soaking my grimy
feet in the cool water, washing the dirt off my hands and trying in vain to get the grit out from under my fingernails. Carrying my sweat-soaked riding boots, I came into the sleeping
porch through the back screen door. Through the window I
could see Conor had taken my place out in the garden, awkwardly trying to help my mom finish watering and weeding
the corn.

A half hour later Conor came into the semidarkness of
the sleeping porch.

"Your mother is a piece of work," he said.

She was a piece of work. Just about anyone would say that. I sat down on the edge of the bed, afraid to ask what he meant.

"She tried to tell me about what you were like in high school, how you were such a druggie slut. She tried to give me details. I wouldn't let her. No one should say things like that about their own daughter. I just left."

I was shocked that Mom would do such a thing, but it was not outside the realm of possibility for the woman who had nicknamed me the Washington Whore. Maybe she was trying to drive him away. Maybe she was jealous. Neither made much sense. After sitting with Conor for a few minutes, I headed for the main house to see if I could find anything out.

Mom was back in from the garden now, too. She stood in the doorway to the kitchen, three steps above me, her green eyes blazing as she wiped the garden dirt off her hands onto her cutoff flowered jeans. She had a glass of rum and Coke in her hand.

"Nice boyfriend," she said.

Behind her in the living room I saw my father's back. He pretended to look at some old books on the dusty shelves. He reminded me of a deer among trees, trying to camouflage itself from a hunting party.

"What?" I asked, not knowing what to say.

"Yes," Mom said, looking down at me from the kitchen where she'd cooked hundreds of meals for me as a child. "You always did like to bring home strays."

I turned and left.

An hour or so later, Dad came out to the sleeping porch.

"So, Conor, I hear there was some . . . uh . . . trouble between you and Ann this afternoon," Dad said softly, one
hand on his bony hip. I looked away. Conor folded his hands
across his chest.

"Stan, your wife said some inappropriate, insulting things
about Leslie. I don't know why she would say such things to
me. After she said them, I left the garden. Maybe it was
rude to leave, but it wasn't right for her to say those things
about her own daughter to me."

Dad shook his head. He waved his hands in the air as if
to acknowledge there was no easy way out of this. "Okay, I'll
see what I can do."

He went back to the main house while Conor and I sat
next to each other on the patchwork quilt that covered our
double bed, waiting like defendants dreading a jury verdict.
Dad came back ten minutes later. "Ann would just like you
to apologize," Dad explained to Conor. "To get this first visit
off to a good start, I think it's best to give in."

Give in, like you'd always done, Dad. Where did that get
you, or us kids?

"I'll give you two some time alone to think about it," he
said as he left, the old stall door squeaking behind him.
Conor watched him go.

"She's crazy," Conor said, shaking his head. "She's just
trying to bully you, and to bully me, too. She's saying she's in

charge here. She's trying to humiliate us. Like she's always done to you. And your dad—did you hear him? Leslie, I can't let anyone humiliate me, ever again. I can't let them denigrate you, either. I don't want this to be like my family all over again. It sets a standard if I go apologize."

Shit. He was right. Why couldn't this visit have just gone quietly, peacefully? My crazy family. I loved them. But it was time to stand up for Conor. And for myself.

We quietly packed our bags and straightened up the sleeping porch so that there was no trace we'd been there. Within thirty minutes we were standing on the front porch of my beloved farmhouse, just more than twenty-four hours after arriving. Mom, Hugh, and Dad gathered on the front step under the two biggest spruce trees. Sylvia had retreated to the loft. I folded my arms across my chest and looked straight at Mom, then Dad and my brother.

"Y'all, Conor isn't going to apologize for something he hasn't done," I said, looking from one to the other as I talked. "There are two sides to the story. We still want to see you for the rest of the visit. But we're going to stay at the Pasquani Inn instead of here."

I turned away. The three of them stood dumbfounded on the stoop, the sun in their eyes, either too satisfied or too surprised to respond.

"Dad, will you give us a ride?" I asked him.

He nodded, reaching into his shorts pocket for the keys.

We drove away in his red Mustang, shielding our faces

from the branches of the trees I used to leap over as a small girl. I didn't feel angry. Or sad. What I felt instead was simple: grown-up. Thanks to Conor, I'd finally stood up to the woman I loved, and feared, more than anyone in the world.

*Book
Two*

A FEW WEEKS LATER, ON A CRISP FRIDAY IN SEP-
tember when the edges of the leaves in Central Park had
begun to crinkle into yellows and reds, I came home from
Seventeen to our tiny apartment. I turned my key in the door,
walked into the dark foyer, and set my purse and two grocery
bags down on the parquet kitchen floor. I put my keys and a
pile of mail on the butcher-block counter and started opening
bills.

"Hey, babe."

I jumped. Conor was sitting on the balcony wearing jeans
and a baby-blue Polo shirt, already changed out of his suit
and tie. He had a lit cigar in his right hand, the ash about to
fall off. Normally he didn't get home until after six P.M., even
on a Friday. I'd never seen him smoke a cigar.

He put the burning butt down on the wrought-iron
table and walked in from the balcony. He leaned through the
kitchen pass-through to kiss me. I could taste the cigar on his
breath—kind of like kissing your grandfather.

"Hi, honey . . ." I said quizzically. "What are *you* doing
home so early?"

"Oh, I left work early today . . . because I quit." He smiled
crookedly, like he'd brought home champagne-caliber news.
He winked at me.

"What? You quit? Why?" *I* was not smiling. He looked so cute, but he seemed buzzed, off-kilter, almost like he was drunk.

"I'd just had enough. I had to escape the stress of that job. It's just too intense. Like New York," he explained, looking away, as if of course anyone would understand this logic. "I've been fighting alone my whole life. Babe, now that I've found you, I want the bullets to go over my head for a while."

Oh, boy. I sat down on one of our wooden bar stools next to the kitchen counter, still holding a piece of mail. The warmth and trust in Conor's voice made me feel light and swoony. At the same time it was all I could do to stop myself shouting, *Are you crazy? Shouldn't we have talked about this before you quit?* I tried to be calm and stable for Conor.

"My boss made some calls and there's an opening at one of their subsidiaries. Guess where? Vermont. Can you believe that?"

I looked at him in bewilderment, unable to say anything.

This was all a bit fast. A voice in my head said: *We love New York. I have a terrific job that half the girls in America would push me off the Brooklyn Bridge to get.* A few months ago his lucrative Wall Street trading job—a job his street smarts made him naturally good at—represented the fulfillment of ten years of hopes and dreams. Hell, half the men from Southie would push *Conor* off the Brooklyn Bridge to get his job. Moving to a new company in a new state, he'd face new challenges, different scenery, but his demons would dog him no matter where he went. As much as I loved summers at my mom's farmhouse, I couldn't trade life in New York for rural Vermont. What would we do there?

"Okay, Conor, okay. Give me some time to think this all through."

Instead I tried *not* to think about it as I put away the groceries, changed out of my work clothes, and held hands with Conor as we walked to the gym and then dinner at El Pollo. But another voice broke through, insisting: He needs you. He's much more important than any job or any city. As his lover, his best friend, his soul mate, I had to do what was right for him. This was what love was about. Wasn't it?

———◆———

Sunday. As usual, a late breakfast with lots of coffee at our favorite diner on Madison Avenue. Red leatherette booths, black-and-white subway tiles on the floor, our regular waitress who had a crush on Conor. An awkward silence between us. The choice: him or New York. I couldn't imagine leaving New York and *Seventeen*. I couldn't imagine a day of my life without Conor.

This was all happening unexpectedly fast.

Every woman's magazine warned against being one of those reckless women who gave up everything for a man and got nothing in return. In the back of my head—okay, maybe the front—I'd been wondering why Conor had not gotten me a ring in the months since we'd talked about getting married. I had to bring it up. I took a deep breath to get Conor's attention.

"Conor, you know how much I love you." I wrapped my hands around his on the cheap Formica tabletop. "You want me to go with you to Vermont, I'm there. But it's not right unless we are engaged—officially. It's been four months since you asked me to marry you. I don't need any proof of your feelings for me. But . . . I want to be engaged before we move. I want to get a ring and set a wedding date and tell our friends and family—before I give up my job and leave New York."

Now Conor seemed taken aback. He arched his blond eyebrows and stared into his coffee cup for a minute. He slipped his hands out from under mine and wrapped them around the chunky white ceramic mug. His tanned fingers looked like a teenage boy's. I imagined a gold wedding ring on his left hand. Our waitress rushed over with the pot as if her mission in life was to make sure Conor never, ever went without hot coffee.

"Okay," he said resolutely when the waitress left, giving me a big smile, exactly what I wanted and needed from him right then. As if his eyes were saying yes, of course, it was time to tell everyone what we had together. My stomach melted like butter on toast.

"Conor, I'm so glad you understand."

As long as I was with him—in Vermont, New York, or Timbuktu—nothing else mattered.

But then he looked away and took one of those quick inhales, like he was scared.

Did he understand?

"Yeah, babe, but the thing is, with leaving my job, we don't have the money for a nice ring now," he said, looking down at his hands and then up at me questioningly through the blond hair on his forehead.

Lack of money was why he hadn't given me a ring?

"Why don't I buy you a small ring now, one that we can upgrade later, you know, for a special anniversary when we have more money?"

My face suddenly felt made of Play-Doh. I tried to hide my dismay.

I didn't want a diamond as big as a doorknob. It was just— I wanted to be proud of my engagement ring. I wanted something that showed our commitment to each other. What if he went to the Wiz and came back with a diamond chip in a cheap gold setting? I could not wear something that ridiculed how I felt about him, that my family secretly made fun of, that made me feel embarrassed when I put it on.

"Let's think about it, Conor. This is really important."

And we left it at that.

------ ❖ ------

A week later I went into my boss's office and shut the door.

"Kathy, Conor just accepted a job in Vermont."

"Wow, good for him," she said, looking down, shuffling some papers on her desk.

"Kathy, I'm going with him."

She looked up, her hazel eyes suddenly huge.

"*What?*" She stared at me in disbelief. She lit a cigarette to cover her shock.

"Leslie, you love this job. You're really, really good at it," she said, blowing out a bluish stream of smoke. "What could you possibly do in Vermont?"

"Well, I think I'll try being a freelance writer," I explained.

"You're talented, Leslie, but you're young. You're the most promising new editor here. You have a lot to give readers. You worked hard to get this job. Why would you give that up?"

"Conor really needs a break, Kathy. He wants to leave New York and I need to go with him. We're going to get married in a year," I said.

"I know you love him, Leslie. But you can't sacrifice everything you've worked for, just for a man. This is Feminism 101. You know that already."

This made me smile. Conor was not just any man. He needed me. She didn't understand.

"I am completely in love with him. I'd do anything for him. You've been really good to me, Kathy. *Seventeen* has been good to me. But I have to do this."

"Okay, okay." She blew out smoke with a big sigh and shook her head. "We'll give you lots of freelance assignments."

"Conor, how about this?" I said a few days later, standing by the butcher-block pass-through. I was looking up the number for the Chinese place to order mushu pork and moo goo gai pan.

"I could take some money out of my trust fund to help buy the ring. My father always said the money should be used for something . . . permanent. Stitch—you know, the security guard at work—he has a childhood buddy who's a wholesale diamond dealer. I bet he'll give us a deal."

Sitting across from me on a stool, Conor held yet another white ceramic coffee mug in his hand. He shrugged and gave a small, noncommittal smile.

"Fine," he said. "Sounds like a plan."

On Tuesday during my lunch hour I walked ten blocks across Midtown to visit Marty Eiss, diamond merchant. In a small second-floor office, Stitch's "Ice Man" showed me loose diamonds like enormous mica chips glittering on black velvet. I picked one. The Ice Man pinched the small, sparkling stone in his callused, stubby fingers, held it up to the light and said he'd put it in a classic gold setting for me. A few days later I got the finished ring appraised, insured, and gave it to Conor to give to me the next weekend.

None of this struck me as strange. I didn't have to get engaged according to Emily Post. I wasn't my mother. I wasn't Winnie on the beach of a ritzy Caribbean island. Love was like a Persian rug: the backside of the tapestry with all the thread knots and loose ends was meant to be hidden. What mattered was the top side and the quality of the wool. Our love was real. The way Conor had proposed four months ago was incredibly romantic. It didn't matter that I'd paid for my own ring, that he hadn't lifted a finger to get it for me. I was a realist, unusually mature for my age. Right.

That night I called my family. I twirled the phone cord around my finger while I looked over at Conor's blond head as he watched the Knicks game.

First I dialed Mom's number.

"Mom, hi, it's Les. Guess what? Conor and I got engaged. And we're moving to Vermont."

"Oh," Mom said. She was probably in the kitchen, clutching the wall phone that was covered with years of newspaper-smudge fingerprints.

"Well, ah, congratulations."

Her voice had an edge to it, like inbred etiquette alone forced her to go through the proper response to a newly engaged daughter. Did she despise Conor because he had the guts to stand up to her drunken bullying? Did she hate it that I now had the strength to face her, too? *Too bad, Mom. Get used to it,* I felt like telling her.

After an awkward silence, I said good-bye, hung up the phone, and called Dad. What he said sounded even more weird.

"Oh, well, Leslie, that's great," he remarked. The Sunday night Redskins game blared in the background. "He seems like a nice enough fellow. I guess if it doesn't work out, you can always get married again."

What?

Then Dad laughed.

I figured he must be thinking about divorce and remarriage a lot these days. Both of my parents were so screwed up, obsessed with their own problems. I felt like the only mentally healthy adult in the family.

Fortunately Sylvia, whom I called on her bedroom phone upstairs from Dad's TV den, was thrilled. She screamed "All right!" like I'd just slam-dunked a basketball to win the big game. Then she dropped the phone on her foot and I could hear her howling in the background.

A fresh start in Vermont, near the old farm where Mom took us for our barefoot summers, seemed a way to give Conor part of my childhood. How could I say no to someone who had such a terrible life before meeting me? How could anyone else understand this? I wanted him to have everything now that he was with me. He would have no reason to leave me, ever. It felt wonderful and selfless—like nothing I'd ever felt before. I had so much love in me that I never considered what moving for love would mean, what I might leave behind that could never be found again.

Conor's new company was headquartered in the suburban, flat part of Vermont, about one and a half hours from Boston, sixty-five miles from my mother's farmhouse. Conor lived alone in a motel while I tied up loose ends in New York. I gave *Seventeen* four weeks' notice. I wrote a twelve-page memo outlining—in excruciating detail—each project I was working on. I arranged to have our furniture put in storage until we found a house to buy. Going through the motions of each day in New York without Conor felt like quitting heroin cold turkey. Our apartment felt unnervingly dismal, the city itself gray and colorless.

Columbus Day weekend, Conor drove down to New York in a rental car to get me. On Saturday morning we headed north together, giddy with our escape. We cheered as we crossed into Vermont, where the trees had faded to a dull russet, the finale of the fall foliage parade.

"Do you mind if we stop? I need to pee," I said just after we'd left Massachusetts. The parking lot at the next fast-food-bathroom-gas station complex was jammed with cars. Conor had to circle around to the back to find a space.

"I'll just come in to get a Coke and stretch my legs," he said.

I sat down with him for a minute in Arby's while he got his drink. It was close to two P.M. and the place felt like everyone was leaving just as we arrived, as if we were out of sync with the tourists visiting Vermont to see the trees. Under the dim lights, Arby's cheap plastic chairs and tables were a slippery black covered with ugly gray scuff marks, as if the employees had been playing soccer with them after-hours.

"Would you watch my purse while I go to the bathroom, hon?" I asked as I walked away from the table.

"Mmm . . . sure," Conor said midsip.

When I came back a few minutes later, my hands still wet from the bathroom dryer, he was hunched over the table, small pieces of crumpled colored paper spread out before him.

"Hey, what are you doing, Conor? That's all the junk that was in my purse. . . ."

He looked up, his eyes yellow. I stopped at the table's edge.

"I was looking for some Carmex in your bag . . . and I found all this stuff. What the hell are you doing keeping this crap? It's Guy all over again. Do you need to have someone else always waiting in the wings for you?"

"Conor, what are you talking about?"

I looked down in disbelief at the contents laid out on the Arby's table. Why would he go through my purse? What could he have found that would make him this angry?

I laughed. "Honey, I have nothing to hide. You can look in my purse anytime."

"What's this, then?" He shook a tattered piece of red cardboard at me furiously. His broad chest and muscular arms were coiled tautly like a lion poised to spring off a *National Geographic* cover. My brain flashed back to that fight in our New York apartment when he'd slammed the glass door to the balcony so hard I thought it would shatter.

"Oh, that." I laughed again, remembering how I got the torn red paper. "I never told you that story? Some guy working at the Bennington airport during Christmas last year— he must have been about fourteen—wrote me a love note on the claim tag on my skis. . . ."

Conor stared at me, furious. I sped up my explanation like a record on the wrong speed.

"It rained on Christmas—there was no snow—so I didn't

discover the note until three months later when I went to Vail. Isn't it cute? He says I'm the most beautiful girl he's ever seen, and that although he doesn't have his license yet I should call him the next time I come to town. He hadn't even started shaving. Oh, Conor, I kept it because it was such a sweet note . . . from a *boy*. . . ."

Conor was still not laughing. I started having trouble breathing.

"Don't keep shit like this if you want to be with me," he said coldly, not looking at me.

"What do you mean, if I want to be with you? I am with you. We're moving to Vermont together. We're engaged. Come on, Conor. I love you."

I waggled my hand to show him the ring, trying to get him to smile.

He held out the red luggage tag. "Throw it away if you want to get back in that car with me," he ordered.

"What? It's just a sweet note that always made me smile. I don't even know his name."

"Your choice."

I grabbed the tag and threw it into the black Arby's trash can a few steps away.

"Fine, Conor," I said, pissed. Who cared, it was just a note. I'd remember the boy, even without the red tag.

"And what's this?" he asked, smoothing out a piece of very crumpled, stained yellow legal paper.

"Oh, that must be . . ."

Holy shit. It was that piece of paper on which I wrote

"I am not a whore" over and over during our first night together in New York. I thought I'd put it in the kitchen trash. Instead I'd been carrying it around at the bottom of my purse since that horrible night.

"Are you fucking crazy?" he said, standing up, flapping the paper in front of my face. "Who are you writing to? What's your problem? You're a nutcase." He folded the paper and put it in the back pocket of his jeans.

"Give it back, Conor. That's mine," I pleaded through gritted teeth as he walked away.

An overweight woman taking her young daughter to the bathroom stared at us and then hurried by, grabbing the girl's hand. I couldn't bear the thought of Conor having that paper, like a dark piece of my soul, in his back pocket to pull out whenever he felt like it.

"Damn straight it's yours," he said, reaching into his pocket, crumpling the folded paper into a ball, and throwing it at me. I grabbed it in midair and ran back to the restroom. I flew through the door so fast, the handle smacked into the bathroom wall with a loud clang. The mother and daughter were washing their hands. The mother looked at me sideways, like I might be a kidnapper-cum-crack addict, and said softly to her daughter, "It's okay, honey. Let's just dry your hands and go back to Daddy."

I locked myself in the handicapped stall and sat on the oversized toilet tearing the sheet of paper into small pieces and flushing them away. What had set him off? He was so insecure and jealous—sometimes. If I'd shown him that

LESLIE MORGAN STEINER

boy's note another time, I swear, he'd have teased me about robbing the cradle. Or if I'd explained about the yellow paper, he'd have rocked me in his arms. How could someone I loved and who loved me be so cruel, so randomly?

I washed up and patted my face with wet paper towels. Amazingly, my reflection looked normal in the mirror. I headed out to the main entrance, not sure if Conor would still be there. He was waiting in the rental car, the engine running. I got in without saying anything. We drove away in silence.

After twenty minutes, Conor made a comment about how many evergreens there were—he called them "Christmas trees"—this far north. He called me "babe," smiling as if nothing had happened.

At first we lived in the Vermont Star, a motel on the side of a highway between two small towns. The carpet had cigarette burn marks I covered with a bathroom towel. The bedsheets were dingy gray.

I spent my days house-hunting, the local realtor my new best friend. Our plan was that when Conor got into Harvard Business School next year—of course he would with a year more of what the admission committee considered "real" work experience—we'd resell whatever house we bought for a good profit and move down to Cambridge. Compared to the mountainous lakes region of my childhood, the part of

130

Vermont near Conor's new company was far more suburban, and ironically (because it was much less nice by my standards) far more expensive, due to its relative proximity to Boston and to companies like Conor's.

I'd dreamed we'd live in an old farmhouse like Mom's on acres of hilly land. Instead I looked at worn-down tract homes in our price range until my fingernails felt dirty. Then one day I found a 1950s ranch house in a sprawling small town dominated by a Pizza Hut, a Mobil station, and post office. The split-level ranch in a quiet neighborhood of half-acre lots about a mile from the turnpike was the best house we could afford. We put the property in both our names, despite the fact that the down payment and money for repairs cleaned out my trust fund. Conor's company paid to have all our furniture moved from storage.

I never imagined I'd spend my dad's hard-earned money on something as modest and unexciting as this ranch house. But I was happy to do it. After his lifetime of rental apartments and eviction notices, I wanted Conor to have a home. With me in it.

The house was spacious and airy, with good flow from room to room, structurally sound, but run-down and badly in need of cosmetic improvements. The plan was I'd tackle the surface work, steaming off old wallpaper, repainting some walls, replacing the linoleum in the kitchen and bathroom.

I'd held a hammer only three or four times in my life, but how hard could cosmetic repairs be? We'd sell the place for a profit in a year or two to pay Conor's business school tuition. After Conor left for work each morning, I walked around the empty rooms feeling very smart to have come up with this easy, clever way to make money.

In New York, having no furniture was normal and kind of chic. Here it made me feel like we lived in a trailer park. We spent five hundred dollars at a neighbor's yard sale to buy a few pieces of used furniture. We put an old wicker couch in the living room and a laminated maple dining set in the kitchen. I set up a white table and cheap bookshelf in a small back bedroom, my new office.

The walls throughout the house were a dull green, probably the original paint job from the 1950s. They were covered with years of cigarette smoke. My finger left a clean streak through the accumulated grit on the walls. I'd learned from a neighbor that the previous owners had both died of lung disease.

I rented a fifty-five-pound metal steamer from the hardware store on the main street of our new town. Wearing old jeans and long-sleeved T-shirts, I attacked the cancer walls in the kitchen, hallway, and bathroom. I spent hours alone in the empty house dragging the steamer around, loosening smoke-stained wallpaper off the kitchen and living-room walls, holding the steamer nozzle like an elephant's trunk. The days felt like years. As the water ran down the walls it turned brown from smoke residue. By early each morning I was covered with dirty brown cigarette water thickened with old sticky wallpaper paste. After a week of steaming and scraping there were still scabs of wallpaper on the plaster walls.

The place looked and smelled worse than when I'd started.

One morning I pulled off my yellow gloves to read the paper and then moved on to the kitchen floor: scarred yellow linoleum which looked like an easier, more rewarding job than the walls. I tried mopping the floor clean. After two hours of scrubbing, down on my hands and knees, my fingers were deeply wrinkled and my body coated in sweat and lemon Mr. Clean. The green mop head was still coming up brown with fresh grime. I gave up.

After a quick lunch of Kraft Macaroni & Cheese out of a box (yum), I tackled the dirty, musty basement. The real-estate agent had called it "half-finished," which meant it had a cement floor and Sheetrocked walls. Old furniture and dozens of boxes of rusted tools, cracked jelly jars, and decrepit sewing supplies were piled in the corners. Some boxes were so heavy I had to drag them outside using Conor's leather weight-lifting belt. After two hours of dusty subterranean work, the afternoon broke into a glorious Indian summer day, turning the thick basement air into a golden yellow fog like Tinkerbell's fairy dust, only not all that magical.

I needed to open a window to let in the crisp fall air. To reach it I stood on tiptoe atop a small pipe sticking out of the furnace oil tank. Before I could reach the window latch, the pipe snapped under my feet like a dead branch.

Black oil gushed out the spout, splashing the walls, creeping black and silent toward the electrical outlets. Would the house blow up when the black river reached electricity? My feet looked like they were covered in gooey, slippery black socks. I pounded up the wooden basement stairs, leaving black sneaker prints on each step. There was no time to call Conor. I grabbed the kitchen phone and dialed the number of the oil company which—thank God—was posted on a magnet on our crappy refrigerator.

I screamed the fiasco to the nice lady who answered the phone for the oil company: "The oil is *gushing* out! You have to come *right now!*"

"Ma'am, go outside," she told me calmly, sounding as if she got calls like this every day. "I'm sending the truck."

In less than ten minutes the oil company truck came tearing down the street like an ambulance. Men in jumpsuits and high rubber boots burst out each door, leaving the truck parked crookedly in front of the house.

"In there!" I gestured wildly toward the basement door. The men rushed through the garage entrance to plug the oil tank. I wanted to laugh, cry, and scream.

The house did not blow up. With my oil-stained fingers I signed an estimate for six hundred dollars for the company to suck up all the oil and repair the tank. The money was all I had in my checking account.

I picked Conor up from work at five o'clock in my oil-stained clothes, smudges on my face, oil in my hair, my sneakers slipping on the clutch. In a rush I explained about the damage, the narrowly averted risks to me and the house, the money to clean the basement.

Conor did not find my idiocy funny.

"You smell like oil," he said with disgust, sitting in the passenger seat, staring at my oil-stained body. "You know, that smell reminds me of my stepfather."

New York seemed impossibly far away.

———◆———

November. The bright red and orange fall foliage was gone. So were the tourists on the highway. Each morning the withered grass in our neighborhood was covered with a layer of white frost.

"Hi, this is Leslie Morgan. I'm a freelance writer and I'm calling to suggest a story . . ."

Introducing myself to strangers had been easier when I'd been able to add "from *Seventeen* magazine" after my name. Now I had nothing to add.

The editor from *Vermont Sunday* interrupted me.

"Sure, I'm definitely interested," she said quickly, surprising me before I was through my spiel about my New York magazine experience and English degree from Harvard. "Why don't you send me the pitch in writing and I'll call you in a week or so?"

I hung up the phone and leaned back in my chair in the

sunny former bedroom off the kitchen. Outside the two windows grew an old gnarled lilac tree. The neighbor across the street told me it blossomed beautifully in the spring, that it would fill the house and street in front with sweet perfume. Conor rarely came in here.

In my first several weeks as a freelance writer, I'd found an editing job two days per week at an irreverent weekly magazine in Bennington, gotten a gig writing restaurant reviews for *New England Monthly,* and had been hired to write articles for local publications about pagan witches, singles facing Christmas in Vermont alone, and teen sexuality. Ironically, now that I lived in Vermont, New York magazine editors seemed to think I represented a Middle American perspective. In addition to *Seventeen,* editors from *Mademoiselle* and *Ms.* magazines had hired me to write for them. I was on track to make as much as I'd made at *Seventeen,* still about half what my Harvard classmates in consulting and investment banking made, but I was proud. Of course, I knew I wouldn't have checks to deposit for months—I used to put through freelance paperwork at *Seventeen* and I knew how erratically writers were paid.

When we moved to Vermont, Conor and I had set up a joint checking account at the local bank. Seeing both our names and the address of our new home in black ink on the rectangular paper slips had excited me at the time. Then Conor had, without explanation, left all bill-paying responsibilities to me. Every two weeks, he handed me his paycheck, which after taxes, utilities, and our mortgage payment, was astonishingly meager. The little checks I earned from editing barely covered groceries. The bigger ones from my national magazine articles came in sporadically with the glitter of late-arriving, beautifully wrapped Christmas presents.

I pushed my chair back and looked out once more at the twisted lilac. The skies had clouded up; the forecast was for our first snow. I thought of my view from the hallway at *Seventeen,* where I could see Manhattan skyscrapers looming out Kathy's window. I thought of her and the other editors putting together the January book without me. What if I called Kathy to ask for my old job back, and she said no, there wasn't a spot for me any longer?

Conor got dropped off around 5:30 P.M. by a coworker who lived three blocks away. He sat in the living room reading the paper while I fixed dinner. We ate in our bare kitchen with dark green walls, our elbows poking into the hard maple table because we didn't have place mats.

"I never told you this? Come on, I did so!" he grinned, his whole face lit up, fresh and smiling. He looked like a carefree man-boy, Oscar Wilde's Dorian Gray. Conor's unlined skin showed no trace of his childhood beatings at the hands of his stepfather or the emotional pain his mother had inflicted on him.

"Back in October, after my first day here, after I met Greg Mouse Brain, the other execs. It was that same day I had to wear those two left shoes."

Conor cracked up. I burst into laughter, too, remembering his first morning, how getting dressed for work at the motel he'd discovered he'd packed only a mismatched set of black wing tips. He had to limp around the office all day, trying to impress his new bosses with his intelligence and New York business acumen while wearing two left shoes.

"I hadn't called the movers. You hadn't left *Seventeen*. You had just started that mongo memo. So that night I called the apartment in New York to tell you not to quit, that I was coming back, that it was all a stupid mistake. How could we ever be happy in rural Vermont? My boss was such a bozo. I couldn't find a deli for lunch or a restaurant open after eight P.M.

"When I called you, the phone was busy. You know what happened? I fell asleep!"

Conor threw his head back. The walls of the empty house echoed with his laughs.

Damn you, Conor. I gave up *Seventeen*, my life in New York, for this? I looked at our half-eaten spaghetti dinner. I was a terrible cook. I looked around the half-renovated empty house. I could hear cars roaring down the turnpike every time I stepped outside. It would be at least three months before I got paid for the jobs I was working on now. We'd barely be able to cover the mortgage and my health insurance until then. Heavy snow was falling silently outside. I would have to shovel it before Conor could back the car out tomorrow.

Easy for him to laugh. Part of me felt as trapped as the miniskirts and high heels put away in my office closet.

"Funny, Conor. Real funny." I got up and started to clear

the dishes. I wanted to break one over his pretty blond head. Conor laughed again and went back to reading the paper.

--- ✦ ---

December. We needed a car. Conor's human resources department wouldn't stop hassling him about having a rental car for more than ten weeks, which they protested was longer than any new hire in company history. Conor wanted a stick-shift Volkswagen like the used one he'd driven in college. There was only one VW dealership in Vermont. We haggled with the dealer and then plunked down a down payment for a black Jetta with gray cloth interior—my first real car.

Of course, we didn't have the money to buy a new car. With Conor being employed fewer than three months and my erratic freelance income, we didn't qualify for a loan from the dealership.

I called my father at eight A.M. at the office, knowing he'd be there.

"Dad, hi, it's Les."

As usual, we tackled a safe subject—the weather. I could hear Dad stand up from his desk and walk to the picture window overlooking Pennsylvania Avenue and the White House.

"It's quite humid here. I played tennis this morning. If it keeps up like this, we'll play outside till Christmas!" he drawled, delighted, as if the good weather were a present just for him.

"It's snowing here again. You should see our front yard—the snow looks like a cement wall. But Dad, I'm actually calling to ask if Conor and I can borrow money to buy a car. It's not much—just for a Volkswagen. And I do mean a real loan, not a wink-wink-nod-nod parental disbursement."

He laughed.

"Okay, no problem. I'll charge interest, too. And you both have to sign a promissory note."

Ever the lawyer, my dad. But hey, it was his money, he more than earned it. A fair-and-square loan was the kind I wanted anyway.

"Sure, Dad. And thanks a lot. We both appreciate it."

"And, ah, don't forget about the oil, babe. I want you to protect my investment."

"Ha-ha-ha, Dad. See you later."

The last car I drove was a dinky secondhand white Chevette that all of us kids shared in high school. My father let me take the car to Cambridge my junior year. He did not tell me about checking the oil. I guess he thought intelligent beings were born knowing when to put oil in cars. One day as I was driving down Mass Ave. the engine blew up with a loud bang. I looked out my rearview mirror and saw a trail of neon green ooze lining the road behind us. I sold the car to the towing company for twenty-five dollars. My father retold this story with glee every single time I mentioned automobiles in his presence.

"So, babe, why don't you get some car mats for the car today?" Conor asked when I dropped him off at work a few days later. "I want to keep the car really clean."

I nodded automatically. Car mats—those rubber things? I'd already promised to get the car washed every week because Conor explained that the Vermont winter and heavy salt on the roads corroded a car's undercarriage. I was happy to comply with Conor's requests; he knew far more about cars than "I blew up a Chevette" Leslie. Fair enough.

Of course I bought the wrong car mats.

"Too cheap," he said, kicking them over with the toe of his leather loafer when I picked him up at work that afternoon and showed off my purchase. "Too thin. Too short."

So the next day I went back to the car parts store and bought the only extra-long, extra-thick car mats the clerk had in stock. I could not return the first forty-dollar set of four, so I threw them in the trunk.

"How could you buy *brown*? The car interior is gray and black." Conor made me sound like a moron when I picked him up at work that afternoon.

"I've had cheap things all my life," he explained, as if this were news to me. "Some things, you really have to spend money on and do right."

I looked at him, astonished, thinking of all the things, like my engagement ring, our house, that we couldn't spend the "right" money on.

"You're an asshole," I said. Righteous, 100 percent justified anger—strangely pleasurable—flooded my body. "I've driven around getting these goddamn car mats for you for the past two days. Who gives a shit! I've got better things to do than find you the perfect set of car mats! Go get them yourself!"

I unclipped my seat belt and stormed off into the maze of the employee parking lot. God knew where I was going.

I threw the keys to him. Well, okay, I threw the keys *at* him.

Then Conor did what he did best: He laughed. Dodging my throw, he caught the keys easily, and tossed them in the air a few times while looking at me. His blue eyes flashed and the corners of his mouth twisted up in small inverted Vs.

"Hey, Retard, I'll make a deal with you. Let's never, ever argue about car mats again, as long as we live. I love you."

He shook his head and laughed some more. My shoulder blades melted down my back, like I'd just gotten a Swedish massage.

"No more car mats, Retard, I promise."

He put his arms around me. He laughed again and kissed the top of my head.

Most Saturday mornings we headed two towns down the highway to our new weekend fort, a crowded breakfast-all-day place called Jake's. One day a Doberman sat tied with a red nylon leash outside the diner. Conor stopped to pet him. The dog looked up and whined with pleasure.

"Reminds me of Knight—you should have seen him," Conor said, shaking his head as we walked inside. I'd heard plenty about Knight, the big brown Doberman who'd been Conor's best friend during his twenties. "You'll love this—I remember once I had to leave him alone for twelve hours straight. When I got home and tried to open the front door, it wouldn't budge. I finally forced it open. Turned out Knight was blocking the door. I got in and saw a huge pile of dog poop on the floor that Knight was trying to cover with a towel he'd dragged in from the bathroom."

He laughed uproariously, overpowering the small, crowded diner. Conor was wearing a pale pink pin-striped shirt, perfectly ironed jeans, and expensive Italian loafers. Every other man at Jake's had on work boots. I doubt any other man in the diner—maybe all of Vermont—had a pink shirt in his closet.

"Another time, I'd been helping my stepfather on a job at the gas station—don't ask me why. I got home in the middle of the night, covered with gas and oil. I had to come in through a window because I'd left my key somewhere. I stuck my leg through first and Knight, without a single bark, swear to God, silently clamped his jaw around my shin. I yelled at him and he let go when he heard my voice—I guess the oil masked my scent."

Conor laughed again. Joy took over his entire face, his hands flew in the air, a tear appeared in the corner of his eye. Patty, our middle-aged waitress, was smiling at him from across the room, her arms folded over her blue apron.

I knew already that the story of the perfect dog had a

terrible ending. I remembered the first time I couldn't help ask, "So what happened to Knight?"

Conor had shaken his head and looked down like a kid without a costume on Halloween.

"Well, when Knight was five, I got into college. I couldn't take a dog. So I gave him to a former police officer who'd worked out at my gym. Had a big farm in western Mass. His kids thought Knight was like an older brother. He had the run of two hundred and fifty acres. I stopped by on my way home during spring break a year later and the farmer told me that Knight had been shot by deer hunters just after Christmas."

At the diner now, five years later, Conor sighed and leaned closer to me. He took my left hand, looked at my pretty engagement ring, and then glanced up at me.

"You'd love a Dobe, Leslie," he said softly. "They are such loyal dogs. You need someone to keep you company during the days that you're working at home."

I was not lonely working at home. We lived in *Vermont,* which last time I checked had a burglary rate one-hundredth that of Manhattan. For company my cat Criseyde would have been ideal, and she would have loved our rambling ranch house and the mice in the basement. It was useless to even bring up getting her back from my sister. Conor would just say he was still allergic, right?

"I love dogs, honey," I told him. "But I've always imagined a black Lab or a golden retriever. A Doberman, Conor? I am terrified of them. Everyone is. What will our friends and family, even our neighbors, think? I don't want to have a dog that everyone is afraid of."

A few days later, Conor found a local breeder and took me for an afternoon to check out puppies. The father had huge, peaceful eyes and an easy grace to his action. The mother, smaller and darker brown, wagged her stub tail so hard it blurred.

On our way out to the car, puppy smell still on our hands, we saw a double rainbow arched over a stubbly cornfield across the road from the breeder's red ranch house. The colors, especially the yellow and violet, gleamed against the gun-metal gray of the sky. A sign of something good coming our way.

"See, Leslie? I knew you'd love them. You should trust me," Conor teased on the drive home. It wasn't that I trusted or didn't trust him. It was that I had no idea how to oppose someone as determined as Conor.

There was only one male in the litter. Conor insisted that a male would bond better with me. The puppy had patient brown eyes, too large for his head, and a coat so silky it had a blue-black sheen. We brought Blue home the day before our first Christmas together, our present to each other. The three of us huddled alone in our empty living room, the center-piece a scrubby tree decorated with a strand of lights from the hardware store. We bought Blue more presents than we bought ourselves, although Conor did surprise me with a big square box from Filene's that contained an elegant wool coat with a raccoon collar. The coat was more expensive than anything I would have bought for myself. I loved it. At the same time I dreaded our January credit card bill.

Blue became my small, uncoordinated shadow. He slept on the floor of my office while I worked, chewing on a blanket he held between his huge paws as if it were an oversized baby bottle. I spent hours in the backyard teaching him to wear a collar and leash, to sit, lie down, come when called. I took him for long walks in the snow around our ugly little town, past old decrepit farms that had been neglected because the owners, whose families had cleared the fields stone by stone a century ago, couldn't afford repairs after paying property taxes. Blue waited on a blanket in the passenger seat when I visited clients or worked at the magazine in Bennington. Sometimes I even took him to New York when I had to meet with editors. After every absence, no matter how brief, he wagged his slinky body as if I were the savior he'd been awaiting his entire short life.

January. Conor and I stood in two feet of snow in our backyard with our hands on our hips, looking at the rotting wood of our back fence and the scraggly bushes that were taking over the yard, figuring out how to fight a half acre of Mother Nature. Suddenly a gruff voice called out over the wooden fence, "Don't be surprised if you hear my shotgun going off in the backyard. I'm after that goldurn groundhog there." A few seconds later, a white-whiskered seventy-year-old man who looked like a skinny Santa Claus lumbered around the fence and introduced himself as our next-door neighbor. He carried a long, heavy gun, which he pointed toward the snow-covered ground. Red flannel long underwear peeked out under his belt. He hitched up his pants and stuck out his free hand.

"A shotgun?" I asked after we'd introduced ourselves. "For the backyard?"

"Sure, sure," Santa said, looking at me like a young 'un who didn't know any better. "Almost all of the neighbors 'round here have guns. Two retired police chiefs down the street. Guarantee ya they got more 'an one."

He gestured in the neighbors' direction with the long black nose of his gun.

"Aya, it was nice meeting you folks. Don't be scared if you hear that crack. Hope I get him this winta'." And he trudged back to his side of the fence.

I raised my eyebrows at Conor. "Whew!" I said quietly so as not to offend our gun-toting neighbor. "Can you believe that? He's got a gun! Do you think he's right that lots of people here own guns?"

"Well, it should be that way, Leslie," Conor said resolutely, almost excitedly, as if he'd been waiting to argue this new opinion. "It's cold as hell out here. Let's go inside." He turned toward the house. I mechanically followed him, stunned by this strange new reality: guns in our backyard.

"Everyone should have a gun if they want to protect

themselves," he said over his shoulder. "That's what this country is about. Guns are easy to buy here. You gotta love Vermont. My company even has a gun range for employees to use."

"What?" I looked at him like he was a two-headed snake. In New York, company perks were health clubs and taxi rides home if you stayed later than eight P.M.

"I actually have been thinking we should get one, too. I know how to shoot. . . ."

He did?

"I've always wanted to be able to practice on a regular basis. It would be good for you, too, so that you could protect yourself when I'm not around, all those days you spend alone in the house."

I looked at him sideways. He was holding onto the railing of the back porch, stomping his snowy sneakers on the wooden steps.

"Conor, I thought we moved here so you could escape the bullets. Why would you want to bring them into our life?"

Now he looked at me like I was deranged.

"Retard, I don't want some criminal to come in here and take away everything that matters to us, to humiliate and degrade us. You should have protection when you're home alone. Just you wait, you'll see that I'm right."

I was too surprised to say anything. God, I hoped he was not serious.

Turns out he was. On Saturday I stayed home to finish

an article for *Seventeen* while Conor drove to the Brattle-
boro Trading Post and bought not one but two guns. Just
like that. He laid out a Colt .45 and something called a
Glock on our kitchen table, complete with four cardboard
boxes of bullets, at least ten little brushes and several plastic bottles of cleaning fluid and oil and special chamois
cloths. He also had an application to join the National Rifle
Association.

Saturday night we stayed in for dinner. The kitchen table
smelled like the lubricating oil from the guns and Conor's
fingernails were rimmed with black grease.

"Those bullets I got?" he said, his mouth full of leafy let-
tuce. "Hollow points. They explode upon impact with flesh.
And I think I should probably get a shotgun, too, next time I
go to the Trading Post."

Hollow-point bullets? A shotgun?

"How much did those guns cost, Conor?"

Maybe logic about our finances would get through to
him. We had no money for *guns*.

"It's a small price to pay for your safety, babe."

He had no idea how disturbing this topic was to me; or
did he?

"If you make guns criminal, only criminals will have
guns." He said this like he thought it up himself. Had he forgotten I knew how to read? This pithy NRA slogan was plastered all over the yellow application form he'd asked me to
sign so we could get the family discount.

I got up from the table, unable to say anything more.

This was not a conversation I had ever imagined having with anyone in my life.

Conor never bought a shotgun, fortunately. But he put the Colt .45 under his pillow and the Glock into the car's glove compartment behind the owner's manual. Often he'd stuff it into his pocket when we went to breakfast at Jake's or walked around the neighborhood at night. When I was fluffing our pillows in the mornings after he left for work, sometimes I'd come upon the .45 like a scorpion in our bed. Who was this man I loved?

— — —❖— — —

March. As we sometimes did on weekend mornings, one cold, overcast day we drove to Boston to escape the paralyzing quiet of Vermont winter weekends. On the way down, bundled in my new wool coat, I drove while Conor sipped his coffee in the passenger seat, the car filled with the blooming voices of Anita Baker and Sade. Blue sat in back with his head poking between us.

I nosed the car into one of the tiny, crooked spaces in Cambridge that I'd discovered as an undergrad when I knew every brick in Harvard Square. First we walked across the cobblestones to Memorial Church, where in June Conor and I would be married. We tied Blue's leash to the railing at the bottom of the steps.

Conor and I walked up the smooth wide stairs, between four elegant white columns into the empty one-room brick building. The narrow crimson carpet led to a mahogany altar. In three months I would be on my father's arm walking past guests sitting in the simple wood pews underneath the creamy white walls inlaid with the names of graduates who died in World War II.

The last time I had sat in this church was during graduation two years before. All the English majors had gathered here, our black gowns heavy and awkward, the air in the Yard thick as fog with the pride and nostalgia of the thousands of parents, including my own, assembled to witness our coronation. A few weeks later, I'd moved to New York and *Seventeen*.

So much had happened in two years.

At the altar, Conor put his palms on my shoulders and kissed me softly on the lips. "I love you, babe," he whispered. "Thanks for loving me so much." He rested his forehead on mine. The altar became the world all around, Conor at the center.

We crossed the snowy, wind-whipped Yard arm in arm, the raccoon fur of the coat warm on my chin. Conor held Blue's leash. We walked to the Fogg Art Museum, where our wedding reception would be held in the inner courtyard. I took Conor through the Fogg's collection, pointing out my favorite Van Gogh self-portrait with green and yellow insanity swirls around his head; a delicate Degas dancer; a florid nymph by Titian. I showed him where the florist would place the bouquets, where the photographer wanted us to pose, the special changing rooms set aside for us.

"It's all gonna look great, babe," he said, looking around in awe. "You're gonna make us a beautiful wedding."

Although today was freezing, raw and gray, the early June weather would be sunny, I knew. I had luck in making everything look perfect on the outside. My graduation from high school was on a cloudless blue day. College, too. Every birthday. All perfect days. No one had ever told me that rain on your wedding day was supposed to mean good luck.

After leaving the Fogg we walked the crowded streets of Cambridge arm in arm, Blue trailing behind us. I kept my eye out for Winnie. Their HBS dorm was right across the Charles River. I hadn't called her much lately because Conor became enraged every time I did. He'd rant for an hour about Harvard's half-wit quota that made it easy for the richie-rich boys to get in instead of him. To make matters even worse, Winnie had taken a part-time job working in the HBS admissions office, which Conor took as an insult designed just to gall him. But I would have loved to run into Winnie, to see her smile, to hear her use a few inappropriate swear words in telling us about her life as an HBS spouse.

Conor, Blue, and I walked along Brattle Street as it curved through Harvard Square, window-shopping, passing the Brattle Theatre, which had been a church until my father and a classmate converted it to a movie theater in the late fifties and Dad hired Mom to be the candy girl. The loony, dynamic energy of Cambridge was a drug compared to the isolation of the empty ranch house with green cancer walls in snow-covered Vermont.

We ended up at the Coffee Connection overlooking bustling Mt. Auburn Street. We spent two hours drinking strong black coffee and silently reading the papers, our legs just touching, Blue asleep under my chair. We spent the rest of our cash on coffee beans to take home—one of our few luxuries.

Conor put down *The Boston Globe*—*The Glob,* Mom always called it.

"So, where should we go for dinner? The North End?"

We were only a few miles from Southie but going to see Conor's family was out of the question. We'd been there once, for a brief, horrifying visit to Chickie and Wade's essentially unfurnished apartment near the Expressway. I'd tried not to stare at the bare rooms, more like a cheap motel than a home. It was true, what Conor had said that day back in my Chelsea apartment so long ago—there was not one book, magazine, or newspaper in the entire place. Nor much of anything else, nothing on the walls, no personal knick-knacks or framed pictures of family, nothing but a television set on the cardboard box it came in. Wade and Chickie kept the TV on the whole time we were there. Conor said one day he'd take me by his grandparents' old apartment, show me his former gym, his favorite haunts when it didn't make him too angry to go back.

"Honey, we really should just go home," I told him.

I pictured the latest statements from our credit cards. Each balance was at or above the limit.

Conor gave me a cold stare.

"We literally cannot afford to go out to dinner tonight, hon," I tried again. I wanted to stay here, too. At times I wanted never to go back to Vermont and the house and our life there.

"Fine. Let's go then," he said brusquely, childishly, throwing his empty coffee cup into the trash. As if our credit card balances were my fault. Blue jumped up, shook his body to wake himself, and looked in puzzlement from me to Conor as if trying to figure out what the problem was here.

Conor took the wheel as we drove home. The roads going north in the early evening were empty. Southbound, they were crowded—everyone was going in the opposite direction, toward Boston, to dinner, the movies, a hockey game. Conor gripped the steering wheel with both hands, staring straight ahead. His ominous silence ate away at me more than words could ever have.

"Conor, God, it's not my fault."

He didn't say anything, didn't even look at me.

"We just don't have the money."

Again, nothing.

"I'm just trying to be responsible. We need cash for the mortgage, the car insurance, my health plan. American Express is going to cancel my card if I miss any more payments."

Conor still did not respond. He stared straight ahead at the empty road.

I leaned into the gray cloth seat and looked out the passenger window. Old farms lined the quiet country roads. The sky was black overhead, carpeted with brilliant white stars. An ideal setting for the bullets to go over Conor's head. And mine.

"So who gets the car this Thursday night?" I asked, trying to change the subject. "You've got your finance class, right? And I have a puppy obedience class with Blue."

Conor barely glanced at me. Staring straight ahead, face expressionless, he shifted gears and the car decelerated smoothly down a long hill past an abandoned dairy farm, the white fence paint peeling off in long jagged strips.

Suddenly he spoke.

"I don't think I can marry you."

I stared at him, stunned.

He sounded defensive. He sounded scared. Worst of all, he sounded honest.

I held my breath. He couldn't marry *me*?

Conor kept driving, his strong hands steady on the wheel, his blond hair glinting in the light thrown off by the occasional street lamp. The white painted lines at the side of the road slipped by as I looked out the window, away from Conor's face. He said nothing.

After a few moments, I crawled into the backseat to get as far from him as I could. I wrapped my coat around myself, hugging Blue's warm body. How would I tell my family, my *Seventeen* coworkers, my friends, that he'd left me after I'd done so much for him? I started to cry quietly. Blue licked the tears off my face for a few minutes. Then he gave up and went to sleep in my arms. Crying only made me feel more frantic and more desperate. I couldn't stop.

By the time we pulled into our subterranean garage, my throat ached and my face was swollen and cracked from the salt in my tears. Conor pulled in carefully and then got out and opened the back door. He stuck his head in.

"Come on, baby, stop crying. It's okay. I love you."

I heaved a huge sigh of relief, cleansed, saved. Forgiven—but for what, I didn't know. I smiled as I looked up at him. I let him help me get inside. All that mattered was being close to him. I never brought up what he'd said, or what it meant. Conor didn't, either.

———❖———

Tuesday after Memorial Day weekend. Five days to go. Mom's thirty-year-old wedding dress lay folded in tissue paper in its original Saks Fifth Avenue box, perched atop Frankie's dresser in our bedroom. I'd found a six-foot-two German seamstress named Brunhilde—she looked uncannily like the hungry witch from *Hansel and Gretel*—to hand-sew intricate lace flowers into the original neckline and train. The caterer, the florist, the photographer all waited impatiently like shoppers outside Bloomingdale's art deco doors the morning of the summer white sale, except that my marriage to Conor was the white sale.

The early-morning sun slanted into my office, a yellow streak on Blue lying on the carpet. On my cheap wooden desk sat a slim, modern laptop computer, more expensive than we could afford. UPS had delivered it the day before.

"I need a laptop," Conor had insisted six weeks earlier. "For my financial management class. A nice laptop is gonna show people at work that I'm serious."

"But Conor, we can't afford it. We can't even afford a new washing machine. We don't buy more than three dollars of gas at a time."

"Come on, honey. Can't you just charge it to your AmEx and expense it as part of your writing business?"

I couldn't say no to Conor. So there I was in my nightgown, trying to get the new machine to work. I had to finish one last article before the wedding—for once, *Vermont Sunday* had agreed to pay me on the spot when I turned in the article. We needed the cash for the honeymoon. Two rooms away I heard the spray of water that meant Conor was getting into the shower.

This small thin machine seemed overwhelmingly complicated. What if I couldn't get the computer to work? What if I couldn't finish the article? How would we eat on our honeymoon?

To break the spell of my own panic, I stood up and slammed my open hand on the table.

"Shit! You stupid machine!" I yelled just after the noise of Conor's shower stopped.

Suddenly the house felt unexpectedly quiet. Conor burst into my office dripping wet, wrapping a blue towel around his waist. Hunched over the computer, I froze.

He grabbed my shoulder and turned my body to face his. His skin was stretched tight across his cheeks.

My heart seized as if I'd stumbled upon a snake on the path behind our house. I saw the pink blur of his hand as he slapped me hard across my face. My skin stung as my teeth cut through the soft, wet flesh of my mouth. My head jerked back. Conor grabbed my throat, pushed me up against the wall, and tightened his grip. He shook my whole body back and forth.

"Don't. Scream. Like. That," he spit through clenched teeth. With every word my head hit the office wall, my neck bending like a Gumby doll.

I couldn't take my eyes off his face. I could smell his shaving cream but I could not breathe.

"My mother screams like that," he said. "Don't ever scream like that again," he said as if begging me. He pushed me to the floor and left the room. The front of my flannel nightgown was wet from his body.

I stayed on the cold wooden floor until I heard Conor go down the steps to the garage. The car engine rumbled. The garage door clattered open. The tires squeaked on the cement as he backed the Volkswagen out to go to his office.

Once I knew he'd gone, I took the yellow pages off my office bookshelf and looked up an 800 number for an abuse hotline, the kind of advice I'd offer in a sidebar for *Seven-*

teen. Wasn't this what you're supposed to do if your husband hit you? Your fiancé who was going to be your husband
in five days? If any man hit you?

I was shaking from my fingertips to the pit of my stomach, feeling as if I were going to throw up. I dialed the 800
number from my office. Hot, hard tears like flax seeds sprang
from my eyes as I gripped the phone and stared out the window at the lilac tree that smelled so sickly sweet.

What would I say when a voice answered? That it was
7:30 A.M., way too early for this to have happened? That
Conor was the only man I'd ever loved this deeply? That he
had driven off in our only car? That if it came to a choice between him or me I didn't know who I'd choose? That I might
have bruises on my wedding day? That I was sure he was
very sorry?

Did I tell the voice that although I was scared, I was not
surprised?

The line was busy.

I let out a breath that I did not know I was holding. I
walked through the house to make sure Conor was really gone.
The house was quiet. I would take a shower to calm down and
then call again.

I drank my coffee. I dressed and walked to the local library
to finish the article on the public computer. I didn't call the
hotline again.

I didn't call Conor either and I didn't answer the phone
when it rang that afternoon. That was my big punishment
for him. I left the house purposefully dark when he was due

home, to scare him into thinking I was halfway to Dad's house in Washington. Because no one hit me, ever, right?

In reality I was sitting in my office with my small lamp on, hunched over my desk, proofreading the article with my face five inches from the paper and my pen clutched tight in my right hand.

I pretended I didn't hear the Volkswagen pull in around six P.M. He came into my office holding the car keys, head down. I could smell fear on him, panic that I was going to vilify him for what he'd done or announce I'd canceled the wedding.

The dread on Conor's face offered a spider's thread of hope. If he were afraid, he'd never attack me again, right? I could leave anytime. And anyway, he just grabbed my throat. He couldn't have *hit* me. We were getting married.

Three days later, when my family and our wedding guests started arriving, the ten small reddish brown bruises around my neck were so faint no one noticed them.

As our wedding day accelerated toward us, it was easier than you'd think to avoid what had happened. Pulling off a flawless wedding for one hundred guests provided constant distractions—last-minute questions from the caterer, photographer, bridal party, minister, out-of-town guests who called to express their trepidation about Cambridge's notorious

maze of one-way streets and demonic drivers, the mainte-
nance man at the church, the concierge at the hotel.

Yellow Post-it notes littered the kitchen like autumn
leaves. Winnie: Hold bouquet during ceremony. Sylvia: Needs
Bible for reading. Photographer: No pictures of Mom and
Dad together! Aunt Nellie: Happy to wear lucky penny inside my right shoe. Minister Preston: Take "obey" out of the
vows.

The gravitational force created by friends, family, and
near-strangers, including myself, who expected me to get
married seemed nonnegotiable. The fact that it was me marrying Conor, the man I loved who'd just choked me and
bashed my head into a wall—in other words, the rest of my
life that was at stake—seemed basically irrelevant.

What seemed far more pressing was that every detail
fall into place. A fairy-tale wedding seemed like insurance
against a turbulent marriage. There was no space for enjoy-
ment or regret, reflection or reconsideration. It all happened
too fast.

Conor did not apologize. Not a word to acknowledge
what he'd done. I never caught him looking surreptitiously
at the bruises on my neck. He carried himself exactly as if
he'd never attacked me, never held his hands around my
neck, never thrown me down onto the floor like an old rake.

My side of the family settled into the Embassy Suites on
Storrow Drive, across the Charles River from the blue,
green, and red spires of the Harvard River Houses. Conor's

family lived close enough that no one needed a hotel, fortunately, sparing Conor their proximity. The rehearsal dinner
was held at the Union Oyster House. Afterward, amid the
Friday night hustle of Fanueil Hall, Dad and I waited for
taxis to get the guests back to the hotel, awkwardly saying
good night to Conor's mother, Wade, and his stepsisters and
brothers.

"Dad, could we have breakfast tomorrow, maybe around
eight?" I suddenly asked him, my throat swelling, my stomach feeling liked I'd swallowed a tennis racquet. I wanted an
hour just with my father. Maybe I'd tell him what Conor had
done to me, if I had enough guts.

"Sure, babe," he said, smiling, a bit tipsy from his Old
Turkey bourbon, throwing his arm around my waist. "What
a perfectly lovely idea."

I felt like weeping with relief.

Conor and I had decided to honor the tradition of the
groom not seeing the bride until the wedding (or until the wedding photos, at least), so I didn't see Conor again that night.
Back at the hotel, I went up to Sylvia's room. She was already
asleep, wearing her basketball shorts and a Harvard T-shirt,
holding the old stuffed elephant she'd gotten for Christmas
when she was six. Conor crashed with his best man, Jed, his
partner from the kung fu schools in Southie, in the honeymoon suite.

Our wedding day dawned clear and sunny, a perfect June
morning. I slipped out of my soft hotel bed and took a quick
run along the Charles River, pounding the same paths I

learned to love in college. The early-morning sky was a powder-blue wash, the bright white sun just beginning to warm the cool, sweet-smelling air. I ran along the twisting dirt trail that skirted the slow-moving, polluted Charles. I thought about what I'd say to Dad. I pictured him telling me I couldn't possibly marry Conor; I imagined him making an announcement on the church steps while I hid in my sister's hotel room crying, devastated but sure it was the right thing to call everything off.

Shaking with adrenaline, I showered and changed quietly, tiptoeing while Sylvia slept. The lobby and restaurant were nearly empty when I went down just before eight. I waited by a window table at the hotel restaurant for nearly forty minutes. I couldn't admit that Dad had forgotten, or simply wasn't coming. A couple of times, checking my watch, I cried a few tears surreptitiously. Now I *needed* to tell him—but how would I find the time, the place, the courage?

On my way out to the lobby to call around, hoping maybe there was another restaurant where he just might be waiting, I spotted him sitting at a table by the buffet with some relatives, the remains of his breakfast in front of him, his thinning hair still wet from the shower. He looked up, his gray eyes like small manholes. He did not say, "Oh, there you are, I was looking for you." He barely acknowledged me. I didn't know what to do. Suddenly I couldn't imagine telling him or anyone what Conor had done to me; the attack didn't seem real, even to me. So I sat down and ate breakfast and pretended everything was normal.

Conor and I and the wedding party met the photographer at Memorial Church two hours before the ceremony was slated to begin. Harvard Yard was peaceful and quiet, the maniacal Cambridge traffic shut out by the high brick walls separating the Yard from the Square. I felt like I was behind bulletproof glass in a New York taxicab. The afternoon sun dappled the lawn outside the church across from Widener Library, where I'd spent many nights in a tiny cubicle surrounded by darkened stacks writing my thesis about twentieth-century vanguards like Edith Wharton, Virginia Woolf, and Margaret Drabble, writers who labored to capture the exquisite splitting-of-self compromises women face.

The wedding photographer looked like Georgia O'Keeffe, a tall, thin woman with a big toothy smile and a graying bun of hair. An artist who couldn't take a cheesy wedding picture if she tried. She arranged the dress, my hair, my flowers, my flowing ivory train, Conor and me in perfect symmetry.

"Okay! I've got enough. Beautiful shots!" she announced thirty minutes before the ceremony was supposed to begin.

I went inside the church to fix my makeup in the tiny upstairs bathroom. After about ten minutes, Winnie and Sylvia came to tell me that Conor had disappeared. Sylvia looked to me, uncertain, scared like she was on the nights Mom was reeking by five P.M. and getting to soccer practice meant risking her life with Mom behind the wheel.

"Every groom is late, last-minute cold feet, right?" I joked. The three of us made a face at our reflections in the full-length bathroom mirror. The absence of a groom on your wedding day had to be just a minor detail.

A quiet voice inside said maybe *this* was the way out. Maybe Conor wanted to dodge the wedding as badly as I did. Perhaps if I hid in the bathroom, this wedding would vanish like a cloud wisp on a summer afternoon. From the tiny rectangular bathroom window, I looked out on my guests parading up the church steps in colorful wedding attire, decorating the white stone entrance like flower petals. To make myself stop shaking, I imagined they'd come to honor someone else's union.

Mom came in to tell us that Dad had gone off, too. Fifteen minutes after the ceremony was supposed to begin, I saw my father come up the steps, his face down. From my perch I saw his back bent over, his slightly pigeon-pointed toes, reminders of our Cherokee ancestors. Behind him walked Conor and Jed in their rented tuxedos and slicked-down hair. Conor looked as numb as I felt and he did not see me peering out the window as he passed below.

Mom returned to confirm that Conor was now waiting at the church altar.

"Look up," she said, giving me one final hair and lipstick check. She looked beautiful in her beaded blue mother-of-the-bride dress. A mother anyone would be proud to have.

"Mom?" I asked, hoping she could sense my distress through the same kind of mother-daughter osmosis that had prompted her, from four hundred miles away, to pick up the phone the night my junior year when I'd gotten food poisoning so severe I'd been hospitalized. She'd also known something was wrong the afternoon I'd found out my creative writing thesis had been rejected by the English Department's stuffy, all-male review committee. These moments alone with her were my final toehold. But I couldn't begin to say any of that.

Instead I asked, "Do you have any last-minute advice?" My voice sounded like I was begging.

"Don't smile too much as you walk down the aisle," she said, looking away.

We were married. The ceremony took twenty-five minutes. It felt like twenty-five seconds.

You could hear the harp chords floating out from the Fogg courtyard like a princess's herald. The tablecloths were fuchsia, the flowers a medley of pink, white, blue, and purple, the champagne endless, the menu graced by delicate asparagus, salmon rounds, puff pastry shells. Our chocolate wedding cake would have held its own on a *Gourmet* magazine cover. My stomach felt like a locked safe. I didn't have time to eat or go to the bathroom and I hardly talked to Conor. The reception felt like a video where someone had pressed the fast-forward button.

There was a moment when time paused. The photographer, inspired by the dramatic setting of the Fogg's Italian Renaissance architecture, asked me to pose on the edge of the second-story balcony overlooking the courtyard below. Behind me, the marble walls were lined with paintings by

Titian, Ingres, and Cabanel, dark oils of frolicking nymphs and depictions of Venus in heavy gilt frames, celebrating the glory days before Manet's shocking *Olympia* and the explosion of Impressionism. As I sat on the wall feeling like Juliet, my ivory train fluttered almost ten feet below me into the courtyard space. The guests gathered to watch the photo arrangement. They were silent, clutching their drinks as they looked up at me, their eyes like matched sets of dark coins. Conor was not among them. The photographer told me not to smile, but to imagine I was Mona Lisa looking into the distance, into the future. Half a smile was probably all I could muster anyway. After a dozen clicks, the photographer helped me climb down. "This will be the one," she said, tapping her camera. "The perfect shot."

Later, after the photos and toasts and first dance and cutting the cake were all over—beautiful, everything—all I could fathom was that my feet were killing me and I needed to pee badly. I came out of the bathroom trailing my long wedding train to find the courtyard half empty. Many guests had left without saying good-bye. Why would anyone leave such a beautiful reception so early?

Mom followed me upstairs to the changing room where my green silk "traveling suit" was laid out. She unbuttoned the back of my—and her—wedding gown nimbly. Her dexterity made me realize she wasn't even tipsy. It'd been years, more than a decade, since I'd spent an evening with Mom where she was so tense that she'd refrained from getting drunk. Was every single person at the wedding, including me and Conor and my mother, pretending this marriage was not a horrendous mistake?

"I'll take it now—that'll be easier," Mom said. From under a couch she took out the cardboard Saks Fifth Avenue box. She must have hidden it there earlier in the day, planning to take back my wedding gown even before I'd put it on. She covered the dress, still warm from my body, with tissue paper. She carefully closed the corners of the old box like a tomb.

Sylvia and I filled a taxi with flowers from the reception and we drove back to the hotel together, squeezed in the backseat with pink and yellow roses on our laps. Conor could not fit with us, so he left with Jed. I hugged Sylvia and headed up to the honeymoon suite carrying the biggest vase. The hallway was quiet and empty. I set down the flowers and slipped the keycard in the door, my hand shaky, not knowing what to expect.

Inside, Conor and Jed were sitting under the covers in the massive king-size bed, waiting for me. They had their arms around each other and huge grins on their faces. Jed stank of whiskey. He was wearing one of my long-sleeved flannel nightgowns, a Lanz sprigged with pink rosebuds, white lace and pearl buttons against his black chest hairs. He had my wedding veil on, too.

Conor sat next to Jed smoking a cigar, his broad chest stretching the ruffled front of his rented tuxedo shirt. As I took in the tableau, they burst into guffaws like teenage boys in high-school French class. Laughing so hard the huge bed shook, Conor finally told me the story of why he was late to the ceremony.

"This guy"—he shot Jed a hard glance and burst into fresh laughter—"talked me into going to a bar across the street from the church. We had no idea what time it was. Don't know how your dad found us," Conor explained in the awed tone he always used when talking about my father. "Somehow he did. He sat down at the bar, chatted us up, said he didn't really have time for a drink because the wedding was about to start. So we went back with him."

"Ah, Les, you looked like an angel up there," Jed said, smiling like I was his little sister.

"Yeah, babe. You are the best. Come here," Conor chimed in. My body uncoiled. He slipped his arm around my waist and kissed me. "We're married." He had the same touch of awe in his voice.

He and Jed looked at each other and started laughing again. I changed into a pair of peach silk pajamas, a gift from Nellie. We bounced on the bed and took pictures of each other in my veil. Jed drank every miniature whiskey in our minibar, breaking the tiny gold seals with his large workman's hands, carefully lining up the empties on top of the burled wood TV console. They told me stories about Southie that made me laugh until the corners of the sheets were wet with my tears and stained with black streaks of my mascara.

At midnight Conor and I kicked Jed out and fell into bed. We didn't make love. It was a glorious relief just to forget the events of the day and the week, to sink into the thick white hotel pillows and fall asleep with Conor's arms and body wrapped around me, warm and soft as a sheepskin coat.

—◦—◦❖◦—◦—

People complain—with enthusiasm—about the stress and expense and family tantrums that make up the drama of most weddings. But admit to an awful *honeymoon*? It'd be easier to open up the PA system at the local Wal-Mart and announce that your husband gave you herpes.

More than anything, Conor and I required a *cheap* honeymoon. In April, sitting at my white desk, I'd opened a distinctly unfriendly letter from the mortgage company about our myriad late payments. My American Express card had been canceled in May, via a form letter ordering me to cut up and return my card. I still kept the little green rectangle in my purse, a talisman from my New York life. But I knew it was useless. Our dire daily cash flow meant I could only take out twenty to forty dollars from an ATM at once, hardly enough to get traveler's checks for a romantic sojourn to Italy. I'd scoured my brain, scanning for affordable places that would still be marginally romantic.

One day a few weeks before the wedding, as I drove to pick up Conor from work, I'd thought of Martha's Vineyard, the secluded island off the Massachusetts coast. We could drive there, and take our car on the ferry. We'd continue the twenty-dollar-per-day local cash machine habit instead of taking out lumps of cash in advance. We'd rent a cottage instead of an expensive hotel room. We could still make it sound and hopefully feel like a real honeymoon.

Once, with Winnie and her family, I'd come to the tiny pile of rubble at the tail end of the massive glacier that slid down from Canada. As a twelve-year-old, I took my first flight alone in a puddle jumper, up and away from the tiny Vermont airport near our cluttered, noisy farmhouse to Winnie's family's enormous Victorian estate, complete with tennis court, a pond with an island, a private beach, and a little bakery at the end of the winding, tree-lined driveway. Winnie and I and her babysitter stayed in our own guest house, listening to "Hot Child in the City" on her babysitter's boom box, French braiding each other's hair, talking about boys from school until we fell asleep in our sleeping bags. Winnie's family sold the estate when we were thirteen. She'd never been back. But as a college student, I took a bus from Boston and then the ferry to the Vineyard by myself, to spend a day visiting the island, going to the bakery, the private beach next door to her old house, standing at the bottom of the winding driveway to catch a glimpse of the house's peaked shingle roof above the trees.

Conor had never been to Martha's Vineyard, despite living his entire life less than three hours away. The treeless streets and gray concrete of Southie might as well have been two million miles from the Vineyard's private white beaches and Victorian "cottages." Conor, who had never said a word about our honeymoon or how we'd pay for it, agreed Martha's Vineyard would be fine.

The morning after our wedding, we packed up the Volkswagen in the driveway of the hotel on Storrow Drive, said our good-byes to our families, and drove south along Route 93. We risked missing the ferry due to Conor's insistence that we stop at multiple fruit stands along the way in search of great corn and tomatoes.

"Would you just relax and let me enjoy my own honeymoon?" he yelled from the passenger seat, his eyes hidden behind his dark sunglasses. "What is wrong with you? You're a bundle of nerves, you're killing me. I want to eat lunch at a real restaurant. We're passing all these great fruit stands. Chill out!"

"Conor," I said sternly, feeling like a schoolmarm, taking one hand off the wheel to point my finger at him. "I had to make these ferry reservations five weeks ago. You don't understand the way it works. If we miss our ferry to Martha's Vineyard in the peak summer times, we won't get there. We'll be spending our honeymoon by the side of the road."

"Yeah." Conor spoke like a rebellious ten-year-old determined not to take me seriously. He reached for the radio tuner.

I grabbed his hand, hard.

"Look, fuck you, *buddy,* for both your insults: that I don't know what I'm talking about, and that I'm a nag for trying to rush you. I planned every minute of this honeymoon and I'm not going to let you screw it up."

I couldn't see his eyes behind his sunglasses. He turned and looked out the window for the rest of the drive.

We arrived at Woods Hole three minutes before our ferry left and three seconds before I duct-taped Conor's mouth. But on the rollicking ferry ride across the ocean, the outline of the Cape Cod coast as well as the fight in the car receded in the background. Conor took my hand as we stood together at the front of the ferry. The salty wind, warm and fresh, blew our clothes and hair. The Vineyard came into view and I felt like skipping down the ramp. The island earth felt different, more solid; the sun was strong and bright, as if we were closer to it now. Conor pulled the car off the ferry ramp and we drove the few miles to our rented cottage, me pointing out all my favorite landmarks. Our little shingled house was neat and sparse, sitting atop a grassy hilltop in Gay Head, the deserted, wild tip of the island near Jackie Kennedy's estate. There were four tiny, barely furnished rooms and a long romantic porch with a view of the ocean. If you didn't look closely, you missed the rotted wood along the house's foundation and the white paint peeling off the porch swing.

Conor lay down for a nap. I started unpacking. I couldn't find his suitcase in the car or the house. I tiptoed into the little yellow bedroom, where white curtains embroidered with buttercups blew gently in the afternoon sea breeze.

"Conor? Are you awake?" I whispered from the doorway.

"Yeah . . . kinda," he said.

"I can't find your suitcase, honey. Did you bring it in from the car?"

"What suitcase, Retard?" he said groggily. "I thought you packed all my stuff in yours."

I stood in the doorway, astonished. He didn't pack for his own honeymoon. I thought of what he'd worn so far. The clothes he had on when we left the house in Vermont—the same button-down shirt and khakis he had on now. The only other clothes were the rented tuxedo he wore to the wedding.

"What are you talking about, hon? I never said I was packing your stuff."

"I just assumed you'd packed my clothes. Isn't that what a good wife does?"

"Oh, Conor," I said, turning away. Is that what a good wife did? There went another two hundred dollars we didn't have, just to buy him a bathing suit, some shorts, and a few shirts to get him through this week. But it was such a funny and stupid thing to have done, I forced myself to laugh as I carefully shut the door to the bedroom so he could go back to sleep.

When he woke up, we went into Edgartown and bought a few essentials. Then we took some old bikes from the cottage shed and went for a long ride along the narrow, winding country roads in search of Winnie's old summer home. That night after dinner I read short stories from F. Scott Fitzgerald's *Babylon Revisited* to Conor on the cottage front porch. He loved "The Diamond as Big as the Ritz" so much, I read it to him twice. In the twilight, the sky's red, pink, and orange streaks faded into the purple and blue night, the horizon disappearing as the ocean merged with the night sky.

The days went by slowly, lots of sleep and daytime sex in

the hammock out back and many cups of coffee on the front-porch swing. I sent pretty postcards to my family, Conor's family, Winnie, the minister who married us. We found a tick on Conor's forearm and put it in the microwave oven. We were little kids again. We ate out twice—all we could afford—but it was enough.

One afternoon we came home from a walk on the beach to find a handwritten note stuck under the cottage door from a woman we'd met outside a coffee shop in Oak Bluffs the morning before. She'd looked at us with longing as if we were a golden couple; she seemed personally elated that we were on our honeymoon. We discovered that she had rented our honeymoon cottage once many summers ago, before she bought her own small bungalow. The note was an offer to ride her horses on the deserted beachfront of her family's farm.

"C'mon, Conor. Let's go. This will be great!"

Driving there, trying to follow her little hand-drawn map, I got lost among the narrow dirt roads leading to the farm. I hated getting lost.

"Fuck," I yelled.

Before I saw his fist go up, Conor had punched me on the right side of my face. My head hit the glass of the driver's side window like a pinball. *Thwonk* went my skull against the re-inforced glass. I started to cry but I didn't even pull the car over. I just kept driving. Damn him. Not again. Not on our honeymoon.

The worst part was my lack of surprise.

A few minutes later we found the farm and our friend waiting by the weathered gray horse barn, the two ponies saddled and tied to the fence. I wiped my face and practiced a few quick grins to get my muscles going. I popped out of the car, a fake smile in place.

"Oh, thank you for letting us ride! Sorry we're late, we had a little trouble finding it."

I was pretty sure she wouldn't notice that my eyes were swollen and that there was a red mark on my right cheekbone the size of a fist. What was I supposed to do, jump out of the car and tell this total stranger, "Help! My husband just hit me because I got lost trying to find this place. Dial nine-one-one!" Unlike Mom's verbal attacks, which I blamed for years on myself, at least I knew what Conor did was wrong.

Conor didn't say anything.

We got on the pretty brown ponies, waved good-bye and rode off down a path to the ocean. We took beautiful, idyllic pictures of our long ride, the shiny ponies prancing in the foamy ocean in the afternoon sun. The sky turned orange and gold with the coming sunset. The light was purple by the time we came back to the barn and put the animals in their stalls.

The last three days went by and then our honeymoon was over. On our way back to Vermont, I drove while Conor slept. Everyone agreed getting married was stressful—maybe that was why he'd hit me. He always hated seeing his family—maybe it made him have flashbacks from the times his stepfather beat him. Was he acting out like the little boy he used to be? Our money problems, too much free time on his hands, the unfamiliar surroundings, all seemed like plausible excuses. I loved him. He loved me. He did not mean to hurt me. That made it okay.

Didn't it?

About thirty minutes before the Vermont state line a small neon-blue car that was going so fast it was shaking like a tin can appeared in my rearview mirror. The car pulled directly behind me and the driver started honking. Surprised, a little frightened, I looked in the mirror again. In the car were two young men dressed in ratty sweatshirts. I slowed down. They pulled up alongside me. The driver flashed a bronze badge that looked real. He kept pressing on the horn, gesturing wildly, his beat-up blue car rattling along the highway like it was made of aluminum.

If these two guys had taken on Massachusetts policemen and gotten away with a badge, I could picture what might happen if we pulled over on the highway for them. So I carefully moved to the right lane, slowed down to fifty miles per hour, and kept driving steadily, looking ahead. Conor woke up in the middle of this. The men badgered our car for a few seconds like a frustrated yellow jacket after a peanut butter and jelly sandwich. Then the car sped away.

"What the hell did you do to make those guys so angry at you?" Conor, barely awake, yelled at me. When I didn't respond to his accusation, he reached down to the floor. What was he doing? Something red, white, and yellow came toward me. After the object hit me and fell apart, I realized he'd thrown the cold remains of his Big Mac from lunch at me. Small bits of onions and special sauce stuck to my hair, my ear, the steering wheel, and stick shift. This debris hardened during the rest of the drive. I left it there.

I didn't mention these details when friends and family asked how we enjoyed our honeymoon.

June, July, August. The summer passed.

We drove to the lake near Mom's farmhouse one time. She was away on a trip with her tennis team. We had to sneak onto a private beach because no dogs were allowed on the public one, and Conor wanted to let Blue splash around.

The lake was cerulean-blue. Its fingers spread into broad sandy beaches and dozens of secret coves. The moss-green mountains surrounding the water reminded me of Frankie's velvet ballroom couch that was so massive three kids could hide between the seat cushions. Only a few people besides my family and the local residents knew this lake. No place I'd seen—not Lake Como in Italy, not the alpine lakes in Switzerland—was more breathtaking. As a kid, I'd gotten eighteen summers here.

Conor complained that he needed to get home to study for his financial management class.

He would get sunburned because we (I) forgot sunscreen.

The sand bugs were biting his legs.

There was no place nearby to buy a sandwich, a good corned beef deli sandwich, like he used to get in New York. We left after an hour and a half.

On the way home, we stopped by a spring I remembered near the highway. The water at our ranch house tasted like rust (and worse). Conor wanted pure water, even for Blue's metal drinking bowl, even for brushing his teeth at night. We couldn't afford bottled water. We filled up and tightly capped a dozen gallon milk jugs I'd rinsed out and brought along. I was a good and frugal wife.

One night, sometime that summer during a fight I can't remember, Conor pinned me on the pink futon in our little guest room and held the cold muzzle of the Colt .45 against my temple. He threatened to pull the trigger. I don't remember feeling scared. I did not believe he would fire the gun, although I knew it was fully loaded with hollow-point bullets.

The muzzle left a perfectly circular bruise on my skin for two days.

A bright Tuesday in September. I'd sold a big job to a Bennington printing company that afternoon, doubling my year's earnings. Conor made dinner to celebrate. He set out candles and cloth napkins that I didn't think he knew we had. He charred a steak on the rickety grill the previous owners had left in the garage.

I leaned against the yellow counter in cutoff jean shorts and a University of Vermont sweatshirt, watching him look for the baked potatoes he'd put in the oven an hour before. They were definitely not in our 1950s oven. He opened cabinet doors and even the trash can. All the while he hummed his favorite Three Stooges ditty ("La Da Dee, La Da Daa"). "Hey, Retard, where'd you hide the potatoes?" he asked me, grinning. He finally looked in the freezer. The two potatoes were gently nestled next to the ice cube tray, at eye level with the top rack in the oven he had heated for the spuds.

Over the candlelit dinner, sans potatoes, he told me that his boss refused to let Conor buy coffee for him that morning in the company cafeteria.

"Greg just looked at me like I was crazy. Wearing his ninety-nine-dollar suit from Sears. Like in Vermont, you upset the world order if you spend thirty-five cents on your boss."

We looked over at Blue, who was gnawing on the bone from the steak, lost in dog nirvana. He noticed us looking at him, stopped chewing, eyed us suspiciously, and then got up and carried his bone out to the living room. Conor and I burst out laughing.

By nine, our street was quiet and dark. Conor cleaned the kitchen while I changed into one of my flowered nightgowns and washed up in the house's lone bathroom, tiny and narrow, covered in faded pink tile, with a small broken window that hadn't opened in several years.

I crawled under the covers to read in bed. The lights were on only in our bedroom, a first-floor room with three large windows that faced the street. Directly across from us was the neighbor's three-story white colonial, the largest house on the block, filled with two parents, three teenage girls, two hyperactive dogs, and an arthritic old Siamese cat. The husband had a subscription to *New England Monthly*. He read and liked my restaurant reviews and an article I'd just written about Frank Lloyd Wright's Usonian residences in New Hampshire. His chipper, sturdy wife wore red lipstick when walking the dogs at seven A.M.

We kept the shades pulled down in our stark little bedroom even during the day. Otherwise we could watch the neighbors' TV from our bed, which actually would have come in handy if our electricity got cut off. Conor came into our bedroom naked, his usual bedtime habit. He fumbled with the shade closest to the street. He hated the thin little crack of light in the morning. He jiggered the shade, trying to get it *perfectly* pulled down until—as if in defiance—it wildly, loudly rolled up.

Across the street, the faces of all three girls and their father, plus the red eyes of the Siamese, stared right at him, the TV flickering in the background of their living room. Conor had gotten a bit fat here in Vermont. "Enjoying married life," he often joked as he patted his belly. His skin was a damp, pale white because he rarely had time for the nature and outdoors he told me he wanted to move here to enjoy. His profile in the lamplight looked like a naked Homer Simpson.

"Conor!" I shouted. He stood like a Popsicle frozen on a stick.

Like the Road Runner in a Looney Tunes episode, I tore to the light switch and flicked it off. Then I pulled the shade down myself. In the darkness we fell on the bed, holding onto each other, laughing until our cheeks and stomachs ached.

—–◆–—

October. Winnie was driving up from Cambridge. I couldn't wait to see her, the first time since the blur of the wedding. A part of me wanted to hide from her, from everyone in my life. I didn't want to lie and say married life was great, even though sometimes it was.

"Doesn't she have anything better to do than drive all the way up here?" Conor asked as we walked Blue around the neighborhood in the morning before he left for work. "I want you to come have lunch with me. I'm your husband. She's just some friend."

"I haven't seen her since the wedding, Conor. She's one of my only friends around here," I explained, not for the first time. Winnie was planning to arrive in the morning, after he'd left for work. She was leaving in the late afternoon to visit some college friends in New Hampshire. I was grateful she wouldn't see Conor at all. Conor lobbed ambiguous insults about Rex in front of Winnie until I wanted to devour myself from shame. I was never sure whether he did it because (1) he was envious, (2) he wanted to push Winnie away, or (3) he knew it drove me crazy. Maybe all of the above.

Conor, Blue, and I turned the last corner of our walk and came upon our house—still puce green on the outside although I'd made sluggish progress repainting the inside walls a calm, unopinionated eggshell white. We walked into the dusty garage. Cobwebs hung from the old roof. I unclipped Blue's leash. Blue raced past Conor up the wooden basement stairs to the kitchen—one of his missions in dog life was to be first to the top of any stairs and out any door. A few weeks ago he'd jumped through the back door, shattering the glass and severing the tendons in his front legs but miraculously not killing himself. Sometimes I felt the same way myself, like I could understand jumping through glass to get to—or escape from—your family.

"This place still smells like oil," Conor said to me accusatorily as we passed through the laundry room on our way to the steps. The complaint was so routine, I missed the undertone that signaled he was still angry about Winnie's visit.

Watching my footing on the creaky, unpainted wooden stairs, I was about two steps behind him. Halfway up, he turned and said over his shoulder in the same coarse voice, "My laundry done yet?"

"No," I said, still looking down. "I think it's in the washing machine."

He turned again, blocking the stairway. He paused and gave me a look of hatred. I stopped, suddenly off balance. With a light push on my chest with both of his hands, just as he pushed his stepfather Wade so many years ago once he'd learned martial arts, he shoved me.

"Get it, then," he said through clenched teeth.

I stumbled backward, clutching for the handrail. My feet, clumsy in Birkenstocks, tangled. I fell halfway down the steps. As I caught my breath on the cold concrete floor, I thought, in amazement, that nothing hurt enough to be broken. Suddenly the basement went black.

When he'd gotten to the top of the stairs as I lay near the bottom, instead of coming to see if I was okay, Conor turned off the basement light.

— —◆— —

I was sitting on the front steps drinking my second cup of coffee, listening for her car, when Winnie arrived in her old diesel Mercedes. She got out and we both start laughing because we were wearing identical yellow sundresses. I hugged her long and hard. My back was stiff from the fall and so the hug hurt. At least I didn't have any bruises to cover up. I wouldn't—and did not want to—tell her the truth. But if she saw bruises, I could not have lied.

We talked over a long lunch of salad and pasta in the Indian summer sunshine on the back porch, surrounded by golden trees and green grass and chirping birds, like blond twins who'd stepped off the cover of a romance novel. Not one set in rural Vermont on the back porch of a cheap ranch house that had no furniture and smoke-stained, hospital-green walls.

"How did I get here, Winnie?" I asked incredulously. "Yesterday, I was single in New York working at *Seventeen*. Now I have a husband, a house, a dog. . . . How did this happen?"

She put her arm around me and laughed, but I meant it.

Conor had taken the VW to work, so Winnie gave me a ride into Bennington that afternoon before heading to Hanover. Conor was planning to pick me up around six P.M. at the magazine's offices. As we drove down the turnpike, Winnie's car coughed a few times and went silent. She pulled over and tried turning the ignition, but the ancient Benz wouldn't start. I walked to the pay phone at the nearest toll-booth and left a message for Conor at work. He left work to rescue us, but Winnie and I had already ridden away in the front seat of the tow truck by the time he got to the highway.

We sorted all this out when Conor picked me up at the entrance to *Bennington Magazine* that night. As soon as I was inside the car he started yelling.

"Goddamn it, Leslie, where were you? I had to leave work, I couldn't find you. I cannot do this kind of thing, Leslie! It's just not done."

He sounded like a kid stamping his feet in frustration. He was so angry that I was afraid to answer.

He got out of the car and said, "You drive," without looking at me. I took the highway to get home as quickly as possible. As I drove sixty miles an hour on the turnpike, he punched the right side of my face. I kept the car in its lane, looking straight ahead, cars all around me in the heat of rush hour.

"Are you crazy? I'm *driving.*" I put on my blinker and eased the car to the far right lane and slowed down. He looked at me and smiled.

"I'll show you crazy," he said with something akin to pride. I watched, unbelieving, as he pulled the keys out of the ignition.

The steering column froze. The steering wheel made a soft click as it locked. The speedometer read fifty-five miles per hour.

"Conor!"

He was still jeering at me. I pushed the emergency flashers and applied the brake with caution. The car veered gradually to the breakdown lane. Cars whizzed by on my left, honking furiously. The Volkswagen slowed to a stop. I gripped the steering wheel to hide my shaking hands.

"Conor, give me the keys," I said as calmly as I could manage. When he handed them over, I held them in my sweaty palm, taking deep breaths. "That was really stupid, Conor. Do you want to kill us both?"

His plastic smile faded. "Just drive home," he ordered in a tone I had no desire to truck with. I started the car, eased our way to the next exit. I drove home slowly on back roads. Once in the house I quickly started making a pasta dinner. I tried not to think about what he'd done.

While the noodles were boiling on the stove, the phone rang.

"Winnie, hi, where are you? Did you make it to Dartmouth?"

I looked over my shoulder. Conor was in the living room, stroking Blue's back. I didn't think he could hear me.

"Yeah," she said. "I'm at Tamra's apartment. The bus came a few minutes after you left the station. I'll take another one home tomorrow. The mechanic says there's some problem with the engine that he can fix but it's going to take a week. Is there any way you can drive the car back to Boston the next time you come down?"

"Sure, sure, no problem." Did my voice sound normal? "I'll make it as soon as possible."

The pasta boiled over.

"Shit, wait a sec, Winnie." I grabbed the pot and set it in the sink.

"Hey, are you okay? You sound . . . distracted."

An understatement.

"No, I'm okay. Thanks so much for coming to visit. I'm sorry about all the problems with your car."

"Oh, it's not your fault," she said.

Conor had stopped petting Blue and he rustled the newspaper in annoyance that dinner was not ready. I was talking on the phone too long. I'd better get off before he realized it was Winnie. What if he thought I'd told her about the car keys or him pushing me down the stairs? He'd done so many things in such a short space of time. He seemed on a tear he couldn't control. No way I would chance making it worse.

"Oh, no, I'm fine, Winnie," I said loudly so Conor could hear. "Just tired. Long day. Hey, it was great to see you. Thanks for coming. Thank you so much."

I hung up and dumped the overcooked pasta into a colander. The noodles hung like strands from a limp mop. I was too "distracted," as Winnie would say, to care.

When I served Conor dinner, he took one bite and then brushed the bowl off the table with the back of his left hand. Stunned, I stared at the pasta and vegetables lying on the stained yellow linoleum floor.

Through clenched teeth, fists at his side, he said, "Leslie. I can't eat this shit. It reminds me too much of what my mother made me eat after Wade's kids were all done."

Without saying anything I went out to the porch to eat my cold dinner on the back steps, breathing in the cool fall air, trying to recapture the happiness I felt for a few hours with Winnie. Trying not to think about what could have happened on the highway with Conor. Our life would get better. It had to.

Conor was asleep by the time I'd finished cleaning up the mess.

— — —❖— — —

I drove Winnie's car back to Boston the next week. We sat in the small living room of Winnie and Rex's apartment at Harvard Business School. Rex was in class.

With no preamble I said, "Winnie, I have to tell you something. Sometimes Conor hits me." I said just that—not that in a two-week period he'd choked me, pushed me down the stairs, taken the keys out of the ignition on the highway. I couldn't bear to recount the details.

Winnie gasped.

"Fucking bastard. Right now, Leslie, leave him now. Stay here."

I blew out a mouthful of hot air. "I can't, Winnie. I just can't. I love him. We're married. He doesn't mean it. He just does not know how to deal with his childhood. We're going to go see a therapist, to deal with it."

She was my friend. She knew about love. She tried to understand. She looked miserable.

"Okay, Leslie. I'm just so scared for you. It has nothing to do with him. I like Conor, and I know how much you love him. But he's sick, he needs help."

I could feel her fear. It was terrible to burden her with

the knowledge of what Conor did to me. She put her hands over her eyes.

"Winnie, I had to tell someone. You're the only one I can stand to tell. But I can't leave him."

Every other woman had given up on Conor. I wouldn't. He needed someone who loved him enough to help him. That was me. That's what Winnie couldn't understand, what no one would ever understand.

Winnie sighed and looked up at me.

"Just do this, okay, Leslie? Call me the next time. Come here anytime."

"I will, Winnie. I promise I will."

———❖———

When Ed Horrigan walked through our front door, I knew right away he was different from the other men Conor worked with—as different as Conor himself. Ed had given Conor a ride home after work. He came inside to say hello; everyone else from the company who'd given Conor a ride dropped him at the end of the driveway. Tall and lanky with close-cropped dark hair and no-nonsense wire-rimmed glasses, he reminded me of my father, in a good way.

"Leslie, it's nice to meet you," he said, politely reaching out his hand.

"Come on, Ed, let me show you around the place," Conor said, waving around. Ed nodded to me as they left the room.

"Wait just a sec, Conor," I interrupted. "Ed, do you want some water, coffee, a Coke?"

"Oh, yes please, pop would be fine."

Pop? He must have been from Boston, too.

It turned out he was. I invited him to stay for dinner. He eyed the spaghetti I'd prepared hungrily. If he was salivating over *my* cooking, he must eat at Burger King and Pizza Hut. He didn't notice that we had no place mats.

I peppered him with questions as he ate.

"Next one over from South Boston, a neighborhood called Roxbury. Roxbury was just like Southie when I grew up. My parents still live in the same house. Ask them," he said, grinning, "they'll tell you nothing has changed. But the truth is our house is the only thing that's the same. Today our neighborhood is filled with graffiti-covered buildings and rusted-out cars. They're too lost in their books and my father's languages to notice a difference."

"Languages?"

"Oh, sorry. My father is a linguist. He speaks over ten languages. Most he taught himself from books. One or two, he doesn't know anybody else who speaks them, so he talks to himself. We hear him carry on conversations in his study for hours. You know that kind of ethereal brilliance that precludes mundane matters such as paying the mortgage or buying his children shoes that fit properly?" Ed laughed. I sat back in amazement to have heard *ethereal* and *preclude* used in the same sentence in the state of Vermont.

"Did you go to school in Roxbury?" I asked, puzzled by how the son of two intellectuals, with glasses and a beanpole frame, could have survived the Boston public school system.

"Well, when I was fourteen, I passed the entrance exam to Boston Latin. You've heard of it? Then I got a scholarship to Harvard. You went there, too, right?"

I nodded. "Class of '87."

"After my time. And anyway, I lived at home during college—to save money. I was probably the only Harvard student in history to pass from Roxbury to Harvard Square twice a day. I was a Dud."

"You were? You must be kidding! I was, too!"

Conor hadn't said a word the whole time. Now he was really lost. A Dud meant Dudley House, the Harvard dining hall for students who lived off-campus. Home of the eclectic, wacky transfer kids, foreign visitors, and shaky twenty-year-olds coming back from nervous breakdowns or rehab. An eccentric group even by Harvard standards.

"I knew there was something I liked about you, Leslie." Ed smiled. "When Conor told me you'd gone to Harvard, I was worried. But now that I know you're a Dud, you're okay by me."

Conor would get really pissed if we kept up with this Harvard-speak. But I couldn't help myself.

"How did you ever find your way to this outback?"

"I've been thinking the same thing about you and Conor. It's a long story . . . Nickelface . . . the Quand . . . a letter from Harvard Business School that sat on my father's desk unopened for five months . . . I'll tell you the whole sordid tale when you've got nothing better to do. I've worked here—I'm the company's accountant—for the past five years. I send out résumés all the time but no one else wants me."

He smiled again. I felt like I'd found my long-lost brother. Ed turned back to Conor.

"Pal! Sorry about all this Harvard b.s. You married a good woman. You didn't show me the basement yet." Ed winked at me.

Conor took the bait and jumped up, man's work to be done. I cleared the dishes while Conor showed off his tools in the garage, his chain saw and circular blade. Tools he'd insisted on buying but had never, would never, put to use except to demonstrate to other guys.

After that night, Ed and Conor often came home together. The three of us spent long evenings around our dinner table in the ugly, half-renovated kitchen, which faded as we talked and laughed and told stories about work and Harvard and Ed's latest girlfriends. Ed brought me books by the bagful. He read all my article drafts.

One night he started laughing as soon as he saw me.

"Do you have a green dress?" he asked, cracking up. Conor gave him a wary look.

"Well, as a matter of fact, I do, Ed. But I hardly ever wear it around here."

What had Ed been doing? Looking in my closet?

"Mmm, well, last Friday I had lunch in town with Greg Mouse Brain."

Friday was the day I drove back from Manhattan wearing the tailored silk coat dress I had put on as my "traveling suit" after our wedding. I'd worn it last week in New York for my meetings with my new editor at *Seventeen,* the one who replaced Kathy when she went over to *GQ* the previous month.

"We were walking back to his car from the diner. I'd left my glasses at work and you know, I can't see three feet without them. Out of the corner of my eye I saw a blond woman in green, carrying a big pile of mail. 'There is only one woman in Vermont with a dress like that,' I told myself."

We were all out of place here.

⸻ ❖ ⸻

I wrapped my scarf around my neck as I left *Bennington Magazine*'s offices after a long afternoon proofing the issue about to go to press. The cold October wind whipped a few shriveled brown leaves off the trees as I walked the two blocks to the big double-door entrance to the public library, which stayed open until eight P.M. on Thursdays.

That day was the one-year anniversary of my last day at *Seventeen.* Our second fall in Vermont. Winter was coming. We'd started seeing a new couples therapist, our third in three months. The first was an intake to get a referral within our health insurance network. Conor hated the second, an older woman who reminded him of Chickie. Now we'd found a third, a man who seemed acceptable. Neither of us had told any of the therapists about Conor's attacks on me. We'd never spoken to each other about it, either. Amazing but true. Talking about it might have made it real; we both badly needed to believe the attacks were aberrations rather than predictable events that weren't going away by themselves.

I came to the library to conduct research. Some people believe abused women provoke the violence from their spouses. Not true. I'd conducted my own experiments.

Nothing I did made Conor hit me. Nothing I did made him stop. He acted like he knew what he was doing. I was sure he'd hit other girlfriends before me.

Conor always threw the first punch or kick. Sometimes, I hit him back as hard as I could. My one or two solid hits probably just made him angrier and violent faster, if he even noticed them.

Sometimes I purposefully said nothing, did nothing. He'd wind up. I'd shrink back, eyes open, body bracing. Passivity never stopped him, either. It didn't even slow him down.

"Do you have any psychology books on domestic violence?" I asked the middle-aged librarian. My voice cracked, surprising me as much as the librarian. A pink flush crept up my cheeks and down my neck. Without comment, she pushed her glasses up the bridge of her nose and looked at me. She led me to a stack in the back. She ran her wrinkled index finger along a row of thick, heavy books.

What a stupid euphemism. My situation wasn't "domestic violence." I grabbed four books and walked to a small, unoccupied reading room in the back of the library. I sat at a Formica table and opened one of the books.

I flipped through the introduction and the first few chapters, page after page of black-and-white type. I guess for obvious legal reasons, the book didn't have any photos of women who'd been abused or the men who'd abused them. No pictures to make the people real like me and Conor.

I read the opening to one chapter, looking for some connection:

> Despite the intensely apologetic "honeymoon" period following each domestic violence incident, every time a man hits a woman he's saying "I hate you."

Honeymoon period? I put the book down. Conor never apologized. It would be beneath him to acknowledge the violence was his problem by doing something predictable and sentimental like bringing me red roses with baby's breath the next morning. And hate? Our relationship was about love, not hate.

"I love him beyond words, Winnie," I'd said to her a few days before when she called to check on me. "I am lucky to feel this way. He's brilliant, funny, fascinating. I want to be with him *forever*. His mother never protected him, Winnie. Who can blame him for being so fucking angry? He needs help, my help. You don't abandon your soul mate."

Winnie breathed heavily on the other end.

"I know, Leslie. I think you are lucky to have found someone you love so deeply. But that doesn't make it okay that he hits you," she said firmly. "He has to take responsibility for that, and to stop the behavior."

"How am I supposed to get him to stop, Winnie?"

"I don't know, Leslie, I don't know. Sometimes I think the only way you can get him to stop is to leave him. Not for good, but just until he figures this out."

"Maybe, Winnie. That actually sounds like a good idea. But it will never work with him."

Conor would cut me out of his heart forever if I left him, even "temporarily." He'd see it as abandonment. I didn't want to join the long list of women who'd left him.

I went back to my reading in the quiet library.

All the statistics were about women. Why wasn't any research done on why men became abusers? Did the world think violence in a relationship was the woman's fault? Because she caused it? Because she stayed?

I'd heard the question a million times: "Why would any woman stay in a violent relationship?" As if only someone really stupid, or with utterly no self-respect, would take that kind of abuse repeatedly.

Why did I stay? I had tried to leave. I'd gotten in my car in the middle of the night and started to drive away plenty of times. Leaving was easy. Then I'd get a few blocks and have no idea where to go. He lived in my home. He needed our car to get to work in the morning to earn money to buy groceries, to make our mortgage, to pay his student loans.

But the real reason I stayed was that I loved him. Leaving

meant abandoning our home, our life, our dreams, the best part of me, that part that was not afraid to love unconditionally. I couldn't leave that part of myself behind.

None of the books asked the question I thought about all the time: Why did Conor attack me? He knew I loved him and wanted to help him. Yet he was destroying what we had together. Conor still had trouble putting on a tie every morning because the tightness brought on flashbacks of Wade's hands around his neck, he'd told me. Now the turtleneck sweaters I wore to cover my bruises made me choke, too. The poison from Conor was spreading to me.

A single point in the books made sense: Many abusive men tried to isolate their partners in order to prevent them from leaving. Was that why Conor had wanted to move to Vermont? To get me away from New York, where I had friends and neighbors and coworkers? One chapter also warned that the most perilous time in an abused woman's life was when she decided to leave, because her abuser had nothing to lose by killing her then.

The librarian came into the reading room quietly and then whispered, "Did you find what you need?" I slammed the book closed and jumped up. "Yes, thank you," I managed to blurt out. She smiled and backed out of the room. I put the heavy books back on the shelf and then called Conor from the pay phone next to the bathroom.

"Hi. Just calling to check in. I'm at the library looking some stuff up."

I didn't tell him what stuff. And I didn't tell him how alone, and how scared, reading the books made me feel.

━━━◆◆◆━━━

A few weeks later, after finishing up at the magazine, I went to the big Stop & Shop in Bennington and then it took thirty minutes to drive home in the frigid starry night. The moon was full and shockingly bright in the black Vermont sky. I drove with the sunroof open. Bracing cold air filled the car. I'd gotten adept at maneuvering through the tolls on the country highway. I glided through, flipped a coin into the basket without stopping, and started accelerating just as the gate rose. Hey, sometimes you had to take fun where you found it.

I parked the black Volkswagen in the basement garage and trooped up the wooden stairs in my winter coat and boots, my arms full of groceries. Yellow light spilled out the windows but the house was silent.

At the top of the stairs I heard the soft rustle of a page being turned. The sound came from my office. Curious, slightly bewildered, I put down the food at the top of the stairs and walked into my office, a place Conor rarely went, especially when I was not there.

My heart froze. Conor sat behind my desk, in my chair, with my tattered blue teenage diary open in front of him. I had not written a word in that diary or any other since

the night I was sixteen and Mom told me she'd been reading it. For the eight years since Mom had read that diary,
I'd kept another in my head where no one could read it
but me. But I'd never hated myself enough to throw the
first one away.

Conor did not look up when I walked in.

My first confused question: How did he find it? I'd never
mentioned this diary. I kept it in the bottom of my file cabinet along with a few letters and souvenirs from high school,
an article I wrote for the graduation issue of the school
paper, my yearbook filled with friends' signatures. I hadn't
looked at it in five years or more. He must have been looking
for something (but what?), and then stumbled upon this. I
felt like his dog Knight, trying to hide the shit on the carpet.

I could only imagine what Conor would say and do to me
as a result of reading descriptions of my rampant drug use,
drunken adventures, and sexual experimentation, culminat-
ing with losing my virginity at an age I was sure he'd consider
way too young (fifty would probably be too early in his mind).
He sat quietly, contemplating the scuffed blue diary as if it
were an original da Vinci notebook. Was he so angry that he
was refusing to acknowledge me? He turned another page.

Memories of Mom screaming at me flooded my body like
hot water from a tub faucet.

"No, no, no! That's *mine*!" I grabbed the diary from him and
held it to my chest like a stuffed animal. It was so small my
two hands covered it completely. I sank into the rug in front of

the desk, still wearing my coat and boots. Conor looked at me, stunned.

All I could think to do was call Dr. Joseph, the new therapist Conor and I had seen twice. He'd tell me to get in our car and leave, drive to a hotel, get away fast. I grabbed the phone off my desk and looked up his home number, written on the business card he'd given us. Conor stared at me from behind my desk, not saying a word.

The doctor answered the phone after two rings.

"Hello?" I could hear classical music playing in the background. I pictured him with a glass of white wine in his hand.

"Dr. Joseph, it's Leslie—you know, your new patient? I just got home from the supermarket and found Conor reading my diary . . ." I could barely stop crying long enough to get the words out.

"Okay. Okay," he said firmly. "Take a deep breath, talk it out."

I took a few breaths. Conor wouldn't hit me while I was on the phone with a doctor, would he? Once I calmed myself enough to start explaining what had happened, Dr. Joseph interrupted.

"Leslie, I think we should get you a prescription for tranquilizers." He sounded mildly annoyed. "I can call it into your pharmacy right now. We can all talk about this next week during our appointment."

"No! You don't understand. This is an emergency! You

don't know what he's going to do to me after reading
this—"

I turned my back to Conor and moved as far away from
him as the phone cord permitted.

"Now, come on," he interrupted again. "We're all adults
here. What's going to happen between now and the appointment? We're going to have plenty of time to talk all of this
through. I'll schedule you a special appointment for tomorrow or the next day if that will make you feel better."

Any mental health professional who assumed I was fine,
who couldn't sense the danger I was in, who tried to invali-
date my panic, who thought a tranquilizer would help, did
not know much more about domestic violence than those
idiotic books. I was alone. Again. Damn it.

"No, Dr. Joseph, that won't be necessary," I told him.
"Don't bother with a prescription. I feel better now just talking to you. Thank you."

I wish I'd had the guts to say what I really felt: Go to hell,
Dr. Fucking Joseph.

I hung up the phone. My tears were dry, my face tight
from the salty residue. Conor was still sitting behind my desk,
his arms folded in his lap. What was I going to do now?

"Leslie, just listen to me for a second." He was surprisingly calm and rational, the nice Conor. "I came across your
diary when I was looking for some paper in here."

Right.

He kept explaining.

"I was actually reading the diary to try to help understand

you better. Isn't that what we're trying to do with this couples therapy? Understand each other better?"

Not exactly, I felt like saying. I thought we were aiming to get you to stop hitting me. I eyed him warily but he seemed sincere.

"Okay, Conor. Thanks for your attempt. But don't ever, ever read anything of mine again without asking me. I don't want you to mention to me what you read. It's off-limits, like evidence gotten in an illegal search."

"Okay, okay, fine." To my surprise he agreed, nicely, his face open and sympathetic. Something was fishy here; was he on Valium?

Then it dawned on me. Given that he was a fairly slow reader, he probably never got to the parts in my diary about losing my virginity. I felt like throwing my head back and laughing at my escape. He probably spent an hour reading about my fights with Sylvia and Winnie and Mom, my early drug experimentation, taking the SATs with a third-degree sunburn and open blisters on my face following a spring break tanning fiasco, the highlights of the 1982 Rolling Stones concert at the Capital Center during which I fell asleep. There was nothing that would set him off in the first thirty pages—the first two years I kept the diary. He did not realize what he'd missed.

I waited until Conor was in bed, then hid the diary in a file labeled "Maps and Travel Info" and crawled into bed quietly. The next day I called Dr. Joseph's office and canceled all our future appointments. I started thinking about how to find someone or something that could really help us. It did not occur to me that I had to start with myself.

- — ❖ - —

Ed Horrigan and Conor and I sat around the kitchen table, chairs pushed back, the remains of dinner in front of us. While we were drinking coffee, Conor got up to go to the bathroom. Ed turned to me suddenly, as if he'd been waiting all night for a moment alone. His eyes clicked onto me like a Nikon camera lens.

"Leslie," he said quietly, putting his long fingers over my hand on the table. "Do you know that your voice trembles when Conor comes into the room? What is going on? Can I help?"

My eyes widened but I couldn't get any words out. I tried to pull away but Ed increased the pressure on the back of my hand slightly, the way a teacher would if confronting a child about something she didn't want to admit.

"Listen to me, Leslie. It's a Pavlovian experiment. When Conor's here, your voice shakes. When Conor is out of the room, your voice holds steady."

"What?" I managed to squeak out. Holy shit. He *knew*.

"Are you okay, Leslie?" Ed asked steadily, unafraid, glancing down the hall to be sure Conor was still in the bathroom. He didn't mean was I okay now. He meant was I safe, day in and day out.

I looked away. My face felt hot. I snuck a quick look at him. The concern in his eyes startled me.

"Believe me—the last thing I'd do is undermine Conor. I thought long and hard before bringing this up. But I need to know—are you okay?"

How could it be so obvious that I was afraid of Conor? So fearful I couldn't even say what I thought in his presence without trepidation? Ed said my voice trembled. Who else had noticed? What else was I oblivious to? Before I could ask Ed any questions, Conor came back.

"Hey, buddy," he said loudly, slapping Ed on the back. Ed winced involuntarily. "Let's go smoke a stogie on the back porch."

I turned away before Conor noticed my face, which I figured must be totally crimson or ashy white, I hadn't a clue which. I cleared the table quickly, head down, and started washing dishes. On the metal sink I broke Ed's Coke glass and nearly cut the side of my hand.

I couldn't stop thinking about what he'd said. It was true: I was terrified of Conor. Being afraid had become my normal state. I was always tensed for my next mistake, his next attack. The only person I was hiding the truth from was myself.

I left a message at the farmhouse on Mom's answering machine, an electronic antique with a minicassette inside.

"Hi, Mom. We'll drive over for Christmas but I think it'd be easier—you know, with the dog and everything—if we just slept here. We'll get there as early as we can Christmas morning. See you soon! Bye."

I hung up the phone in our kitchen. My family was converging on Mom's Vermont farmhouse for Christmas—and sleeping miles apart. The rambling house could easily sleep more than a dozen people but all of us refused to stay overnight. My father couldn't—Mom didn't know it yet, but Dad had begun to date a young divorcée in D.C. Although Sylvia felt guilty about hurting Mom's feelings, she and Dad had reservations at a bed-and-breakfast about a mile from the farmhouse. Hugh had flown with a college friend to California, a place he was thinking of moving to after graduation, so he was off the hook. Conor had flatly refused to sleep at the farmhouse since the fight two summers earlier, so we would drive the ninety minutes back home Christmas night.

Just after ten A.M. on Christmas morning, we arrived at the farmhouse, which looked tiny perched up on the hill, surrounded by snow-covered blue spruce trees. The snowdrifts had piled up almost five feet in some places, covering Mom's empty flower boxes. We brushed off our boots in the rough-hewn summer kitchen, which felt even colder than outside. I stamped my feet loudly so Mom would know we were there. No one came out to greet us.

I pushed open the winter door to the kitchen, Conor trailing a few feet behind me. I could smell the roast beef Mom had in the oven. Frankie's old, handwritten, batter-stained recipe and the ingredients for Yorkshire pudding—practically the only recipe my grandmother could follow—were laid out on the counter next to the cast-iron sink. Through the doorway to the living room, I saw a branch of the small Douglas fir Mom had decorated with a handful of favorite family ornaments, a fraction of the hundred-year-old hand-painted angels, doves, and Santas she kept in the attic in Washington.

"Hello?" I called from the kitchen. "Merry Christmas?"

"Oh, they're here," Mom said, as if to someone else in the living room. I walked into the room, stepping over the warped floorboards, to kiss my mom on the cheek. The fireplace was crackling even at this early hour. Mom didn't get up. She turned her face away and half-hugged me with her forearms.

"Merry Christmas, Ann," Conor said politely, without warmth. She leaned toward Conor and gave him a peck on the cheek, carefully holding him at arm's-length so he couldn't hug her back. She raised her eyebrows at me and took a sip of her coffee.

"Your father and Sylvia are out back, chopping wood," she said.

I tried ignoring her frostiness.

"Mom, the tree is beautiful," I said. "And that roast smells incredible!"

She smiled for the first time and looked around the room, thawing just a bit with pride. Beneath her thin-lipped exterior, I could feel that my mother was pleased I had come.

Christmas had always been her favorite holiday. She shopped year-round for presents, which she then hid under her bed and in the linen closet. During our childhood, every year the pile of presents grew more and more stupendous—proof that she loved us, despite the fact that Santa's wrapping skills and penmanship looked a little more sloppy-drunk each year.

I unpacked the presents we'd brought for everyone and took a deep breath of the sweet Christmas tree needles as I placed each gift under the tree. The house had its own smell—old wood, candle wax burnt down during summer nights playing Clue and Spades, wool blankets. It was good to be here.

At noon we crowded around the pine table Dad made more than twenty years ago, which was set with heavy silver and the blue-and-white china my parents received as a wedding present thirty-four years before. We dug into the roast and Yorkshire pudding and green beans and salad and little red potatoes my mom made every Christmas. She had always been a terrific cook.

After eating, we politely exchanged presents. Conor and I gave everyone gifts with a Vermont theme—maple syrup, hand-knit wool caps and mittens, sweaters from the White River Crafts Fair. Sylvia opened a camera with a series of heavy black lenses, a joint gift from Mom and Dad that probably cost nine hundred dollars. Then Mom handed me my unwrapped gift: a cheap watch with a fake black snakeskin band that looked like it came from the discount drugstore she went to in Bethesda. She gave Conor a polyester tie with shiny black-and-gray stripes. The presents were so meager and ugly that I looked at her to see if this was a *Candid Camera*–type joke. Maybe she had our real presents hidden elsewhere. She gave me a look in return that said: *A lump of coal is all you deserve this year.* God, she could be so mean.

"Oh, thanks, Mom," I said, smiling. If nothing else, growing up in my family had taught me how to hide the hurt. I tried to look as if she'd just given me a string of matched pearls.

Dad didn't give us presents. "Ah, I'm sorry, Les, Conor. I was busy with a trial this week. I'll send you a check when I get back to Washington."

Later in the afternoon we piled into separate cars and headed to a nearby family-owned ski resort, a long Christmas tradition. We had the mountain to ourselves. Conor had never skied. My father tried to give him a lesson, attempting to ski with Conor between his long legs as he had when he taught us to snowplow as little kids. Despite the underlying awkwardness and Mom's crappy gifts, I was happy and grateful to see my family, even for a day.

We sat around the lodge after the chairlifts closed, our woolen socks resting on our chunky ski boots, the roaring fire warming us, drinking hot chocolate, a ritual that captured the happiest moments of my childhood. With a laugh, Sylvia looked at me with her blue beach-ball eyes.

"Les, do you remember that time I got lost?"

"Hmm, of course," I said, laughing.

Oh, to hide behind the past, when all was well with this family, when these stories were in the making.

Since Conor was the only one who hadn't heard the story, Sylvia told it to him.

"I was about eight," she explained, looking at Conor, beginning to laugh. "Taking the last run on a really cold day. It started to get dark around three-thirty. I took one more run when the rest of my family went inside." She wiped her nose with a napkin emblazoned with the red ski lodge logo. "I was going down Rattler—Conor, you didn't go down that one today, it's an expert—when I saw a roped-off trail. I don't have any idea why, but I decided to ski it, which was really stupid, because the ski patrols get mad if you go down closed trails. But I figured, last run, all they'd do was take away my lift ticket if they caught me. So, I was skiing down this run, all by myself, the drifts high as my knees, when I fell into a huge snowdrift."

She started to laugh so hard that tears slipped down her cheeks.

"I couldn't get up and it was getting dark and I just lay there moaning, thinking I was going to die."

By now she was laughing so hard her chair shook. I burst into laughter, too, because I could still picture what she looked and sounded like when I found her by following her tracks on my last run. Her eyelashes had been frozen with tears but she was too mad at her own idiocy to be grateful.

I could hear Conor's choked, polite laugh a half-second behind everyone else. A few minutes later, we all got up. My face felt hot and chapped when I hugged everyone and piled our gear into our salt-dirty car in the empty parking lot.

I drove home through the steep, winding highways that led down from the mountains to our ugly little industrial town. Conor claimed he was too wiped out to drive. He dozed for much of the ride.

We pulled into the garage and trooped stiffly upstairs to the cold kitchen, our heavy snow boots clunking on the wooden stairs. Blue was overjoyed to see us after our twelve-hour absence. His happy body wriggling under my hands melted away some of my exhaustion and the ache of nostalgia, what my family used to be, what I wished it still were.

I let Blue into the backyard and then started rummaging for something for dinner. As I stood on a chair searching for matching types of spaghetti among the many half-empty boxes of pasta in our cupboards, Conor leaned against the stove with his arms folded.

"You know, how could you have just taken me to the top of that mountain without even teaching me how to do that snowplow thing?" His accusation might have sounded like an angry three-year-old's, if not for the edge to his voice. I knew better than to make light of his words. Underneath my ski sweater and turtleneck, my shoulder blades knitted together like wings sticking out of my back. "You set me up to be humiliated in front of your family! Your father actually tried to put me between his legs to teach me."

Still on the chair, I twisted to face him, my hands behind my back in tight fists.

"Conor, I really didn't do it on purpose. I am sorry. I didn't mean it."

I *was* sorry. He had a point. I learned to ski when I was two. It didn't occur to me until right that second how hard it would be to learn at thirty-three when the distance to the hard ground was considerably farther. It must have been terrifying and humiliating to be at the top of the hill wondering how to ski down by himself.

All this was irrelevant now.

With Conor in a foul mood, it was wiser to say little, to hope he blew himself out before he found a target. The best thing to do was to keep saying I was sorry, over and over. I stepped down and back.

Tonight my apologies did not slow him down.

"Just like my mother! You expect me to be able to do everything by myself!" He was shouting now. His face was red. He couldn't even see me. I stepped as far away as I could without being obvious.

"Do you know how that feels? Do you know how stupid I felt in front of your father? You just left me there all by myself! I would never do that to you!"

The pasta started to boil. I opened a plastic container of store-bought pesto and spooned it into a bowl. Breathe, breathe, I told myself. I just wanted to be at the farmhouse, with my family, safe, not alone here because he refused to even spend one night at my favorite place. Damn him.

"Look, Conor—you're right. I'm sorry. I said so twenty times. I've had enough!"

This was all the excuse he needed. He grabbed me and shoved me against the half-painted kitchen wall. The bowl, the pesto, the wooden spoon, one of the pasta boxes, all clattered to the floor. He grabbed my neck and started to squeeze. The water boiled over.

He shoved me to the floor and paused to catch his breath, wiping his nose with the back of his hand. While he was figuring out what to do next, I picked myself up, rigatoni stuck to my palm. I grabbed my car keys off the kitchen counter and ran down the basement stairs. As usual, it was beneath him to apologize, to follow me; he'd yelled many times that if I wanted to leave then he didn't want me anyway. The engine in the Jetta was still warm. I backed out of the garage and started driving.

Where to? Leaving was easy. The hard part was figuring out where to go.

Within a few blocks I had to make a decision, even if it was just to drive around town. I had no coat, no wallet, no money, no driver's license. Blue was outside in the cold night. Conor might or might not remember to bring him in. I wanted my dad. I longed to drive the two hours back to his bed-and-breakfast, wake him up and tell him what Conor had done to me. I stopped the car in front of the little bakery that sold homemade rhubarb muffins and leaned over the steering wheel, crying as if my whole body would break apart, thinking about how good it would feel to tell my dad everything and to hear him say, "Okay, babe, I'll take care of you, come back to Washington with me tomorrow."

Right—the man who'd forgotten to get me anything for Christmas. I imagined what my father's reaction would actually be if I showed up at his bed-and-breakfast at one A.M., waking the owner to get him out of his room. Shaming my father with my mistakes was worse than facing Conor. I couldn't stomach his disappointment and annoyance if I were to bring my problems to him instead of solving them on my own. And the ugliest possibility: What if he didn't believe me, or refused to help? Keeping Conor's attacks secret seemed my only way of preventing the violence from being real, the only piece of this ugly situation that I could control. I was alone again with the truth. I would be alone forever.

I straightened up, stopped crying, and slowly turned the car around. I drove home at five miles per hour, going slow, hoping that Conor would think I'd been gone a really long time, ashamed I'd only been gone a measly twenty minutes. I pulled into the driveway and waited until the light went off in our bedroom. I slipped back into the house. The stove had been turned off but the mess was still on the floor. I cleaned up as quietly as I could, let a shivering Blue in, and warmed him up with a long rub with a kitchen towel. I crawled halfway into his crate with him for a few moments. Then I got into bed next to Conor.

———◈———

January. Frozen snow everywhere. Sidewalks covered with a permanent glaze of ice. Salt marks, like dried powdered sugar, streaked every car on the highway. Time for Conor to reapply to business school. He said this time maybe he'd consider a few other schools in addition to Harvard, to hedge his bets.

"You should apply, too, babe," he said to me one night over dinner in our kitchen with Ed. I'd finally gotten to the point where I could conjure up a decent marinara sauce over al dente spaghetti. "You've got good business sense. I can see it in the way you've grown your writing business and advised your clients. Trust me—you'd do great at b-school."

He'd said this before. I'd always been suspicious that he just wanted a companion in this endeavor. But I had to admit the idea had grown on me.

Then Ed repeated the same thing. I was a natural for business school. He said maybe he'd go with us, too. Maybe he would—to watch over me, to stay close to Conor, to buffer the tension between us. He'd never said anything more about my fear of Conor since that night he'd held my hand down on the table.

"But the thing is," I told them, "I'm just not sure business school is right for me *now*—I don't feel quite ready to go."

They both looked at me like I was the big party pooper. Ed went so far as to stick out his bottom lip.

"Okay, okay, maybe I'll apply, too."

———— ❖ ————

I spent most of the snowy winter in my office, proofing Conor's application essays in addition to my own late into the night while Conor slept. Stripes of snow lay draped like long skinny blankets along the gnarled gray branches of the lilac tree outside my office window.

Late one night, like most nights when I couldn't write another word, I pulled on my boots and zipped my down parka over my flannel pajamas, and took a midnight walk down the middle of our snow-covered street with Blue. There were no streetlamps in our neighborhood. The pale orange glow of the moon behind the clouds provided eerie illumination for our walk. Our neighbors were long asleep, snug in their beds. The streets were so quiet I could hear the snow falling. The houses Blue and I passed looked like indigo shadows. The fresh powder was so white that the pine trees looked as if their branches were weighed down with frosting.

"The woods are lovely, dark, and deep . . ."

I crunched along in my boots, hands stuffed into my warm pockets, while Blue raced in front of me, behind me, all around me, a speedy brown locomotive blowing fluffy snow in his wake.

"But I have promises to keep, and miles to go before I sleep . . ."

Ed and Conor had bet I'd get in everywhere. At least one good business school had to take me, as proof that God or something in the universe believed in me and was directing me to leave this dark place, beautiful only when covered in virgin powder.

In early spring, when traces of dirty melted snow lined the mud of our front yard, we started receiving decisions from the schools we'd applied to. Every afternoon, I walked to our mailbox feeling like an altar boy heading to the front of church while a watchful but invisible congregation looked on. Fat envelopes meant yes, thin ones no. As it turned out, Ed and Conor were right: I kept getting fat envelopes. I had to hide my pride because Conor kept getting rejections. More unfairness in the world. The worst was the day he got the thin envelope from Harvard. I left it buried in a pile of bills on the kitchen counter. I called Winnie at her part-time job in the HBS admissions office and asked her to withdraw my application before Conor got home from work and opened the mail.

"Christ, Leslie, are you *sure*?" she asked. "Harvard. Business. School. You know exactly what admission here would mean to your life."

I wanted to scream at her.

"Winnie, please, process it before the end of today, before the next mail drop."

"Okay. Just wait. I'm going to get your file."

I clenched my teeth and waited for her to come back to the phone to confirm she'd thrown away my forms.

Even so, I checked the mail with new urgency until I received the letter from Harvard confirming that my application had been withdrawn, which I waved quickly in front of Conor the night it came and said, "See, I didn't get in either, honey."

He finally heard good news from one of the schools that had accepted me. Fortunately it was one of the top programs in the country. Not Harvard, but in the same dazzling universe.

It would have been a way out, to insist that I had to attend one of the schools he had not gotten into. Instead we decided—I decided, he decided, somehow we decided together—to go to the same school. He also convinced me to take out loans for his tuition in my name, because his spotty credit history meant red tape and higher interest rates. Did this prove that most of me wanted to stay with Conor? That I loved him despite his attacks? Was I a pathetic battered woman? Or was I scared, rightly so, of the rage my abandonment would provoke? Was I an idiot? A coward? A good and loyal wife?

Was I afraid of admitting the truth? That my so-called soul mate, the man I had chosen among millions of single men in New York City, the man my friends and family had suspected might be trouble, had turned out to be a man who held a gun to my head—when not telling me I was the wonder girl of his dreams?

I could not leave Conor. Even though I had no hope he would stop beating me down. Even though my voice shook when he entered a room.

When it came to a choice between him and me, I chose Conor.

Book
Three

---※---

THE WHITE AUGUST SUN IN THE VERMONT SKY made it hurt to look in the rearview mirror of the U-Haul as I drove away from the old ranch house. Blue sat next to me on the truck's bench seat. The furniture, clothes, books, wedding presents, kitchen paraphernalia, Blue's crate, bowl, toys, dog bed, and Conor's guns—the sum of my and Conor's life as a married couple—didn't even fill the small U-Haul we'd rented.

Conor drove the Jetta behind us, the wind from the sunroof ruffling his hair. His left hand, gold wedding band glinting, hung out the driver's window. He looked like Jack Kerouac, except that Kerouac would have driven a car far cooler than our VW.

Ed had helped us pack. He'd decided to stay in Vermont to wait for his next promotion. Maybe he'd apply to business school or a Ph.D. program the next year. He'd bent over to give us both identical good-bye hugs the night before, as we stood in our cracked asphalt driveway next to the U-Haul, finally locked up after a long day packing. I knew he was still worried about me. Maybe he thought, or hoped, I'd be okay at business school.

I'd called Winnie a few nights before, while I was packing

dishes and Conor was out walking Blue, to tell her our moving date and our new number in Chicago.

"You excited?" she'd asked.

I looked around the empty kitchen and living room. The
walls were finally white, and there was a new blue-and-
white-checked linoleum floor under my feet in the kitchen.
Even the outside walls were spanking white, the shutters
and doors slate-blue. Now that we were leaving, the place
looked great.

We'd tried to sell it. The depressed Vermont real-estate
market kept sinking lower. So we'd put an ad in the local paper and rented the place to a nice lesbian couple with two
dogs. The key was already in the mailbox for them.

"Relieved, I guess. But Winnie, what about leaving him,
too? How can I? Do I just walk in one night and say, nice
knowing you, let's get a divorce? Where would I go? Who
would get Blue? Would I take our car? Leaving . . . it's a
concrete wall."

Silence.

"Maybe our relationship will get better at business
school."

"I fucking hope so, Les, I do," she said.

So we left Vermont. The road flew by underneath the
U-Haul tires. Fewer than five hours later, we crunched into
the gravel driveway of Aunt Nellie's house in Upstate New
York a few miles from Strawberry Hill. Blue spent the night
in the U-Haul on his blanket. We got off by nine the next

morning and made it to Chicago by nightfall. As we crossed from Indiana into Illinois, the lights of the Chicago skyline jutted up on the horizon. All told, it took less than two days to leave our old life behind.

As we drove through the South Side, I thought about my dad, who moved here fifty years before. In Oklahoma one day, while his father was at his electrician's job, his mother piled Dad and his brother and two sisters into the family's beat-up car. They stayed a year in Kansas City, then moved to St. Louis, then Denver, then Birmingham—I don't even know if I've got all the cities straight. One day, his mother opened her Bible and decided Chicago was next.

What did Dad think the first time he made this drive?

His mother found a job on an assembly line at a manufacturing plant. They moved into cheap company housing on the factory grounds. By November, they were so poor, Thanksgiving dinner was a handout from their church. "We wouldn't have had anything to eat otherwise," Dad told me when I was in tenth grade. One day when he was about eight, my father rode his bike home from school to find that his apartment, with his mother and three siblings inside, had been quarantined for six weeks due to chicken pox. Somehow Dad found a place to sleep, in this unfamiliar Midwestern city where he had no relatives, until the quarantine was lifted.

He also told me that his older sister, Marilyn, was diagnosed with leukemia here. Marilyn died when she was fifteen, alone in a public Chicago hospital. Alone because my grand-mother would have lost her job if she'd taken time off to be with her.

Conor and I parked the U-Haul and the Jetta on the street in a leafy neighborhood filled with stately 1900s mansions with large front porches. A massive low-income housing project built about ten blocks away had precipitated instan-taneous white flight three decades before. In the b-school newspaper we'd found a listing for an old Victorian split into six dirt-cheap apartments. We'd rented one on the second floor with twelve-foot ceilings, crown moldings, expansive bay windows, a fireplace. Conor hired two young guys walk-ing by to help us unpack the truck. The dishes were in the cupboards and our bed made by midnight. We put my desk in the living room.

Now, instead of a view of the lilac tree, I looked out at a busy street corner glittering with a carpet of broken glass, used syringes, and condoms. The city grit and graffiti—and the people behind the spray-painted hieroglyphics, even if they might be thugs and homeless people—made me feel safer than I'd ever felt in the idyllic isolation of Vermont.

But what did I know about safety?

———❖———

Classes began ten days later. My first two were finance and accounting. Gibberish spewed out of the professors' mouths—credits, debits, burn rates, turnover. The other students had spent the last few years working eighty-hour weeks in Wall Street investment banks and consulting companies. *They* knew what alpha, beta, and delta meant.

My work experience at *Seventeen* and an undergrad degree in English left me at a stunning disadvantage. I scrambled to learn odd new rules: the laws of supply and demand, the psychology of marketing and advertising, the balance of accounting. I scored a 52 on the first accounting test—out of 800 possible points. Afraid I'd fail everything, I read every assignment, sat in the front row for every lecture, turned in every paper on time.

Each day I got up early, dressed quickly (and quietly), and snuck out to walk Blue around the block before I left for campus. Conor—sexy under the white sheets, but surreally distant and impersonal, like a Calvin Klein underwear model on a billboard—stirred in bed. Due to his Wall Street experience and economics background, he placed out of most first-year classes, and thus could sleep in.

I always had the same thought as I locked the apartment door before he woke up: *Phew*.

I usually had a muffin and coffee with my new friend Cherie in the sunny atrium of the business school, skimming *The Wall Street Journal*, which I struggled to comprehend, reviewing my notes with ink from the *Journal* staining my fingers. My section was 50 percent female, a bonus, because my year overall had fewer than 30 percent women. Business school felt like the first week of freshman year in college: Everyone was effusively cheerful and outgoing.

Soon I felt surrounded by more friends than I could keep track of. There were endless study group meetings, small mobs going to lunch at the local deli, intramural soccer games, corporate receptions almost every weekday, spontaneous raids on Baskin-Robbins, Thursday nights at the campus pub, where no one noticed or cared that I didn't have a plastic cup of beer in my hand. I stayed on campus as long as possible every evening, studying with classmates who knew I was married to someone at school but had never met him. Because of our different schedules, I rarely saw Conor during the day.

Night was different.

One evening close to Halloween, I stopped in front of our Victorian with its peeling paint and a dozen different mailboxes cluttering the front porch. Trash and dead leaves piled up on the sidewalk and street gutters. When Blue saw me from the second story he practically leapt out the window. The lights were on in the living room. Conor was home.

I turned my key in the door and put my bag on my big white desk. Blue nosed my pant leg, looking longingly at his leash on a hook by the door. I heard the TV in the bedroom; Conor did not come out to say hello.

After an hour I heard the shuffle of his slippers on the wooden floor. I stayed bent over my desk, highlighting a forty-page finance case it was unlikely I'd ever comprehend.

"Hey, babe," he said to my back. I turned around in my chair.

"Oh, hi, Conor. Didn't realize you were home," I lied. He

hadn't shaved or washed his hair. He held a coffee cup in his hand. Had he even left the apartment?

"How are you?" I turned back to the case.

"Hey. I want to talk to my wife," he said, coming to stand six inches behind me, like a subway panhandler about to ask for money, too close.

I paused, my highlighter poised, trying to gauge the anger in his voice.

"Sure, what's up?" I said, smiling, putting the pen down.

"I heard you joined Mike's study group for macroeconomics."

I nodded. How had he found out?

"Yeah, they just asked me today. It's a good group—Mike and Jim both worked at Lehman. You know how bad I am running numbers. I need those guys."

"I told you I want you to be in my study groups. This is the only class we're taking together."

He crossed his arms over his chest and locked his knees.

"But Conor, you said joining a macro group was a waste of time. You know that stuff from undergrad. I need a group that can help me out. That's what this school is about—teamwork and students teaching each other, right?"

"Well, then you can be the only one in my group."

"Oh, that will be fun. Winging a Nobel Prize winner's two-hundred-question multiple-choice exam. Not me."

He ignored my sarcasm. Conor aced every test, missing at most one or two questions, even though he did little homework and didn't take notes in class. "I don't write any of that stuff down," he'd said when I'd asked why he didn't even take a pen to campus. "If I can't remember it right away, it's not worth knowing."

I was different. I wouldn't, couldn't, fail macro just to mollify him.

"Conor, I didn't come to b-school to be in a group with you. You hate teaching me this stuff, anyway."

I turned back around to the open case.

"Hey!" he barked. "I'm not finished talking to *my wife*."

My wife. He said the words like he owned me.

I turned around and raised my eyebrows. We weren't in Vermont anymore. Part of the unspoken contract at b-school was that no one came to class without deodorant; no one argued with professors; no one fell down drunk at the Thursday night pub outings. Those with tattoos or socialist leanings or a penchant for beating their wives hid these failings.

In business, reputation meant everything, so something as innocuous as "I didn't know him well, but he had a reputation of having a bad temper," could doom one's chance of getting a job, could make an entire industry or career off-limits. I bet Conor knew it, too. He didn't want it to get out that he hit me; it would've destroyed our façade of the successful married couple who'd come to business school together.

I crossed my arms over my chest. From the corner of my eye I saw Blue put his head down and slink out of the room, his toenails clicking on the wood floor.

"I don't want you to be in any study groups with men," Conor explained, as if he were repeating something he'd made clear before.

I gave a short laugh, shook my head, and shrugged my shoulders.

"This school is seventy percent male, Conor. Over ninety percent of the professors are men. What are you talking about?"

I looked up at him. He could hit me tonight and I'd still escape to the safety of campus tomorrow. I stayed seated; I'd learned it was harder for him to go after me in a chair, especially a wooden one with arms. I grabbed the seat bottom, digging my nails into the wood so hard they gouged half-moon marks in the varnish. I tried to keep my voice breezy.

"We both need to network with other students, professors . . . it's an amazing program, that's why we're here."

"No!" he yelled, bending over me, his back curved, shaking his finger inches from my nose. "There can be only one person in charge of a family. That's me, *babe*. I am king of the castle here." He leaned closer; I could smell coffee on his breath.

The freedom I'd found at school had loosened his control over me. He was trying to find another way to tighten his grip. For a second, disgust trumped my fear.

"I can't believe I'm married to someone who believes such a stupid thing, Conor. What the hell? Should 'the king' set the time on our alarm clock, answer the phone when it rings, decide what we eat for dinner? Or does being 'king' mean I am supposed to do all those things for you?"

He stared at me, furious, his eyes red. Then he leaned over my desk in front of me. Beads of sweat dotted his forehead. He still looked amazingly handsome, alive with anger.

He paused and looked around the living room as if trying to get hold of his rage with slippery fingers. He uncoiled his right arm and in one clean, purposeful sweep he brushed all of my finance notebooks across the living room. The metal binders snapped. Hundreds of pages of my notes and case study analyses scattered along the hardwood floor like an oversized deck of cards.

"Is that all you're going to do tonight, Conor? Or are you going to hit me, too?"

My voice broke, just a little. I tried to sound sarcastic but I guess somewhere in me I was still afraid. *You've got me now,* I felt like saying to Conor as he stood there, hands on his hips, while Blue huddled in his crate in the kitchen.

But you won't have me for long.

In one final gesture, he threw the massive finance textbook at my feet and then grabbed his leather jacket off the couch. He unlocked the front door and slammed it open. The brass knob went through the plaster of the foyer wall and stayed there, impaled on the cheap drywall.

I watched him go. He still had on his slippers.

"Leave," I whispered to his back disappearing down the

hallway, past the cheap pineboard paneling. "I don't know if I love you anymore."

I didn't say it very loud. He gave no sign that he heard me. Or that what I'd said made any difference. It wasn't true, anyway. I would still be there, waiting, when he came back.

* * *

It is strange what you don't forget.

In May, with money Winnie inherited from her grandmother, she treated me to a rendezvous in New York. The first night we stayed up until two A.M. talking nonstop in our room at the Palace on Madison. The next day we shopped nonstop until two P.M. At Bergdorf's we found a smoky blue Ferragamo interview suit on sale, something I couldn't dream of on a grad school budget. Winnie wanted to buy it for me.

"Oh, Win, you shouldn't," I pleaded, torn by guilt and delight, looking at myself in the three-way mirror. Like a wand from a fairy godmother, the suit transformed me into a confident, promising female executive.

"Oh, come on, Grams loved you, too. She'd want me to."

I graciously accepted.

Dead-eyed from too much shopping and blabbing, we ate lunch at Bergdorf's outrageously expensive little café on the fifth floor. We were mostly quiet, chewing our salads. She looked around like she had some juicy gossip about one of the women at the table next to ours, and leaned toward me.

"I'm eight weeks pregnant," she whispered.

"Oh, my God!" I shouted. I half stood in my chair. She turned red. "Congratulations, Winnie!"

I felt so happy for her, I didn't notice that she wasn't smiling.

"What's wrong, Win?"

She looked like she was going to cry. Winnie hadn't cried since seventh grade. She bit her lip.

"It's just . . . you're the first person I've told, besides family. There were some tests, we thought there was something wrong with the baby. That's why I didn't tell you before. But I just found out Thursday that it's healthy. I'm so happy. But I'm still so scared that maybe there's something wrong."

I took her hand. "Winnie, it's going to be fine. You're pregnant! Wow."

Suddenly she asked me if I was going to stay with Conor for good. A complete non sequitur. But to me, the question made perfect sense.

"I can't have children with him," I said. "I have no idea what it's like to be pregnant, but I just could not do that to a child."

Looking down at her frisée, almost as if she was talking to herself, Winnie said quietly, "Well, then you have to leave him one day soon."

I knew she was right. But I had no idea how to say good-bye to Conor.

After lunch she told me she had to pee—that she'd been peeing a lot lately. We went down to Bergdorf's tiny bathroom under the curved marble staircase in the basement. I spotted a pink baby's sock on the black-and-white subway tiles under the hand dryer. Impossibly tiny. I looked around for a baby girl in her mother's arms. When Winnie was washing her hands, I bent down and slipped the sock into my raincoat.

Back in Chicago, what stretched before me was a lifetime of contortion to avoid tripping Conor's temper. At times I'd succeed. I'd fail occasionally because how can you dodge something as unpredictable as rage?

I could not imagine being beaten while carrying a baby inside me, like Conor's mother had been beaten with him inside her.

I pictured jobs I couldn't take, lies I'd tell my friends, a life without children.

Mostly, though, I tried not to think about the future. The frantic acclimation to b-school distracted me plenty.

Then it would rain. I'd feel the sock in my coat pocket and remember that day at Bergdorf's and think: Would I ever have a baby girl too precious to be left at home on a rainy afternoon? What I was asking myself, I knew, was simple: Would I ever have a life without Conor?

—————◆—————

Winnie's blue Ferragamo power suit—which I wore to every job interview—became my Cinderella ball gown. Every time I put it on, poof! I could smile, shake hands, answer tricky interview questions with aplomb. I changed into a woman who couldn't imagine the day when Conor turned cold shower water on my naked body as I lay soaking in a hot bath. Or the Big Mac he threw at me as I drove home from our honeymoon on Martha's Vineyard. Or the time the previous fall that he poured dry coffee grinds on my head as I was making breakfast in our narrow galley kitchen.

To my surprise, corporate recruiters, a paradoxically picky, lemminglike bunch, offered me two marketing internships, one with American Express in New York City and another with Johnson & Johnson in New Jersey.

Conor did not send his résumé out, did not get invited to any interviews, and ended up with a last-minute summer job in Chicago.

Despite the irony of getting an offer from AmEx (maybe now I'd get my card back?), I took the job with Johnson & Johnson's New Brunswick corporate headquarters. I asked Aunt Nellie if I could live at her beach house on the Jersey Shore for the summer. This meant three months apart from Conor, seeing him only on a few weekends. He was not happy about it, but he didn't protest. I made the thirteen-hour drive to Jersey for the summer, alone with Blue. I could spend a summer without Conor, but not without Blue.

Rules seemed to govern everything for the 150,000 employees at J & J, the world's largest consumer health-care company. All the buildings were as white as a starched shirt. The grass was trimmed as short as a golf course. A dress code specified skirt and sleeve lengths. There was a memo on how to write memos. Every employee arrived before 8:30 A.M.

There seemed to be a policy about what cars you were supposed to drive—no flashy European luxury imports—and what dogs you should have pictures of on your desk (there were many golden retrievers; zero Dobermans). Working at J & J was like drinking a vanilla milkshake.

Every night I arrived home at dusk at the rambling Victorian beach house. Blue and my twelve-year-old freckle-faced cousin Lila, whom I officially chaperoned although she told *me* when her curfew should be, welcomed me on the wraparound porch. After dinner, we'd walk barefoot a block to the ice cream stand and eat our cones on the sidewalk. Conor flew in occasionally on the weekends, along with Nellie, her husband, and my two teenage cousins. There were too many people around for Conor and me to fight. We had a few blowouts in our hot parked car with the windows rolled up so no one could hear us.

Three months alone, without being hit, without having to hide bruises and swollen eyes, brought a tincture of clarity, as well as questions that were too confusing to answer. Why had I never directly confronted Conor about the violence? Where was my moxie, in such abundance in b-school debates and job interviews? Of course, I'd always been afraid of his reaction, but that wasn't my whole excuse. I'd always thought it wouldn't do any good to question him, to tell him the violence was unacceptable, to threaten to leave him. Because I'd never leave him. And I knew it wasn't his fault. He'd been abused far worse as a kid than the stuff he did to me. Naming the violence wouldn't have stopped his compulsion. It just would have made it more real. What was I going to do?

⸺⬩⸺

An article I'd written the summer before ran in *Seventeen's* August issue. When I saw the headline on the cover at a newsstand in New Brunswick near J & J, it occurred to me: I was a writer, I could *research* my future with Conor. Maybe I could find data that unraveled the dynamics of domestic violence, unlike the academic tomes I'd discovered in the Bennington public library.

I tracked down an assistant professor at a large state school in Maryland, working toward his Ph.D. on the behavioral psychology of batterers—a unique perspective in a field where research focused on the victims. I explained that I was a freelance reporter doing an article on abusive men for a woman's magazine. I misled him: (1) because I was afraid if I told him the truth, he wouldn't be as objective and clinical as I needed him to be; and (2) so I wouldn't cry during the interview.

My list of questions lay on a yellow legal pad on my desk at Johnson & Johnson. It was seven P.M. Everyone else had gone home. I clutched the gray office phone tight to my ear, afraid to miss one word of his answers.

I started with an easy, impersonal question.

"Why did you choose to study this population?"

CRAZY LOVE

He sighed heavily. There would be no easy, impersonal answers.

"I'm interested in the question of why men beat women. Not why women stay in violent relationships. I've spent a decade studying abusive men. In addition, as part of my own research, I run court-ordered self-help groups for batterers.

"I care about these men I am studying. They—and their responsibility for perpetuating violence—have been ignored for too long, to our society's detriment. I believe in their right to get help and I believe our society needs batterers to stop being violent."

I used my objective, edgy Barbara Walters voice to ask my first tough question:

"In your experience, why do men batter women they love?"

He sighed again.

"Every man I have ever studied who became a batterer as an adult was physically abused as a child by people he loved deeply. Usually an intimate family member who was also a role model for acceptable behavior. Often his mother or father or both.

"A batterer learns as a child that violence is an acceptable way to deal with strong emotions, and an effective way to dominate others in order to protect himself. The men I work with cannot separate intimacy from abuse. They do not think that their behavior is wrong. And they definitely have no understanding that it is criminal."

I thought of how deeply Conor loved his mother, and

237

what it had done to him when she allowed him to be abused.

"Do they love the women they are abusing?" It was getting harder to maintain my composure. The plastic phone slipped in my sweaty hand.

"Absolutely. They hit their partners *because* they love them," he said confidently. "I have yet to come across a batterer who lashes out violently at strangers. Part of the paradigm is that, to batterers, violence is a normal component of intimate relationships. The men I've studied would not get any emotional satisfaction or release unless they are intimately involved with the object of their violence. Their vulnerability terrifies and overwhelms them because of their learned behavior from childhood. They have learned—as a survival mechanism—that controlling the people they love is the only way to be certain they won't get hurt. And they know, through their own personal experience, that fear and violence are very effective ways to control people."

I always knew Conor's abuse had more to do with love and fear than hate. Finally, an expert who understood.

I looked down at my notebook. Next question:

"Do men who beat their partners, their wives, often abuse their children, too?"

"Yes. Almost always. Again, it's the intimacy and violence paradigm. And even if they don't physically abuse their children, by beating their mother they do two things: They terrify their children with the threat of 'You could be next' and they teach their children that violence against women is okay. Both behaviors ensure that violent behavior is perpetuated in the next generation."

I took a deep breath as silently as I could. It was hard to get enough air in my lungs before I asked the next question.

"What are the positive signs you look for in the men in your group? The signs of hope?"

Now he took a deep breath.

"The most important thing, which frankly is rare, is honesty. Admitting that they have hit their partners, that this wasn't the first time, that they've hit other intimate partners, that there is a pattern of abuse that they have initiated."

Honesty? Conor had never admitted he'd hit me.

"The second thing, also critical, also rare, is taking responsibility for what they did. Saying this is my problem—not my partner's. Most batterers believe their partners provoke the violence. I work extremely hard to break through their denial and to get them to admit that violence is wrong and their fault. If a man can admit this, and truly believe it, then there is hope.

"But for most batterers this verges on impossible, because it requires them to admit that for many years they've been hurting other people, whom they love, in exactly the way they were hurt as small children. For most of the men I work with, denial of their problem has become a survival skill. For them to let go of this defense is devastating. But it's critical."

Conor was galaxies away from taking responsibility for the violence he brought into our relationship. The dull thud inside my chest grounded me. I found my confident anchor-woman voice again.

"You say there is a pattern to the violence that spans different relationships. Could you tell me more about this?"

"Based on my quantitative research and learning from the men's groups I run, my hypothesis is that men who batter are like a subspecies whose behavior, as a group, is highly predictable. A relationship starts. The batterer has an uncanny sense for what the woman wants and needs emotionally, and he meets that need. I hear female partners use the phrases 'Prince Charming' and 'knight in shining armor' with incredible regularity when they describe what their partners were like in the early, courtship stage of the relationship. Batterers are like predators seeking prey."

How did Conor know, the night he met me on the E train, that I was so vulnerable? Was I still?

"You never hear of a batterer who introduces violence early on or too suddenly. No batterer hits a woman on their first date. He always waits until he's secure, which from the woman's perspective means until she is trapped, emotionally or financially, like getting engaged or pregnant, or quitting her job because he 'wants to take care of her.' A batterer intuitively knows when and how to lay the groundwork for a 'successful' violent relationship. The best cons, after all, are the ones that make the victim want to participate.

"Once the relationship is established and the batterer feels secure, he introduces the threat of violence. By a threat I mean something like punching a wall in the woman's presence, or saying, 'If I weren't such a gentleman I'd hit you for saying that,' during an argument.

"If the woman does not balk at the *threat* of violence, then soon the batterer actually hits or chokes or shoves her. Usually, it's something like a pinch that leaves a bruise or a controlled shove, not a full-blown beating. The batterer gradually escalates the violence, and increases the frequency, as the woman's denial and emotional numbness increase. By then, she's trapped and he feels free to do whatever he wants. He works on her emotionally, too, to make sure she does not tell people about the violence. It's critical that he convinces her the violence is somehow her fault or under her control. Her guilt protects the relationship so he can continue the battering."

I could not speak. This stranger on the phone had described my relationship with Conor in dreadfully accurate detail. Our first fight had been the night we moved in together—when I had nowhere else to go any longer. The first time he beat me was five days before our wedding. For two years I had let him beat me, in the name of "helping" him work through his childhood traumas.

I took a minute to write his words down on the legal pad. What I really needed was a decade to collect myself.

I looked at my next question. By this point, I knew what the answer would be. But I needed to hear it from him.

"The men you work with in your recovery groups, do they ever get better? Do they ever stop hitting their partners for good?"

His biggest sigh yet. I could practically see him shaking his head.

"No one I've studied has ever stopped being violent, all at once, for an extended period of time. I've seen batterers make a lot of progress toward controlling their anger and expressing it in more productive ways. But I've never seen anyone who didn't regress and beat their partners at regular intervals, even while making significant progress. There is no one I work with who I could say, this one is done, he'll never batter anyone again."

"Okay," I told him. "Last question. If one of the wives or . . . partners . . . of your batterers came to you and said, 'What should I do? Should I wait for him and help him work it out?' What would you tell that woman to do?"

He gave a short, humorless laugh.

"I would tell her that she is probably the last person on earth who could help him. First she should help herself and her kids, if she has them, to stay away from him—and I'd warn her to be extremely careful, because abandoning a batterer often provokes his deadliest rage. But leaving is actually the best way for her to help the batterer, too, and to help our society, because she is letting him, and the world, know that what he has done is wrong and totally unacceptable. By removing herself from the relationship, she makes it clear that she cannot help him, paving the way for him to realize that the violence is his fault, his responsibility, and that he is the only one accountable for his behavior."

I thanked him, told him I'd let him know when the article came out, that I appreciated his time and insights very much. After I hung up the phone, I sat in the dark of my temporary office, staring at my blank computer monitor. Yeah, I knew *a lot* more now. But I didn't love Conor any less. And I still had no idea what to do.

———❖———

At the end of August, Conor came to the beach to drive me and Blue back to Chicago. We went for one last walk along the empty Jersey Shore. Darkness was falling. We had to step over abandoned children's toys and sunscreen tubes in the sand. Conor's chest and feet were winter white. We moved next to each other in silence without holding hands.

Bringing up the abuse felt like explaining why I'd been speeding to a New Jersey state trooper. *I* felt guilty. I hadn't really talked to Conor in such a long time, my voice felt rusty.

"Conor, I've got something to tell you," I said, not looking at him, afraid I'd cry if I saw his face. The words came out as stiff and unappetizing as a frozen TV dinner on a tinfoil tray.

I stopped walking.

"If you ever hit me again, it's over. I love you and what we used to have together—too much to have . . . this . . . between us."

I looked at him as the wind blew my hair across my eyes. I needed to know he heard me. He looked at his toes in the sand.

"All right," Conor said a few seconds later, blue eyes still down. I could see his long lashes, half-circles over his cheeks. "I hear what you're saying. I promise I'll never . . . I'll never do it again, Leslie," he said, looking up, meaning the words. "I love you. I want to be happy with you and Blue—my little family. Let's go home."

＊＊＊

November. The fall was a crazy blur of job interviews, classes, and study groups. I went through a dozen pairs of panty hose and just as many three-hour dinners with recruiters. The Ferragamo suit got lots of air. At the end of summer, the VP of marketing at J & J had asked me to work two days a week once school began. This meant money, an independent study credit, and two days a week away from Conor. Without talking it over with Conor, I'd said yes. Now I spent two days a week at Johnson & Johnson, flying away from Conor every Wednesday night, bringing in badly needed cash for food, household expenses, and more panty hose. I was so busy, I had no time to think.

Conor kept his promise. Thanksgiving came, marking three months since our beach talk, six months since he'd hit me. A few days later he came home on his bike with a small bag, a gift for me. Painted enamel earrings, two birds to wear in my ears, a matched pair. "Like us," he'd said.

One weeknight, after a fight that stayed only a fight, he

ran out in the rain to get my favorite pizza as a make-up gift. He arrived home with the warm cardboard box, wet hair plastered to his forehead and a smile on his face. Late on a Friday, I stepped off the plane from New Jersey to find him waiting for me at the gate, holding pink roses. When I saw his face, my stomach unzipped like the old days in New York.

A few days later, he left a small package on my desk with this note:

> To My Dear Wife—
> I found this on Saturday at a flea market. It's an antique jeweled peacock pin, a Chinese sign for prosperity and good luck. It's to wear on your interview suit. I just want you to know that your loves and ambitions are shared by me—what you care about I care about for you.
> > Thinking of you always,
> > Conor

I came up with the idea to celebrate his thirty-fifth birthday and Christmas in Paris. "Sure, just us," Conor said, smiling when I told him. "Just us," he said again. His crooked smile flickered. "Just us" had once been everything we'd wanted. Maybe it could be again. I bought charter airplane tickets and found a cheap, hopefully romantic Left Bank hotel in a guidebook at the undergrad library.

The past two years were slipping behind us, a chapter we'd talk about on our silver wedding anniversary: *Oh, yes,*

*those first few years of marriage can be terribly rocky. You have
to get through them, that's what commitment is about.*

———•◊•———

December. The day before his birthday, everyone left campus for three weeks of vacation, the last long break before graduation and our collective return to the working world. Christmas lights and decorations filled the storefronts and the windows of the apartments lining our street. Our neighborhood was deserted and eerily calm, reminding me of Vermont.

That afternoon while Conor was in the Loop buying something—new ties for job interviews, I think—the phone in our apartment rang. The rooms were shadowy in the early winter twilight so I had a hard time finding the receiver by our bed.

"Hello?" I shouted into the phone, breathless from the search.

"Les, hi, it's me, Winnie. I just wanted to say have a wonderful trip. Paris at Christmas? I'm so jealous. Think of me trying to keep Rex's family from pawing my belly while you're strolling the Champs-Elysées."

"Yeah, I am so excited. We'll be there this time tomorrow. Conor's gonna love it. Paris—it's a long way from Southie."

Winnie—almost nine months pregnant now, the baby totally healthy—laughed. It sounded like there was barely room in her lungs to draw a breath.

"Great, Les, sounds like this trip will be wonderful. I am so happy—for you and him and *me*—that you're okay. I have been so damn worried about you."

I looked out the kitchen window at the alley across the street. Someone had decorated her second-floor apartment with a wildly exuberant mishmash of cheap multicolored Christmas lights. I turned my back on the lights to face our dark bedroom.

"Win, you know, he still gets angry. That . . . pact or whatever we made on the beach doesn't stop him. At times it makes him angrier, I think; he's got no release. But there's been no . . . violence. He's trying so hard. I think we're going to make it."

"Sounds like it," she said. "It is fucking huge. He deserves a lot of credit. Sometimes I think the only way your relationship can succeed is if you live in different cities like you did last summer, or like you're doing now, away in New Jersey every week."

Fuck you, Winnie, I felt like saying. Damn her for speaking the truth so baldly. I still loved him, just as much. But if it came to a choice between him or me, I knew I'd choose me. And if you felt that way, didn't it mean part of you'd already decided?

I heard footsteps in the hallway. I half-wished the steps approaching our apartment would continue up to the third floor.

"Win, gotta go—he's back. Have a great Christmas. Thanks for calling—"

I hung up. A fleeting desire to never see Conor again in this lifetime flitted through me like a hummingbird skimming a lavender field. *No, he's your husband. You love him.* His key clicked in the lock. I went to turn on the light in the hallway.

"Hi, honey." I managed a smile.

"I brought dinner from the Italian place. Pasta with pesto. Your fave, babe."

"Yum, let's eat. I've gotta pack after dinner." We ate side by side on the couch in the living room, watching the news on TV like an old married couple. Blue lay at our feet, curled like a Pillsbury crescent roll.

After doing the dishes I went to the windowless bedroom in the back of our elegant but jaded city apartment—ground zero for countless nights of violence and mornings spent putting on cover-up and a high turtleneck. Those memories were fading like photos left in the sun.

Blue followed me, his nails clicking on the hardwood floor. With a grunt he jumped into his red fake-leather chair. I put on a white T-shirt and a pair of Conor's old boxer shorts so I could pack the clothes I'd been wearing. The living-room TV blared, punctuated by Conor's booming laugh at the sitcom's punch lines.

After I'd been packing for about thirty minutes, I looked up to see Conor standing in the doorway watching me. An inscrutable half-smile flickered on his lips.

"I've decided not to go," he said as he folded his arms across his barrel chest, still smiling. His words hung in the bedroom like a kite pausing in midair. At the sound of the edge in Conor's voice, Blue got out of the chair and walked out of the room, his head down, wiggling his body in a half-hearted wag as he slid by Conor. A chill went through me.

The old Conor had canceled plans before, sometimes waiting until I stood at the door, dressed, made-up, perfumed. So I shouldn't have been surprised. But this time I was.

I knew better than to show how I felt. I put down the red wool sweater I was folding. He stood in the doorway, still watching me.

"I said we're not going."

I nodded to let him know I'd heard. I did not ask why he didn't want to go. Or tell him how hurt I was that he wanted to cancel his birthday trip. He went back to the living room.

I imagined holding hands with Conor on a Paris street, laughing while we drank café au lait at a small wrought-iron table, riding the Metro with the colors of the stations flying by.

He returned a half hour later. I was lying on our bed, staring at the inlaid white ceiling of this once grand, now shabby mansion subdivided into apartments. Our almost-packed duffel bags were still on the floor where I'd left them.

"So, have you called the airline to cancel the tickets?" he asked. A stupid question; as if the cheap charter airline was open at ten-thirty on a Saturday night. He meant: *I'm the boss here. Did you do what I ordered?*

I knew why Conor wanted to cancel our vacation. The

trip was my way to celebrate our starting over. But even good news had to be celebrated on his terms only. Even a joyous occasion frightened him if he couldn't control it.

The man I imagined in Paris was not the man in the door-way. That man was gone, if he'd ever even existed. There was no "old Conor." I'd been lying to myself since August. Maybe long before August.

"No," I said. I turned my head away from him, toward the white wall that divided our apartment from the one next door. I found my favorite crack in the wall plaster, the one that looked like a misshapen flower.

"I'm going," I told him, my back still to him. "Even if you're not, Conor. I've worked too hard this semester. We won't have a vacation again for a long time. I'd rather go with you, but I'm going anyway."

I closed my eyes. I suppose it was stupid to tell him the truth. But for the first time in three years I had to know what he would do if I told him how I really felt.

A long silence followed, a moment's pause like when you watch an infant sleeping, swaddled in the crib, and you're not sure whether she is going to take another breath or per-haps stop breathing forever. Silence that mesmerizes you.

A gentle whoosh of air came toward me. The room tum-bled in a slow-motion blur. My head got stuck for a second in my tight T-shirt collar. With a grunt Conor yanked the fabric off. My head crashed into the hardwood floor.

"How dare you." His voice shot across the room like the punch of a fist. "You can't go without me. You selfish bitch."

From the bedside table he picked up my favorite wedding photo in an inlaid silver frame Frankie had given me the year before she died. No time to cover my face as he broke the picture over my head, so I closed my eyes to shut out the glass. Small bloody slits like paper cuts sprang up across my forehead and cheeks from the shards.

No, I pleaded silently as I covered my head with my arms. *Don't let this happen. I do still love him. He is my family.*

I didn't see Conor's foot pull back but suddenly my rib cage exploded as if hit with a sledgehammer. An ominous intensity I'd never felt before characterized his movements. Our small bedroom felt black with rage, as if Conor had been bottling up his anger since August, choreographing each punch and kick in advance, patiently knowing this moment would come even as I had hoped every day it wouldn't.

I looked at him, his jaw clenched, hands in fists, veins raised along his biceps like electric wires. It felt as if a complete stranger had broken into my home and was standing in my bedroom.

The phone. I tried to reach the rickety wooden nightstand next to our bed where I knew the phone lay in its cradle, the same receiver I'd picked up when Winnie called. It was only halfway across the room but Conor moved so fast that getting more than a few inches out of the reach of his arms and feet was impossible. Ludicrously so.

I heard the sounds of my own screams as if there was some other woman in our apartment screaming her head off.

He grabbed my neck with both hands, those fingers I'd

loved circling my windpipe easily. Using my head like a stopper he pulled me up off the floor and back onto the bed, forcing me into the mattress with the weight of his body and his hands around my neck. I could smell his sweat layered over our laundry detergent on his blue button-down shirt.

"Shut up! Shut up! Shut up!" I heard him yell.

He squeezed my throat until I could not make any more noise. What I could see of the room faded until everything before me went starry. I felt a deep quiet, a kind of peace almost, simplicity. My life was this room, this firm mattress, a soft, fading gray-black in front of my eyes.

When I came to, I had no sense of how much time had passed. Ten minutes? Ten seconds? Maybe my entire lifetime?

Conor stood by the head of the bed next to the phone, in front of the doorway. He watched me as if he were afraid to touch me again. He flinched—with relief?—as I opened my eyes and turned my face to him. His underarms were wet with sweat and his muscled forearms were crossed over his chest like a security guard blocking a bank vault.

My stomach and ribs felt as if an enormous hunk of ice lay wedged inside me. The old cliché came true and a parade of faces I might never see again passed before me. My mom. My sister. Winnie.

My love for Conor seemed completely irrelevant.

I heard a faint voice. It came from inside me.

You know this man. Use what you know.

The voice was calm. Its tone suggested a shrug: *Hey, it's*

up to you to decide the outcome here. It's okay if you want to give up right now. Him or you. Your choice.

I breathed. Out. In. I slowly sat up on the rumpled blue-and-white-flowered bedspread and raised my palms, laced with cold sweat, in the universal code for surrender. My body felt small and useless compared to his.

"Conor, I love you," I said softly, looking into his twisted face and red eyes. There were blisters of moisture on his shiny forehead. "I know you don't want to do this. Of course I won't go to Paris without you. Just stop what you're doing. I love you so much I'll do anything for you. I am so sorry."

I bowed my head. I didn't take my eyes off his face.

"We're going to be fine," I pleaded with a half-smile. My knees shook wildly. I tried to cover them with my arms. The iciness in my stomach made me fear I would throw up. He froze for a second, looking at me warily as if I might rush for the phone or the door again. My eyes tracked his. I tried again to smile.

Hope is always good, right?

Suddenly footsteps pounded in the hallway outside the apartment. Someone began hammering our front door, hard enough to splinter the wood. The person did not say anything. But to me the banging shouted out, "Stop it! Stop it! Can't you see you might actually *kill* her?"

The spell was broken. There was a world outside our bedroom again. I could feel glass in my face, a burn around my throat and fire in my ribs.

Conor bowed his face and began to cry. His shoulders

crumpled. His nose ran like a kid crying after breaking a trea-sured toy. He shook his head no as if trying to erase the last twenty minutes. His apartment keys jingled as he took them out of his pocket and carefully placed them on our bedside table on top of the broken wedding photo. A twisted peace of-fering. He picked his blue coat off the rack in the hallway.

"I'll call you tomorrow," he whispered as he left, still choking back tears.

As soon as the front door to the building banged shut, I reached for the phone. I was alive. I took a deep breath and picked up the receiver to call the police.

<hr/>

It felt as if entire years passed during the time I waited in our apartment, shaking with adrenaline, fingering the bruises on my ribs, trying not to throw up. But in actuality the two heavyset cops in uniform arrived surprisingly quickly. They might even have passed Conor on the street in front of the building.

I stood in the living room wearing an old terry-cloth bathrobe. I recounted the beating. The shorter cop wrote a few notes on a little pad, his stubby fingers moving the pen in quick jabs. I did not cry.

"We see a million cases like this," he said, shaking his head in a mixture of anger and disgust. "He'll apologize to-morrow, promise everything. Then we'll be back in a few weeks. Need a doctor?"

Despite the cuts on my face and the ache in my ribs, I shook my head no.

"Well, what ya have to do, is go—tonight, right after we leave—to city hall. Know where that is? You gotta file a restraining order. Tomorrow you gotta call our precinct, make sure a policeman issues the order. You hafta go with one of our guys to serve the order and verify his identity."

The trip to city hall, I might have been able to handle. But seeing Conor again, issuing papers to him, was a prospect too terrifying to contemplate. I shook my head again.

"He's your husband, right? You're married? Well, you gotta get a divorce lawyer. Start divorce proceedings immediately."

I stared at him. I felt the cops' invisible weariness like carbon monoxide filling the living room. They thought they'd be back in a few weeks to break up another fight, that I would be like every other woman who could not leave, women they nonetheless felt sorry for. They cared for me, a total stranger, in a way that Conor didn't—or couldn't.

As they left, the shorter cop paused at the door, as if giving me one last chance, talking to me like I was his daughter.

"Remember this when you think about how much ya 'love' him: He tried to kill you tonight. Next time, we might find you dead here."

He pointed a fat finger to the living-room floor to indicate where my body would lie. He and his partner walked out my door and took the stairs heavily. Like overweight synchronized swimmers, each pulled a walkie-talkie out of his blue uni-form pocket.

As I listened to their footsteps echo on the steps, I looked at Frankie's intricate, threadbare carpet and thought, *No one is ever going to find me dead on that floor.*

———◆———

My throat so tight I could hardly force the words out, I left two identical, stilted messages for Sylvia and my study part-ner Cherie on their answering machines.

"I am okay. But please call me as soon as you get this message. This is an emergency."

I washed the blood off my face and changed into jeans and a heavy Norwegian sweater. I went into the kitchen. "Blue, Blue," I whispered. "It's okay, buddy." Blue walked cautiously out of his crate into my arms. I hugged his warm, silky body and clipped on his leash. We went out together into the cold Chicago night before I could think about what I was doing.

I drove the Volkswagen through the empty streets to city hall, a building I passed nearly every day. I parked at a bro-ken meter in front. Blue curled up on the passenger seat to wait, his brown eyes liquid as I locked the car doors.

Inside city hall, the lone clerk on duty looked at me blankly, cracking her gum, her cornrowed hair decorated with red and green beads.

I robotically repeated my directions from the two cops. "I need to file a restraining order."

The clerk went wordlessly to a filing cabinet. My neck and rib cage and eye sockets ached as I stood at the gray metal counter waiting. She handed me the forms like a cashier at 7-Eleven passing me a Diet Coke.

I stood at a high linoleum table, like the ones in the post office, in the chilly, cavernous government building decorated with grimy plastic Christmas wreaths. One of the fluorescent ceiling lights was out. The clock on the wall said three A.M. Did it take more than three hours to change clothes, wash my face, make the phone calls, drive here? Where was Conor right now?

Forms. The slips of cheap shiny paper were oddly comforting. I was good at this, capturing information with a pen. In black ballpoint I described the kaleidoscope of times Conor held a gun to my head, the day he pulled the keys out of the ignition when I was driving sixty miles per hour down the turnpike, everything that had happened in the past few hours.

I needed to scrunch my words up to get it all down.

Whoever read these complaints would say I was the crazy one. That I imagined such bizarre stunts. It would be natural to think I'd made them up. Or worse, to believe I provoked them.

The day before, I had been taking my last accounting exam. I was supposed to be on my way to Paris with my husband. Instead I was standing in a government building in the middle of the night with cuts on my face describing the myriad times and ways my beloved beat me up during the course of our two-and-a-half-year marriage.

Blue and I climbed out of the Jetta and back up the apartment steps just before five A.M. The phone was ringing as I unlocked the door. The receiver felt like a ten-pound barbell.

"Les?"

Sylvia.

"I got your message when I got home from a party at two-thirty. I've been calling ever since. I'm going to get in my car and drive—"

It took almost an hour to tell her everything as I sat in my living room drinking a cup of lukewarm tea. "Don't come, Syl. I know you want to help. I want you to help. But this is my mess. I've got to take care of this part by myself. I'm . . . okay."

I could almost see her pale blue eyes reflecting the range of emotions I knew I'd inflicted: fear, anger, relief, sadness, confusion, concern. I thought of the time when she was four and I was eleven and I had to remove a cinnamon red hot she'd stuck up her nose. My sister.

Cherie called at seven A.M. I told her everything, too. She drove sixty miles back from vacation to take me to breakfast at the diner near our apartment. Later that day she called with valuable information—that Conor was staying with his friend Matt in the same building Cherie lived in. I needed his whereabouts so that I could direct the police serving the restraining order that afternoon.

I didn't call Mom or Dad or Hugh, Winnie or my cousins, all the people who'd want to know. Repeating what had happened would make the truth stand out like boldface on Page Six: Conor had almost killed me. Our marriage was over. Feeling like a homeowner picking her way amid broken glass after an earthquake, I needed time without an after-shock. Before I could talk to anyone, I had to absorb the damage myself.

Plus I needed to conserve my energy for the afternoon's task.

Around two P.M. I walked in the chilly December sun-shine to the police precinct. It was only six blocks from our apartment. Who knew? I gave the form from city hall to a police officer who looked as young and buff as one of those firefighters who'd whistled at me as I walked home from *Seventeen*. Using two fingers to jab at the keys on an old manual typewriter, he typed up a form labeled TEMPORARY RESTRAINING ORDER.

Then we drove in his squad car to the apartment building where Conor was staying, a building where dozens of other students lived. I prayed Conor would not be there. My palms broke out in a cold, nervous sweat that smelled metallic, of fear.

Conor answered the building's intercom on the officer's first buzz.

"Yeah, who is it?" He sounded like any other man, not someone who beat his wife last night.

"Sir, this is the Chicago police. Please come down to the lobby."

As we waited by the elevator, I noticed the officer had his right hand on top of his gun.

Less than thirty seconds later, Conor stepped out of the

elevator wearing the same jeans and gray sweatshirt he'd had on yesterday. His hair was wet from the shower.

He looked thinner than he did last night, too small for his clothes. Today was his thirty-fifth birthday. Our flight to Paris left in forty-five minutes with two seats empty.

I stood slightly behind the officer, who turned to ask if this was Conor. I nodded yes. He turned back.

"Are you Conor ——— ?"

"I am," Conor said. He sounded like an actor in a play.

The officer unrolled the restraining order and explained it.

"Your wife has filed a temporary restraining order against you. She says that last night—"

He glanced down at the typewritten order. My hands shook in my pockets.

"—at your apartment on ——— Street, at approximately 10:30 P.M., you beat her and choked her until she lost consciousness. She has detailed over a dozen similar incidents that occurred over the past three years. As a result, our precinct has prepared this temporary restraining order. You are not allowed to contact your wife via telephone or written letter or to get within sixty feet of her at any time for the next sixty days. If you do you will be arrested and imprisoned for violation of this order. Do you understand and agree with these terms?"

To my amazement, Conor nodded. He signed the restraining order without protest, without looking at me. My stomach lurched as he handed the forms back to the cop.

The officer tore off the bottom copy and handed it to Conor. Conor looked briefly in my direction and then down at the mottled brown indoor-outdoor carpeting. Less ·than three minutes after arriving, the officer and I left. Conor watched us go, standing in the middle of the mirrored lobby with his legs locked and his right hand clutching his copy of a piece of paper that said he'd tried to kill me.

The officer drove me back home. He double-parked his cruiser in front of my apartment. He handed me my copy of the restraining order.

"Call the police or have someone else call the police immediately if your husband violates these terms. And remember— you can't call him, have contact with him, either. The restraining order applies to both of you."

The officer's poker face as he went over the instructions helped keep my squirming emotions in their lockbox. Not what I would call calm, exactly, but able to limit the shaking of my arms and legs until I was inside our apartment, which felt cold and deserted and way too quiet.

The next afternoon, Christmas Eve, I left for Washington with Blue in the passenger seat. Twelve hours later I pulled up to my father's house. Sylvia's red Jeep was parked outside; Dad had taken his new girlfriend to Europe for Christmas a few days before. Sylvia opened the front door and put her arms around me without saying anything. Her hair smelled of clove cigarette smoke and her skinny body was so warm, so alive, I never wanted to let go. She leaned back to look at me and touched the biggest cut on my face with her chilly index finger, not saying a word.

I spent Christmas Day at Dad's empty town house. My chest felt empty, too, like Conor had taken my heart with him when he left our apartment. Sylvia spent Christmas with Mom just a few miles away. Joining them was impossible for me. I wanted another day before this became real. I couldn't stand Mom telling me, "I told you so." I didn't want people, not even my own mother, to feel sorry for me, or to question my decision, or to suggest, out of malice or ignorance, that this turn of events was my fault or something I could rectify if I just tried harder next time. I felt made of Jell-O, jiggling as I walked around my father's home. I didn't turn on the lights even as darkness fell. Christmas was just another day. Everyone thought I was in Paris with Conor anyway.

On December 26 I sat on a black leather bar stool in the kitchen of Dad's empty house with a list of my closest relatives and friends. Mom's number was the first I dialed.

"Mom, hi, it's Les. I know you think I'm in Paris, but I'm actually here in D.C."

I didn't give her a chance to say anything.

"Conor and I have split up—because he was, ah, physically abusing me."

I stopped talking because I couldn't breathe. I heard her suck in a sharp breath.

"I am so sorry for you, Leslie." She said it like she really meant it. But not like she was completely surprised. "And for him. Because he's lost you now."

This last part undid me. Despite her cruel criticism of me over the years, from where she sat, I was anyone and everyone's prize. My bottom lip started quivering so hard, it was like there was a little motor in there.

"Oh, Mom." I gritted my teeth. "Thanks. I am glad you understand. I really need you."

I couldn't hold the tears back any longer and they dripped down my cheeks. A few slipped into the corner of my mouth. They tasted sweet.

"I'm here," Mom said. "No matter what. Anything you need."

I could tell the words were hard for her to get out, too. Maybe tears were coming down her cheeks as well.

I managed to work my way down the list. I faxed a letter to my father at his hotel in Switzerland. I called my cousin. My three bridesmaids. My best friend from camp. Kathy from *Seventeen*. Everyone sounded stunned, except for one person.

"I am so, so sorry, Leslie," Winnie said when I reached her at Rex's family house in Westchester. "I know how much you loved him. But you're better off now. He was so troubled no one could help him. Thank God it's over. I always thought he was a goddamn ax-murderer."

Oh, fuck, I thought. Was I such a fool?

Ed was one of the few friends I didn't call. He was

Conor's buddy first; it had to stay that way. I needed the division between Conor and me to be like two freshly painted yellow lines on the highway. Our life together, our mutual friends, were off-limits now.

Hanging up the phone, dialing it again and again, repeating the same words to different people, felt like peeling layers of skin off an open wound. Telling everyone was like building a barricade brick by brick, to stop me from giving him another chance, from crossing the yellow lines. The fact that I still loved Conor, would probably always love him, was a grave threat. I crawled into my dad's guest bed that night, afraid of the future. And of myself.

"Stay, Les, just a few more days," Sylvia begged. It was brutal to have someone whose diaper I'd changed worry about me. I told her I needed to go home and prepare for the future. Whatever that meant.

Blue and I drove off the morning of December 30 in the gray, post-Christmas letdown. The highways were deserted. I accidentally left my glasses inside Dad's house and had to drive back to Chicago trying to make out the hazy green-and-white signs along the highway. I nearly missed my exit into Illinois.

I made it home around ten P.M., parked the black Volkswagen in front of our apartment and carried in my duffel bag. Blue raced up the steps in front of me. I propped open the apartment door with the bag while I checked to make sure Conor had not somehow gotten in. I noted with relief—tinged, I was ashamed to admit, with disappointment—that every room was exactly as I'd left it. He had not been there at all. How can you possibly miss him? I asked myself. But I did.

I got Blue food and water and fell into bed.

The next morning, I pulled on jeans and a sweatshirt from a pile of dirty clothes and walked to campus for some fresh air, to buy coffee and to check my mailbox. Afterward I took the cobblestone walkway toward home. I passed the bookstore, the recruiting center, the faculty dining hall, up the wide footbridge that divided the campus from our neighborhood. I cried as I realized it was not me who gave up on Conor or our marriage. I would have never given up. Conor gave up. He knew beating me that night guaranteed I would leave him for good. My worst fear, of Conor abandoning me, had come true long before December.

Tears ran down my face as I muttered to myself, looking down, not meeting anyone's gaze. At two o'clock on the afternoon of New Year's Eve, there were few people around; I couldn't have cared less about the strange looks I must have been getting.

Halfway across the arched footbridge I felt a cold, familiar presence. At first I couldn't quite see who it was because of my missing glasses. As I got closer I saw it was Conor. Of course. He was immaculately dressed in his blue cashmere coat, his throat wrapped in his maroon paisley scarf, his hands thrust into his silk-lined coat pockets. He looked like a carefree young bachelor enjoying a stroll on this sunny winter's day, the last day of the year. *He* didn't have scabs on his face.

He stopped and stared at me in my dirty jeans, equally unsure of what to say. We were trapped on the footbridge, blocking each other's way.

One of the things I'd thought about during the dark days in Washington was that I had never screamed when he'd beat me—until that last night. Even when he held his cocked gun to my temple, I did not feel scared. When he pushed me down the stairs, I didn't remember feeling hurt anywhere on my body. I didn't remember feeling angry at him.

Exactly where had shutting myself down, never getting mad, trying always to see Conor's point of view, wanting to help him, gotten me? Right here on this narrow passageway facing Conor. The only thing good about being here was that Conor couldn't fight back. I would be safe no matter what. So it seemed logical to start screaming.

"You've ruined my life!" I shrieked. My wails echoed off the street below in the chilly winter air. "I fucking hate you!"

It didn't seem essential to go into the details about my lonely Christmas, the bruises underneath my turtleneck, how empty the apartment felt without him. How empty my life would always feel without him. It was enough to scream "You've ruined my life!" and "I hate you!" over and over. I clenched my teeth and stared at his magnificent face as if my anger could obliterate him.

Conor stood still. I felt like a giant wood chipper capable of shredding him into pulp. I imagined bits of his blond hair, his paisley scarf, the cashmere coat, being spewed across the bridge. He seemed afraid to get too close to me.

From my peripheral vision I saw passersby stopping. Nice-looking, well-dressed university people with open, curious faces. As they looked at me their faces darkened with anger. I was the enemy here, screaming at this tall, fresh-faced young man in such a nice blue coat. Mentally I put them through the wood chipper, too.

Finally I walked past Conor, who stayed frozen like a cardboard cutout of himself. I kept screaming and shaking my head like a schizophrenic bag lady released too soon from a state mental hospital. People stopped and stared at me as I sobbed the six blocks home.

By the time I put the key in the door of our apartment, my screams were screamed out. I felt curiously refreshed, better than I had in months. Go figure.

I opened the apartment door and Blue jumped me. I crouched down and he hugged me with his big front paws and licked the tears off my cheeks with relish. No one, not my sister or Winnie or the world's most understanding therapist, would ever sanction the wood chipper. But for once, I'd had the last word with Conor. Surprising how good that felt.

I held onto Blue with my whole body. I closed my eyes.

Then I started to laugh a little. Dry heaves that sounded like sandpaper scraping brick. I felt a shard of hope about my life, my future, the way you do when your fingers discover

something that just might be a Hershey's Kiss at the bottom
of your purse. It never occurred to me that Conor had followed me back to the apartment, and was waiting until he
saw the living-room light turn on so he could watch my sil-
houette from the street. I noticed him an hour later when I
switched off the light. I crouched under the window in the
dark, watching him watch me. When he still didn't leave, I
dragged the dresser from the bedroom to the front hallway,
blocking the door so I could fall asleep.

———❖———

The next ten days dragged by like time spent underwater.

Days passed something like this: Eat breakfast, cry, take
a shower, cry, go rent a sad movie so I could cry some more.
I tried to absorb what had happened—*It's over with Conor,
it's over.* And I struggled with an even dicier concept: What
he had done to me was *criminal.* If our neighbor hadn't in-
tervened, he might have killed me. It didn't seem possible. I
slept from midnight to noon. My face felt like raw corned
beef, salted with dried-out tears.

I had never felt so alone in my life. But stupidly, I wasn't
scared. Despite what I knew about how dangerous it was to
leave an abusive man, I felt far more shock and sadness than
fear.

The few times I ventured out, I took Blue as my guardian,
ridiculous because if we saw Conor, Blue would be delighted,
not ferocious. But his companionship was all I had. One day

we stood together in the drama section of the video store two blocks from the apartment. I teetered between Jodie Foster's *The Accused* and Diane Keaton's *The Good Mother*.

Midway through *The Accused* a few hours later, sitting in our dark bedroom in the red chair, Blue cutting off the circulation in my legs like a sixty-pound lap puppy, I experienced an epiphany of sorts, the first posttraumatic aftershock. Watching Jodie Foster's character reliving the gang rape on a pool table in her local bar as patrons cheered, I dredged up the warning signs I'd ignored during the early days with Conor: the night he choked me during sex, his overreaction to Guy calling me, his possessiveness when other men even talked to me.

Part of me knew about Conor's dark side when we had dated only a few months. I had stifled my own fears, even after the attacks started. Conor had held a gun to my head and I had not been afraid. It was my elemental mistake that I did not listen to my own voice trying to warn me about the danger I was in.

Why didn't I listen then?

Would I listen now?

January. Happy New Year indeed.

I sat in a cushy business class seat on an American Airlines jet. I was headed for San Francisco for my first "callback" job interview. My destination was a large consumer company famous for its bleach and bug spray. The briefcase at my feet was stuffed with the company's annual reports, marketing brochures, and market share analyses I'd memorized for this visit. I was the only one of forty students interviewed who had been asked back for this second round. The bruises on my neck and tiny cuts all over my face had just healed.

An old friend from high school who was getting a Ph.D. at Berkeley met me at the airport and drove me into the city. We stopped by a funky San Francisco coffee bar, all granite tabletops and exotic, aromatic blends. I could not bring myself to tell my friend what had happened with Conor or the decisions I had to make, alone now. That I could be such a good actress seemed a dirty secret. Faker. Liar. I felt numb, an amnesiac.

The worst part was how much I missed Conor. I wanted him there in San Francisco with me. This was loneliness: The only person who would understand was the last person I could turn to. One thought broke through the clutter in my mind: I couldn't let loving Conor destroy the future, even if I had to go into it alone. He chose violence. I chose me. I walked the pastel hills of San Francisco from the coffee shop to my hotel, jerking my heavy roll-aboard suitcase behind me, vowing that I would graduate from business school and get every job offer I could. Damn him.

The company put me up in a spacious suite at the Ritz-Carlton at the top of Nob Hill. I deserved this, I tried to persuade myself, pulling back the gauzy white curtains and looking at a beautiful view of sunny, hilly San Francisco. Not being thrown onto the floor of my apartment by my own husband. Domestic violence? A husband who beat me? The truth just didn't seem possible. At the Nordstrom's a few blocks from the hotel, I bought a red coatdress that proclaimed a confidence I did not possess.

Fake it till you make it, I told myself as I put on my makeup and the new dress the morning of the interviews. Eight grueling hours later, the vice-president of marketing called me into his office. "It's unanimous," he said with a warm grin. "Everyone loves you. We never do this, but we're making you a job offer on the spot." I faced him across his large blond wood desk, the California sun shining so brightly I had to squint to make out the outline of his head and shoulders. I tried to smile. After all, he'd thrown me a life raft to the future, a guarantee that after graduation I'd have a place to go two thousand miles away from Conor. The man's lips moved but I couldn't hear what he said, like someone had pushed the mute button on the TV remote. All I could think was: nothing.

Alone in the elevator on the way out of the building, I covered my face with my hands, took a deep breath, and began to cry. Again.

One rainy, chilly Tuesday morning a few weeks later I sat across from a woman ten years older than I was. I sank into her soft corduroy couch under a watercolor of creamy white calla lilies, blue irises, and pink gladiolas, listening to the unseasonable rain and rush-hour traffic of the Chicago historic district outside. She had brown curly hair, a little makeup, a naturally pretty face. A ready smile. She asked me what I was looking for in a therapist.

"I want someone to tell me, to help me find out, what went wrong here. What I did wrong. I want brutal honesty. I want someone to really help me see why I am so screwed up that I made such bad decisions—"

"What about kindness and respect? Do you want that, too?" she interrupted, the skin around her eyes crinkling with her easy smile.

I managed a grunt in my throat. "Well, some kindness and respect would be nice, too."

From everyone, I thought. Including myself?

I explained my history with Conor. She did not ask a single question about him. She did not dig into why I chose someone like Conor or why I still wore my wedding ring. She did point out that it might be difficult to reunite with Conor, given that I couldn't picture being alone with him for thirty seconds without beginning to hyperventilate.

"Let me give you some kindness and respect right now. First, it is amazing that you survived. Most women don't. Second, you haven't turned back to alcohol or drugs as a way to cope. Incredible. You are far stronger than you think.

"I've got a couple of mantras for you as you go through this recovery," she continued, amused. "Be honest with yourself. Trust your instincts. Ask for help when you need it." She ticked off three fingers. "And you will be fine."

I repeated the mantras silently, as if they were important new rules to follow. Her office was filled with colorful, over-sized books, photos of a small boy and a girl with her same curly brown hair, and a phone that rang quietly in a corner, burbling like water in a fish tank. I imagined that other patients who needed her as much as I did were calling and leaving messages of quiet desperation.

"Last thing," she said. "This is key. Don't *think* about what's happening right now, or what you went through with Conor. Feel it. Let what you feel guide you."

———— ❖ ————

Later that afternoon, Cherie called to tell me that Conor moved into a studio apartment about eight blocks from me, on the other side of the rectangle of dirt everyone calls the Dog Park, because all the neighborhood dogs run free there most afternoons.

I tried to *feel* my reaction. Nothing.

"How's Conor doing, anyway?" Cherie asked.

"Oh, Conor's okay, I guess," I told her. The truth was I had no idea how he was doing.

"Hey, um, I thought you should know . . . people are talking about why you guys split up. People know he was physically abusing you. A few people were talking about how he follows you home and stands outside your apartment. We're scared for you, Leslie."

I didn't say anything. Don't cry, I told myself. All of a sudden, I was feeling a whole lot.

"You know, it's behind you now," she said in a determined, steady voice, as if there were nothing for me to be ashamed of. I was amazed to hear her talk about the devastation of my life so calmly. "I'm relieved that you've broken up for good. Now you have to focus on staying safe."

I didn't push the fact that I didn't feel the "for good" part yet myself.

Instead I took a big sniff.

"Don't you even think about getting back together with him," she said, as if she knew what I was thinking. "You wouldn't let *me* hit you, would you? You wouldn't take any abuse from a friend. So you know what? Apply those same standards to the men you get involved with. Pretend they are me. Don't take anything from a guy that you wouldn't tolerate from me. Call me anytime, anywhere if you even think about getting back together with him."

I didn't tell Cherie I thought about getting back together with Conor every day. I still slept in *our* bed, in *our* apartment, with *our* dog. Alone. And it didn't *feel* good.

February. Now that Conor had his own place just a few blocks from mine, I started finding presents from him on the front porch. A white mohair sweater in a fancy bag from a boutique nearby. A bar of my favorite Swiss chocolate. A bag of freshly ground coffee. Pink roses. I tried to wear the sweater but it was so itchy I had to take it off immediately. I put the chocolate and coffee in the back of the freezer, behind some frozen bananas. The flowers wilted quickly and I was relieved to throw them away without feeling guilty.

He called about twice a week. Hearing his voice on the line felt like the cold suction of a meat locker shutting behind me. But the sound of his scratchy voice also thrilled me—as it always had. Our conversations were brief. No, I didn't need anything. No, I could not have dinner. (Was he crazy?) It was all I could do to refuse him.

He almost killed you, Leslie, I said to myself as I sat clutching the phone till my hand ached. This struck me as a pretty good reason not to see him. A second later it would seem irrational, paranoid—how could I think my own husband might try to kill me? But he had.

I did not ask for his new number because I was afraid I'd call him when I woke up crying in the middle of the night.

One morning he stopped me as I was leaving marketing strategy. He got so close I could smell his breath, feel the warmth of his body under his winter coat. In panic I looked around quickly to see if there was a pay phone nearby that someone could use to call the police. A few students bundled in down jackets walked past us, slowing down in disbelief that we were talking to each other.

"Leslie, wait a second, please. Don't leave. I'm trying so hard to be honest with myself." I could tell from his cottonmouth and slightly swollen eyes that he was taking medication. His blond hair looked stringy and dirty, plastered to his forehead. The expression in his eyes—and his words—seemed sincere. So I listened.

"I have to admit all the wrongs I have done to you . . ."

I had never heard Conor speak about his problems with anger or allude to abusing me. This was as close to an apology as he'd ever gotten. I had to hear this.

"I'm going to a self-help group of men who have abused women. It's hard work."

Was that a teardrop in the corner of his eye? A glimmer of hope—for him, and maybe even for us together—shimmied through me.

"Will you come to family therapy with me? My group really recommends it. I told them I would ask you. Please, Leslie, I need to be with you."

Still in shock, I told him I wanted some time to think it over.

The next day, I left a message in his mail folder saying I'd try the therapy. Was I stupid? Hope was always good, right? Maybe therapy would help him. Maybe it would help me. Maybe I was still crazy enough about Conor to try anything.

— ❖ —

On a Friday afternoon two weeks later, Conor and I arrived separately, but within seconds of each other, at the double doors of a nondescript building near campus for a three P.M.

appointment he'd set up. Conor went first into the therapists' comfortable, whitewashed basement office. He sat
down on a large oatmeal-colored couch, leaving room for me
next to him. I took a deep breath and walked past him and
sat on a cushy white chair with high arms.

There were two therapists, a husband-and-wife team prac-
ticing together. Conor looked like a little kid sitting across
from them. The female therapist, Christine, introduced herself and her husband. "We've found the two-on-two therapeutic model very effective at quickly getting to the root of issues
between couples," she explained. "It helps clarify the central
problems—and whether they can be solved—so that the couple can agree to stay together or end the relationship."

Conor leaned forward with his hands clasped on his knees.
"I love her—I love you, I need you." He turned to look at
me. "You are the girl of my dreams. Please, Leslie." He looked
down at the therapists' woven rug. "I will do absolutely anything if you give me another chance."

We all looked at each other. Small sweat streams flowed
along the fortune-teller lines of my palms and under my gold
wedding band, which I still couldn't bring myself to take off.
Before any of us could say anything, Conor spoke again.

"Therapy is helping me see that I am particularly vulnerable to stress and anger at night because of my childhood,
because Wade used to beat me at night when he got home
from his job," he explained matter-of-factly, leaning back on
the couch, his palms open. "If things are going to work out,
Leslie needs to be more careful in the evenings not to bring

up my 'hot button' subjects. I've made a list—money, academic performance, family stuff. I can't talk about those things. I've got a copy for you right here."

He reached into his shirt pocket and handed me a folded piece of paper.

I took it but didn't respond. I looked at both therapists. How could everything still be all about him? Did he have an inkling of how I had suffered—and was still suffering—because of what he'd done to me? I didn't say anything. Trust me, it was therapeutic enough to sit there.

I was exhausted when the ninety-minute session came to a close. We set a date for the next appointment. All I could think about was getting out of the basement and locking myself in my car before Conor left. I drove home. Miraculously, there was a parking space right in front of our apartment. On my way from the car to the building, I balled up Conor's list of "hot buttons" and jammed it into the trash can by the curb.

Three days after the first therapy session, Conor and I met again. This time the venue was family court, Monday morning at nine A.M. The sixty-day restraining order was expiring soon; a judge who'd never met either of us would decide whether Conor was still a threat to me. The courthouse was a 1960s urban renewal brick building in a run-down downtown neighborhood where garbage overflowed from trash cans at the corners and lined the gutters along the sidewalks.

I parked the Jetta at a broken meter and walked two blocks to the courthouse. It was a bitter, windy day. The trash flew across the sidewalk and up against cars and buildings. A crumpled Dunkin' Donuts napkin stuck to my panty hose, underneath the raccoon fur coat Conor had given me during our first Christmas together.

The waiting room was lined with sad-eyed Hispanic women trying to watch too many children at once, clumps of working-class black men talking and laughing with their hands thrust in their pockets or crossed over their chests, and young cheaply dressed social worker types.

Before I could decide what to do, a thin woman approached me.

"Are you Leslie?" she asked, peering into a worn manila file. She wore no makeup, and had stick-straight, dirty-blond hair like Marcia Brady.

"Yes," I told her. How did she know my name? What else did she have in that file? I balled my coat under my arm to hide the fur trim.

"It says here that you don't have a lawyer," Ms. No-Makeup-Dirty-Blond-Hair Social Worker explained. She had a kind voice and clear, greenish brown eyes. I bet she knew how afraid I was. She was right about my not having legal counsel.

Last week I'd called my father to ask if he could recommend a divorce lawyer in Chicago. I'd seen his Harvard Law

School alumni directory, four inches thick, with graduates listed by city and area of legal expertise.

"Ah, you know, Les . . . I, um, I don't know anyone in *that* line of work," Dad stuttered back, sounding as if I had asked him to recommend a good dominatrix.

Stung by his antipathy, I stuttered, "Okay, thanks anyway, bye, Dad," and hung up the phone quickly. Standing in the living room, I burst into tears, crying so loudly I thought the downstairs neighbors would hear.

Was my own dad that ashamed of me? He sure was proud when I did something right. How could getting divorced, admitting that neither I nor my marriage were anything close to perfect, be *worse* than staying with a man who abused me?

Suddenly, still standing in my apartment, still holding the phone, crying my ass off, I choked on a new thought as if I'd swallowed a piece of gum by accident. Maybe my father *had* known about all my previous problems, Mom's alcoholic tirades, my drug and alcohol use, the anorexia, the terrible boyfriends, even Conor's abuse. Could it be Dad didn't have the stomach, or the heart, to hold me up when I wasn't quite so perfect?

I wanted my dad there, physically there in my apartment, to help me. For a second, through the tears, maybe because of them, I could see clearly: My dad had never been there. Even when I'd badly, obviously needed him. It was terrifying to admit, even as a twenty-six-year-old, that the responsible adult, the only one I could rely on as a child, had actually been the one who was drunk every night. But at least she'd been home. Dad had always been at the office, taking a client to dinner, traveling on my birthday, forgetting about our wedding breakfast, proofreading documents late into the night the time I broke my wrist in sixth grade or the evening Mom first called me the Washington Whore.

Dad had always seemed like the parent I could trust. For twenty-six years I'd misjudged both my parents. My father's love rested on my being perfect far more than my mother's; if I screwed up, he was as reliable as a ghost. Mom had far more obvious faults, but she had always been there for us kids.

Outside the Family court chambers a week later, I nodded to the social worker. She explained that she was a law school student. "An advocate" is what she called herself. She said I didn't need my own lawyer for today's proceeding. Thank God for that.

"You don't have to talk to your husband—Conor? The most you'll have to do is tell the judge what happened to make you file the original restraining order, and why you want it made final. Trust me, it's a brief, routine proceeding. When your husband gets here, I'll talk to him so I can explain both sides to the judge if necessary. I am here to moderate—I'm paid by the Women's Legal Defense Fund—and to make sure the judge hears your side in addition to your husband's."

Although in good legal fashion she was trying to be objective and factual, I sensed that she was trying to protect women like me who might be intimidated by a judge or by speaking against their husband in a court of law. Women like me—whose husbands had tried to kill them.

Conor showed up just a few minutes before our appointment. The advocate went to him and jotted down a few things in her file. Conor did not smile, toss back his hair, or lean in toward her once. Either he was just as sickened by being here as I was, or she was tough enough that she wasn't wooed by his charisma and looks. She came back, her shoes clacking efficiently on the tile floor, and announced, "We're set."

She strode into the court, Conor and I in tow. The judge called our names. Conor and I stood next to each other like penitent children. The young lawyer explained matter-of-factly that I wanted the restraining order made final and that "her husband" had no objection. The judge asked me and Conor in turn if this was correct.

"Yes," I said.

"Yes, sir," said Conor.

The judge waved us away. Dismissed. I picked up my paperwork at a small bulletproof glass window. The Xeroxed form with our names blocked in said that Conor could not come within ten yards of me and must refrain from calling, writing, or talking to me. It was renewable in six months if I proved to the court that Conor was still a threat. It was a thin piece of paper, similar to cheap notices and junk mail letters I threw away every day. I folded it carefully and slipped it into the small wallet I took everywhere. To me it was precious.

I looked around the courthouse waiting room. The young

lawyer was holding another file and talking earnestly to a black woman with a red-and-yellow Caribbean-style head-kerchief who looked about twenty and was holding the hands of a small boy and girl.

I looked around again. Conor was gone.

—◦—

Dogs look at paper clips and candy wrappers and rocks and think: *Sure, I can eat this.* Blue was no exception. He'd always been skinny and prone to vomiting in the car. But lately he'd been throwing up every morning like a pregnant woman with morning sickness.

One Monday, he did not eat the Reese's peanut butter cup I bought him at 7-Eleven, a regular pit stop on our morning walk, his daily treat to go along with my coffee. This dog would eat chocolate in his sleep. What was wrong?

We walked home slowly and I settled him on the red chair, covering him with a blue-green mohair throw. I went to my two morning classes, wondering about him the whole time. When I came home to check on him, he had not moved. I hugged him, shook him, and called his name. Blue didn't even open his eyes. Then I noticed a small pool of di-arrhea dripping onto the floor.

I rolled him into the mohair blanket and somehow car-ried him to the VW, which was fortunately (1) parked right outside and (2) not about to run out of gas. Like an EMT

entering an emergency room, I burst into the vet's waiting
room carrying Blue on my makeshift stretcher.

The vet, a hulking, bearded forty-year-old man wearing
a white coat, appeared quickly.

"He's a three-year-old male Doberman pinscher. He has
not eaten for three days," I told him. The vet wrote it down
on a chart. "He's been throwing up. I found him lying in his
own diarrhea. I can't get him to wake up."

The vet told me to bring Blue into a private room. I placed
him, still wrapped in the blanket, on a chrome examining
table. The vet pinched Blue's silky black coat. "Extreme dehy-
dration," he said. He rolled back Blue's eyelids. "Jaundice," he
continued. He turned to look at me.

"What have you done to this dog?" he said accusatorily. "I
have never seen a three-year-old animal in such terrible con-
dition. How long has he been like this?"

"Just since Friday," I whined, almost unable to speak.
"He ate less and less each day. Then he started throwing up.
I took him for his walk this morning and he wouldn't even
eat his treat from 7-Eleven. Then by noon he wouldn't wake
up. I didn't do anything. I have no idea what's wrong."

The vet's face softened as I talked. "Okay, okay," he said,
patting my shoulder with one hand as he ran his other hand
gently along Blue's flank. "I'll do everything I can to help
him. He is in a coma—he's not in pain. But I need to be
honest with you that he's pretty far gone."

I lay my body over Blue and stroked his beautiful head,
his soft ears, his velvety lips and throat. How could this be

happening? I sent out a short, simple message to the God of Sick Pets, a combination of an order and a prayer: *No.*

———◦—◦—◦◦◦—◦—— —

The phone rang when I'd been home just long enough to make peppermint tea. The vet.

"He held on for about twenty minutes after you left," he said. "I'm sorry. I think he was just sticking it out because you were with him. Once he realized you were gone, he let go. I still don't have any idea what was wrong. With your permission I'd like to conduct an autopsy, at my own expense, just to understand what happened. He was a perfectly healthy dog."

I heard my voice telling him yes, thank you, of course, I have to know why as well. I felt like asking: Did he die of a broken heart, will that show up? As I was about to hang up, the vet interrupted, apologized, he had one more question.

"Afterwards, do you want to pick up his body, or do you want us to take care of it? We could arrange for a private cremation or we could have him cremated with several other dogs."

The words themselves would have been hideous, if not for the kindness in the man's voice. I thought of Blue's happiest moments at obedience school in Vermont and the Dog Park around the corner, places where he was surrounded by dozens of other dogs of all breeds.

"Please cremate him with the other dogs," I said. "He would like that best."

I hung up. While drinking my tea, I realized I had to tell Conor. It came to me unexpectedly—like loud music suddenly blasting from your neighbor's stereo—that I had not thought of him, had not needed him, during this ordeal.

I called information to get his new number. He answered on the first ring.

"Conor, I have something really sad to tell you," I said.

"Yeah, what?" Conor said warily.

"Blue died today. He had been sick for a few days and I took him to the vet this afternoon. He died after I left. The vet has no idea what happened but is going to try to find out."

"What the fuck? What are you talking about? He's dead? Why didn't you take him to the vet earlier? Why didn't you call me a few days ago when he first got sick?"

"Blue didn't seem that sick. I had no idea it was serious. I am so sorry. The vet says that at least Blue didn't suffer. I am really, really sorry, Conor. I know how much you loved him."

Then I was quiet. As much as we loved Blue together, I refused to let grief glue us back into one person, even for a few hours. Another tie to Conor was gone. A strange, beautiful, awful gift from Blue.

"Okay, Retard." Conor's voice held a mix of exasperation, grief, and anger. He hung up.

— —◦❖◦— —

March. Spring had gotten a toehold on the city. Birds chirped outside the basement windows, rectangles filled with pastel tips of crocus buds. Conor twisted his hands as he sat across from me on the therapists' oatmeal couch during our second appointment. I had no words to describe how I felt about being with Conor again.

I perched on the edge of my chair, drying my sweaty palms on my old jeans, which I wore along with ratty sneakers and Sylvia's faded high-school volleyball sweatshirt. Conor looked like he belonged on an Armani billboard instead of a couch in a therapist's office. Pressed jeans, crisp white oxford shirt, polished brown Italian loafers. His hair looked like he just had it trimmed in some expensive hair salon. He'd lost about ten pounds since Christmas, I guessed. He looked like his old self again. In the waiting room before the appointment he'd told me that he'd gone back to working out two hours a day at the gym. *The peacock is starting to preen again,* a voice inside me said.

The four of us mumbled a few inane pleasantries until the male therapist cleared his throat.

"So, you've both had time to think about your relationship since our last meeting. How do you feel? Are you committed to staying together?"

His businesslike candor startled me. He looked at us with his eyebrows arched in a question mark, first at Conor on the couch, then at me several feet away in my chair with the high sides. Conor answered first, without looking at me.

"We want to stay together," he said with a pair of confident nods of his chin. "We've had some hard times, but we belong together. I've never loved anyone so much. I need her—I need you, Leslie."

Yuck.

I had not talked to Conor about our marriage since the last session. How could he speak for me? His face reddened and his eyes watered as he leaned forward to look at me.

Before I even knew what I was going to say, I opened my mouth.

"Well, actually, I don't feel that way."

Both therapists froze. Their eyes turned to me. I couldn't look at Conor but I imagined he was staring at me, too. I was having trouble getting air into my diaphragm. My lips were dry. To my surprise, however, I was too angry to cry.

"I want to get divorced," I said to the two therapists sitting on their couch. I couldn't look at Conor.

The therapists stared at me with identical, surprisingly placid expressions on their faces.

Weren't they going to ask me to explain why I wanted a divorce? To justify my decision with ten reasons? Did they expect me to cry about how Conor destroyed me? To say any woman would be crazy to get back together with a bastard like him? To explain how sorry I felt for him?

I thought they'd at least insist I needed to meet Conor's gaze when I said I wanted a divorce, something I would not be able to do.

Instead, both therapists looked at each other and nodded in unison.

"Okay, Leslie," the male therapist said. Christine smiled

at me and patted my knee. "You can go. We'll stay here with
Conor for now."

As if in a dream, I gathered my pink windbreaker, purse,
and car keys. Five minutes after I'd walked in, I passed Conor
on the couch. I looked down at the gray wall-to-wall carpeting
as I placed one foot in front of the other and walked toward
the door, the shiny nickel doorknob beckoning to me. As I
went by, all I could see were Conor's hands, one closed into a
fist, pounding his other hand like a baseball in a mitt.

— — ❖ — —

I drove home with all four windows rolled down to fill the
car with wind noise and strong gusts of cold spring air. Once
inside my apartment, I locked and bolted the front door.
Checked it twice. Unplugged my phone.

Then I sat in the chair reading a case study for interna-
tional marketing Cherie had highlighted for me. A bit of he-
lium floated in my blood, making me feel light and airy, as
well as slightly trepidatious about what I was going to feel
like when the giddiness wore off. I got to bed early, around
nine P.M. I slept well.

In the morning in the campus coffee shop, I ran into a
friend of Conor's as I stood in line to buy a croissant.

"Is he okay?" the friend asked, clutching a folded *Wall
Street Journal* under his arm. He was dressed in a suit and
tie for a job interview. I got a whiff of his aftershave.

"What do you mean?" I said.

"You don't know?" he asked, looking at me strangely. "Matt found Conor at the train station in the middle of the night. He'd been there for something like six hours, just walking around in a daze like a homeless person. Matt took him to emergency health services. He's gotta stay for an evaluation. That's the last I heard."

"I don't know anything about it," I whispered, stunned. "I'm sorry to hear that."

He's not your husband, I told myself, turning so that Conor's friend wouldn't see me cry. *You can't help him anymore.*

The morning of December 21 Conor and I had sex for the last time. Of course I did not know at the time that it would be the last time. I guess you don't usually know that. It was memorably boring sex. We had a houseguest staying with us, a friend of a friend who was applying to business school. While she was in the shower he insisted we make love. I did it to avoid a fight. I climbed on top of him, did my thing, and it was over long before our houseguest was finished in the bathroom.

April. I spent two hours each week with my therapist. At the end of every session I expected her to proclaim, sadly, that years of therapy were needed to fix me up so I never married a psychopath again.

Instead, we talked about my future, my life going forward. We laughed a fair amount, which always took me by surprise.

As I left one appointment, she gave me homework: I needed to make a list of the top ten things I wanted from a relationship, the next time. "The next time" was a concept that caught me completely off guard. I couldn't fathom going on a date with another man.

So instead of reading cases and studying for tests, I spent long evenings at home working on the list. Sitting at my white desk in my quiet apartment, imagining Blue curled at my feet, I typed on my computer keyboard. I picked out a fancy italic script, as if I were designing a wedding invitation. I revised the list obsessively in my head as I walked the streets around campus.

The day before our next session I printed my top ten list on the creamy white paper I used for résumés:

1. Must be kind, good, uncomplicated, a nice person.
2. Must be successful at life in general (work, relationships, sports, or whatever is meaningful to him).
3. Must be crazy about me.
4. Must have a good relationship with his mother.
5. Would make a good father (acid test: if I were an unborn baby choosing a father, I would choose this person to be my father).

6. Must value independence in himself and in me.
7. Must like animals.
8. Must enjoy watching and playing sports.
9. Must have great friends.
10. Must enjoy books and writing.

Except for being crazy about me, Conor had never fit any of these criteria.

———◆———

Late one weeknight, my phone rang. I was half-asleep in bed. The clock read eleven P.M. I picked up the phone.

"May I speak to . . . Leslie?" a polite, official-sounding male voice asked.

"Yes," I answered, puzzled.

"This is Sprint phone service calling," he explained. "I was calling to confirm that we have permission to release your phone records to Mr. Conor ——— ."

"Excuse me?" I asked, fully charged now.

"Yes, ma'am. We received a request for all of your local and long-distance phone calls from the past six months. Honestly I thought it was an unusual request, so I am calling to confirm. I apologize for disturbing you at this hour, but I had the feeling this might be important."

"Thank you. Thank you for calling. No, you may not release my phone records to anyone," I said, trying to quell the shaking in my voice. What was Conor doing? Why would he want our phone records? Did he think I had been having an affair?

The man paused.

"I'm going through a divorce from a man who physically abused me," I explained, choking out *divorce* and *physically abused*. This Sprint employee, a stranger, was trying to help me, across the phone lines, from wherever he was working, hundreds or thousands of miles away from my dark bedroom. "I think he is trying to dig up information he can use against me."

"Yes, ma'am, I understand. I had the feeling there was something . . . aggressive . . . about his request. I just talked to him a few minutes ago."

"Can you put a note in my account? So he can't try this again? He might call back and see if he can get the records another way."

"I'll do that right away. And don't you worry, ma'am. We won't give out any of your information."

I hung up the phone, still puzzled. Afraid. I didn't sleep again that night, wondering about Conor's next move, his brilliant mind, all the places and people he could call to hurt me in whatever way he could. The next day I had the apartment's locks changed, even though Conor no longer had a key. When I got in my car, I started automatically locking the doors before I started the engine. I stopped leaving my apartment after dark if possible, and when I did I turned on every single light in the place to illuminate a safe return. I mapped every pay phone between my apartment and school. The restraining order was always in my wallet. My new job, the only one that mattered, was keeping myself safe from Conor.

A few days later, I called a lawyer. I had waited, I supposed, because hiring a divorce lawyer was an unambiguous admission that one wants to get divorced. Also I was still hoping that the phone would ring one day and it would be my father.

"You know," Dad would say. "I was thinking you must feel quite alone right now. You probably feel lost and scared. And angry at Conor that he beat you for the past three years, spent all your money, and convinced you to take out all his business school debt in your name. Since I am your father and one of the best judges in the country, I will be your divorce lawyer! We're going to humiliate that bastard for what he did to you!"

Yeah, right. Time to go to the dance alone.

How was I supposed to find a divorce lawyer? I knew no one in this city outside b-school. Who could I ask for a recommendation? One of my marketing professors? My landlord? The Somali guy who I bought coffee from every morning at 7-Eleven?

There was only one person I could think of who knew divorce lawyers in Chicago. My therapist. She recommended someone other clients had used. I called his office and over the phone reduced our marriage to a glib three-minute syn-opsis: I fell in love with this guy, he beat me for three years, he's acting kinda crazy these days, I think it's probably best to never see him again. I cried for thirty minutes after hang-ing up the phone.

Two days later I went in person to the lawyer's office downtown. Before I left my apartment, for the first time I took off my wedding ring and put it in Frankie's old jewelry box. The streets of Chicago were exploding into spring, cherry blossoms, green grass, and dandelions everywhere, people walking around on their lunch hours with silly smiles plastered across their faces. The lawyer's office was in the Loop right next to a dentist I went to once, in one of Chicago's newer buildings on Wacker Drive, thirty stories of gleaming granite overlooking the obtusely green Chicago River.

Greg Bandy, Esquire, came out to the small reception room to greet me with his hand stuck out for a shake. I looked at him in disbelief. He stood six inches below me, Thumbelina's lawyer, fortyish, well on his way to being 100 percent bald, wearing a miniaturized, precisely tailored wool suit and highly shined wing tips. Not a man you'd bet on against Conor, with his muscles, black belt, and Mr. Massa-chusetts title.

Once we were seated across from each other in his office, he asked a few routine questions about where we were mar-ried, when, what kind of ceremony, where our families lived, our parents' occupations, our religions, financial history, and current sources of income. He jotted down the answers in quick, left-handed jerks.

"We'll be able to dissolve your relationship," he told me matter-of-factly, like marriage was an Alka-Seltzer tablet, "in such a way that I'm confident your husband will never have legal cause to bother you again. It will cost you roughly ten thousand dollars plus expenses like notary signings, copying forms, courier services." Even though ten grand about equaled my tuition this semester, Greg Bandy made it sound like I was getting a bargain on a used car.

Where was his outrage? How could he not be appalled, horrified at what I went through? Maybe he just didn't understand.

I took the restraining order out of my purse, unfolded it, and handed it to him like it was an original copy of the Declaration of Independence. He glanced down and handed it back. I launched into a detailed, impassioned description of the last four months, trying to make my outrage contagious with lots of hand gestures. "What I want," I told Greg, shaking my finger at him, "is to *fight* Conor."

I wanted an Oklahoma-sized lawyer who jumped onto his desk and shouted out to the world that we would get Conor back! This groundbreaking domestic violence case would save the lives of thousands of other women! We would take it to a judge, the Supreme Court, organize a March on Washington!

But here I was, stuck with little Greg Bandy, whom I realized had started talking again.

"We're going to convince him that he has won, once and for all," Greg said, as if he hadn't heard me. "That he has truly beaten you, forever. Give him the money he wants. Give in on everything you can afford to give in on."

I leaned back in the wingback chair, agog.

Greg folded his hands in his lap and looked at me humorlessly as if I were a naïve ten-year-old who'd gotten in greater trouble than she realized. He looked pained, as if much against his will, he had become the guardian for a hapless child whom he was obligated to extricate from this mess.

"This is what's going to happen if you go to court. First, it is going to take years. *Years,*" he said emphatically but without raising his voice. He was probably incapable of raising his voice. "The Illinois divorce court currently has a waiting period for unmediatable cases of two to three years. These are cases involving children, complicated assets, thirty-year marriages. These are considered urgent cases that have precedence over simple, no-fault cases like yours."

No fault? I wanted to scream, clutching the restraining order. I bit my tongue, literally.

Greg continued. "You want to move on with your life, don't you? Five years is a very long time to have this man bothering you. It's not a complicated divorce. The best thing is to get it over with.

"Second, get this guy before a judge and this is what might happen—the judge might believe Conor. Young, disadvantaged youth, apparently he must have some powers to charm . . . versus you." He gestured to me with his hands up. I filled in the blank in my head: versus spoiled rich Harvard girl whose father was a big-shot judge in our corrupt nation's capital and whose mother was a gorgeous Wasp alcoholic. "The judge might believe Conor, not you."

I wanted to strangle Greg Bandy right then. I didn't because then how would I find another lawyer? The yellow pages?

Greg Bandy stood up and put out his hand for me to shake again. This time I squeezed it as hard as I could, wanting to break his little bones. Then I headed to the lobby.

Getting divorced on paper was the least of my battles right now anyway, I told myself as I took the elevator down to the street. I could only devote so much time and emotion to the legal side of this self-inflicted disaster. I tried to absorb some measure of confidence from the arrogant, angular skyscrapers rising above me as I left the Loop.

Once home, I called my therapist to tell her about Greg's approach.

"Leslie, I know this is hard to hear. It might take you years to accept, but Greg probably has the right strategy. Conor was abusive and manipulative throughout your marriage. You should expect him to continue to be abusive and manipulative during your divorce. Greg's approach—avoiding hand-to-hand combat—actually sounds pretty rational to me. Pretty wise."

Shit.

Greg and Conor's lawyer met alone a week later. Conor had recovered nicely from his shock that I wanted to get divorced. He'd hired a female lawyer, of course. Someone who had a chance of falling for him, someone he knew how to deal with. Someone whose implicit betrayal of me as another woman would demoralize me even further. It did.

Following their meeting, Greg called me to pass on several new pieces of information. I sat down on our living-room couch like someone preparing herself for dreadful news. I turned off the music on the stereo.

"You might want to know that Conor has listed a new official residence."

My God, I thought. Why? Where would he go with less than two months of school left? Was he going to drop out so close to graduation?

"He's kept his apartment, but he's changed his official mailing address to 12 Main Street in Ocean Grove, New Jersey."

Aunt Nellie's summer house? Impossible. That seaside beach home with its wraparound porches and widow's walk was my refuge during my summer apart from Conor. The rooms were filled with pictures I drew for Nellie as a child, sappily signed "your ever-loving niece," books I wrote for my cousins, pictures of our childhood holidays together. Why on earth would someone who had loved me since I was born let a man who beat me list her house as his residence?

I couldn't speak.

"I also wanted to let you know that apparently Conor visited your father in Washington three weeks ago. Your father gave Conor a thousand dollars to help him get back on his feet. Did you know this?"

"No." My stomach dropped a few floors. I had spoken with my father—the same man who couldn't trouble himself to help me find a divorce lawyer—every few days for the past month and he'd never said anything about seeing Conor or giving him money.

"Conor used that money to hire his attorney."

Sitting on the couch, I shook my head back and forth wordlessly. Getting divorced was turning out to be far harder than getting married. Couples should be read a Miranda-like warning right before they say, "I do":

Any love that you feel at this point may be used against you in the future. Studies have shown that in divorce, the craziest person always wins, regardless of who was harmed most by the relationship. Do you understand that although it takes only five minutes to get married, to get divorced can take years, cost you your life savings, destroy your friendships and family relationships, and forever undermine your emotional health and faith in humanity? Do you realize that you are blind with love and hope right now, and can't possibly know what you're doing?

Greg Bandy interrupted my thoughts.

"There's more?" I asked incredulously.

"Conor's attorney believes that you should be paying him temporary alimony in order to support Conor in the manner he became accustomed to living with you. We can delay this for a few weeks with a counter-request, but it may be wise for you to pay it for a few months just to assuage him—"

"What? I don't even have any money!"

"Well, your father does."

I stopped. "I'm not paying him alimony. What else, Greg?" I wanted this conversation to be over.

"One last request. Conor would like his guns back. He believes you still have them. Is this true?"

"I'll have to get back to you," I told Greg woodenly as I hung up the phone. The pain in my abdomen felt like someone was scraping a rake along the inside of my stomach. My father. My mother's family. A female lawyer. My financial future. He wanted his *guns* back?

And these were just Conor's first moves.

───◆───

As I went through the motions of daily life, reeling from the emotional sucker punches from people I loved, I was struck by the kindness of people I barely knew. The vet. My therapist. All the people at school who did not ask questions.

Would the cops who came that night ever know how grateful I was? Did the family court advocate realize how much I appreciated her respect? Every time I came into my building I thought: Who pounded on the door that night? The Indian couple downstairs? The law school student upstairs? Did that person know they may have saved my life?

My high-school English teacher left a voice-mail message almost every day. The locksmith bumped his wait list and changed my locks the morning I called. Not a single classmate mentioned my sordid situation to a company recruiter. Every time I thought of Blue, I knew I'd had the best dog in the world. Wherever he was now, Blue knew it wasn't my fault, that I was going to be okay when this was all over, Conor or no Conor, perfidious father or not, alimony or no alimony.

I thought of what I'd done with Conor's guns back in February. I couldn't bear to have them in our apartment. Giving them back to Conor had been out of the question. I thought about putting them in a paper bag and dropping them in Lake Michigan. Instead I turned them in at the police station, which of course I now knew was only a few blocks from our apartment. The cop saw my hands shaking as I gave him the shoe box with the guns inside. "I need to give you this. They're not mine." He gave me a short form to fill out. He smiled and nodded. "You're doing the right thing," he told me.

When I'd called the Ice Man, the diamond jeweler in New York, he'd been remarkably kind as well. I mailed him a small padded envelope containing my wedding and engagement rings. He sent me a check I used to pay Greg Bandy's retainer.

A marketing professor I barely knew, a short, plump woman whose red hair was always pulled back in a bun, came up to me in a deserted campus corridor one afternoon. "I've heard some rumors about your situation," she said obliquely, almost whispering. "I was in the same thing a few years ago. You'll get out. You are going to be fine. You won't believe how much better you're going to feel a year from now. Hang in there." She touched my arm and left me speechless as she hurried down the hallway to teach her class.

One night the phone rang while I was trying—and mostly failing—to read a financial accounting case.

"Leslie, hi."

It was Ed.

We talked awkwardly for a few minutes. I hadn't spoken with him in four months. He'd always been best as the funny man, hard to pull off under the current circumstances.

"I called, uh, really to tell you one thing, Leslie," he said, his gravity fitting like a bulky homemade sweater. "I know you probably feel awful now. And I need to be there for Conor. But I want you to know that you are a great girl, any guy would be lucky to be with you. In a year, this will be like a nightmare that happened to someone else. In five years, you're going to be married to a wonderful man, two kids, totally happy. I guarantee it."

These kindnesses did not deaden the pain of Conor's

betrayal, my aunt's puzzling hospitality-cum-disloyalty, and my father's emotional abandonment. But they did give me hope for the future. And, as Mr. Carrola said, hope is always good.

———◦◦◦———

In the midst of the death of my dog, trips to my therapist, and calls from my lawyer relaying Conor's latest kicks to my ribs, good news came into my life daily, links to the future. Job offers. Lots of them. Phone calls, follow-up letters confirming salary, title, and responsibilities, good news on the answering machine and in my mailbox, every single day.

By late April I had five full-time offers. Multiple jobs were rare during the second year of a national economic recession; the school had forecast that only 60 percent of students would get any offers by graduation.

Three different times I overheard classmates talking about my good fortune when I passed in the hallway outside the career development center. I felt grateful they were not gossiping about me and Conor. My friends would probably never understand that luck had nothing to do with my success; anger was the magic ingredient. Each phone call and letter from a recruiter was a vote against what Conor had done to me. A promise that, if I could hold out long enough, I was going to have a future, a safe future, without Conor.

It didn't matter which job offer I took. Each company was hundreds of miles away from Conor, far enough that he couldn't stalk me or impulsively track me down. Back in Vermont, when I'd accepted Ed and Conor's challenge to go to business school, I'd never for one second imagined an M.B.A. degree would be my underground railroad away from Conor. I could hardly believe it now.

If I could have, I would have sewn the thick corporate offer letters to my shirt like armor for the days I passed Conor in the halls, the time I heard he had started dating an old girlfriend who had recently moved to Chicago, the night I spotted him pacing the block in front of my building, looking up at the living-room windows as I drove past him, looking for a safe place to park our car.

The vet called about a month after Blue had died, in the late afternoon as I sat in the living room sipping yet another mug of peppermint tea. On the mantel was a picture of Conor holding Blue back when he was an eight-week-old puppy. Blue's fat belly faced the sky as Conor cradled him in his arms in our backyard in Vermont. Conor smiled down at Blue like a newborn baby.

"The blood work we did last month came back from the lab yesterday. I finished the autopsy paperwork two hours ago. Your dog died of liver cancer. I have never seen such a young, strong, and . . . beautiful animal die of liver cancer, so suddenly. I don't know what to tell you."

He paused.

"By any chance did he eat a lot of grass?"

"Grass?" I ask. "No, not really, we live in an apartment. I've never seen him eat grass. There's no grass around here. Even the Dog Park—you know the one, near the university? It's all dirt there."

"Okay, that rules out fertilizer poisoning. What about chocolate?"

"Yes, every day. He loved Reese's peanut butter cups. I gave him a miniature one every morning."

Long pause.

"I'm sorry to tell you this. But chocolate is a poison for dogs. I assume you didn't know that."

What?

"He . . . he was my first dog. I had no idea. He *loved* chocolate."

"Well, the only reason I can think that such a healthy dog would have developed liver cancer so quickly, and have died so suddenly, is that he might have been poisoned. I was thinking lawn chemicals or rat poison. But even a little bit of chocolate every day might have built up in his system and caused his liver to fail."

My face froze and the tears on my cheeks evaporated.

I thanked the vet in a daze and hung up the phone. I remembered one night in Vermont when Conor threatened to take Blue outside and fire the .45 into his brown head. Instead, I had killed him through a daily treat that I thought showed Blue how much he meant to me.

I got up from the living-room couch, took a sip of cold tea, and went to splash water on my face in the bathroom. I looked in the mirror. My eyes stared back blankly like blood-shot marbles.

———◆———

Out of thin air, my father's older brother Jimmy called to say he was coming to Chicago for an electricians' convention. I hadn't seen him in five years. My dad had never invited his family to any of our graduations or special family occasions, or to my and Conor's wedding. He said it was too far for them to travel, they didn't have the money for plane tickets. So I'd seen Uncle Jimmy sporadically when business brought him to wherever I lived.

Jimmy left a message on my machine, his voice soft in his lingering Okie accent, asking whether he could take me to dinner the last night he was in town. I met him at a small Italian restaurant near the convention center, the kind with red-and-white-checked cloths and marinated peppers in a jar on the table. Jimmy sat waiting for me at the bar, a shorter, stockier, blue-collar version of my dad with his tailored wool suits and cigarillos in his elegant fingers.

We talked about his business, an electrical service company he'd started at seventeen. He was thinking of selling it and retiring. I blushed when he asked my advice. I didn't need the Ferragamo suit any longer. My M.B.A. gave me permanent, instant credibility, even to someone who'd been working fourteen-hour days since before I'd been born.

We both ordered spaghetti and Caesar salad, laughing about how unimaginative our choices were. Over coffee, the candlelight flickering from the small white tea lights on the table, his face softened as he glanced at me.

"Ah, hon, you look just like her," he said, reaching out to cup the side of my face with his worn, callused hand. "She's buried just a few miles from here. I went to her grave today."

I realized he was talking about Marilyn, his sister who had died at fifteen. No one in my family had ever told me I resembled her. My father had never mentioned it, or shown me a picture of her.

"What was she like?" I asked.

"She was the sweetest thing," he said, looking up at the ceiling. "Like an angel." He took a deep, shuddering breath. Fat tears began rolling down his weathered cheeks. He did not wipe them away.

"You know, your father's probably told you, but we had very little money growing up. Sometimes we had no food. And Marilyn, she was so skinny. I know she was as hungry as the rest of us. But she gave us her food, almost every day. Especially your dad. He was a scrawny thing. Still is." He tried to laugh, patting his own gut.

The tears were still coming. He acted like he barely noticed them, as if he cried every day over Marilyn, even though she'd been dead for forty-seven years.

"Our mother used to beat her, I never knew why. Because Marilyn was the least trouble of all of us. Mother had a hard life. She had to take it out on someone. Sometimes I think Marilyn knew that, and she made sure Mother beat her so she wouldn't go after us. But it was terrible to see Marilyn with bruises all over her legs and arms, especially when she was so good to the rest of us."

I sat in paralyzed silence. I'd never imagined violence so similar to Conor's in my own family. How crippling for my father. Despite leaving poverty behind, he had to see me trapped, by love, like Marilyn had been.

"Your father never got over it, Les. You have to understand. It was terrible not being able to help her, not being able to stop Mother, never having enough food, not having a real home. His way was to escape, into his studies at school, to Harvard God bless him, into his law firm. He can't help it if he got so far away from people he forgot how to reach out, even to his own children. He loves you, hon. He just doesn't know how to show it. Since she died, he never did. Especially when people need help the most, like Marilyn did."

Something in me cracked open and spilled out onto the

red-and-white tablecloth as Jimmy talked, his blue shirt collar wet with tears like navy-blue polka dots. A piece of me lay with my teenaged aunt, beaten, hungry, dying alone at fifteen in a public hospital bed. Another piece was lodged in my dad as a smart, sensitive ten-year-old boy, helpless to help anyone but himself, soldering off his heart to survive the pain of growing up the way he did.

Damn it, Jimmy was right. I couldn't muster any more anger against Dad—a boy with a sister who'd died so he'd make it out of a world she couldn't survive. My dad suffered an incalculable penalty for his escape, same as Conor. To leave behind a childhood as traumatic as theirs, most pay with a piece of their soul.

Right then I knew I was done with Conor for good. No matter how sorry I felt for him. No matter how much I still cared. You might have thought, naturally, that I had been "done" when I mailed my rings back to New York or hired a divorce lawyer. But this felt different, subcutaneous, deep in my gut. Almost in a karmic way, I was finished forever, in this lifetime and any to come, with loving bad boys.

I never wanted to be in a relationship with another man who'd shut down part of his heart, even though I understood that neither my father nor Conor had done so voluntarily. I couldn't bear to love another man who couldn't love me back. I wanted someone kind, with a generous heart, one that could regrow itself. Like my uncle, crying unashamed in public about a fifteen-year-old girl who'd been dead for almost five decades.

I had no idea how I'd go about finding such a man. I'd take my sweet time figuring that part out.

———— ❖ ————

May. Two weeks before graduation, late on a Thursday, I drove home blasting R.E.M. with the windows open to take in the fresh spring air. I'd spent the evening with my finance study group. All we did was copy spreadsheet files from one another's computers while everyone but me drank monstrous margaritas. I turned up the radio.

"Losing my religion . . ."

The car felt empty without Blue on the passenger seat.

The street was deserted, no cars on either side of the road.

Except for one. A nice new white Honda, the interior lit, the door open. I slowed down.

A well-dressed black woman about twenty-five years old was walking away from the car, brushing off a tall, handsome young black man wearing a sports coat and jeans. Wet tracks ran down her face. The man walked closely behind her, alternately cajoling her and a second later raising his fists. I could hear the car beeping *ping . . . ping . . . ping* because she'd left the keys in the ignition.

Suddenly she turned and tried to run. He grabbed her with his long arms and shoved her up against a dirty storefront. Even from my car I could see the fear on her pretty face.

Without thinking, I jerked my car over and parked in front of the white sedan.

"Hey, what's going on?" I yelled as I climbed out, jangling my keys like some kind of badge.

By this time the man had let the woman go and she'd slid behind the wheel of the car. He stepped back as I approached, his anger displaced by uncertainty and shame at being interrupted. I didn't look at him. I leaned into the car as she sat clutching the wheel, crying and staring straight ahead. The car smelled like new leather.

"I just left a husband who beat me for three years," I said. "You do not have to put up with this. You do not deserve to be treated like this."

"I know," she whispered as fresh tears poured down her face. She sniffed loudly and shook her head. She wouldn't look at me. Her eyes were rimmed with red, but I could see resolve in them.

"You're right," she said. "It's just taking me longer than I thought."

She bent her head on the wheel. I put my hand on her arm. She squeezed my fingers hard enough to hurt.

"You're going to be okay. I promise." I handed her a clean tissue from my pocket. "No one can treat you like this if you don't let them."

She nodded again, gave a loud sniff, wiped the tears away. "Thank you," she whispered.

As I left, I gave the man a long stare. The spell had been broken and his face was open, sorrowful, filled with hope and fear—a look I saw dozens of times on Conor's face. How long would that look last before he got angry again? I could feel the woman's determination as I got back into my car. I knew she would be all right, one day. The man I was less certain about.

———◈———

Graduation dawned sunny, breezy, a surprisingly cool day for May. Mom flew in from Washington for the ceremony. Although she didn't put it this way, she wasn't flying seven hundred miles merely to celebrate my graduate degree. She was coming to be there, to make certain I closed out my life with Conor, to make sure I did what we both knew I had to do. Despite our problems, she had always been there— physically there—for me.

If that's not love, then I don't know what love is.

I hadn't sent an invitation to my father. He had never asked when graduation was, or whether I wanted him there. He did not offer financial or legal help with my divorce proceedings. Not a word of kindness, respect, or sympathy regarding the dissolution of my marriage and my attempts to start a new life. I tried not to hold this against my dad. Jimmy had been right.

As I stood on stage accepting my diploma, I saw Mom in the audience. With her silver hair juxtaposed with a jade-green silk shift, she created a brush stroke of colors against all the other parents. When I came up to her holding my rolled-up diploma, she embraced me with one of her stiff little mini-hugs and a whiff of lipstick and perfume.

After we left the auditorium, she asked strangers to take pictures of us at various spots on campus. The way she wore her pride reminded me of the day I got my SAT scores back, the time I came home to announce I'd been elected junior class president, the evening I showed her the acceptance letter from Harvard as she stirred a pot of lamb stew in our kitchen. If I became the first female president of the United States, she'd take the same nonchalant pose as the queen of England: Of course, you're my daughter.

The present she handed me while we sat on a bench next to the campus library told me the backstory. Inside the small velvet box lay a gold ring inlaid with tiny green and red stones that formed the shape of a butterfly. I got it right away: caterpillar, cocoon, butterfly. The only way she knew how to tell me I was going to be okay, transformed by ugliness into something more beautiful in her eyes.

How could she see so much sometimes, and so little at others?

I put the ring on my left hand where I used to wear my wedding band. The butterfly felt heavy, an anchor. The stones sparkled in the sunlight. I held out my hand so she could see how it looked.

"Mom, thank you. Thank you for everything."

For giving me the money to finish my last semester of school. For answering fifty late-night calls. For hating Conor when what I felt was far more complicated than hate.

I tried to look right in her eyes so she could know how much she meant to me. She met my gaze for a second and then turned away with a small smile, like a shy eight-year-old girl.

It was just enough.

She took a taxi to her hotel to wash up and change clothes for dinner. I headed home in my black patent leather high heels, still wearing the dark gown and silly headboard with its cheap tassel, my costume for the day. The sunlight dappled the cobblestone campus walk as I slowly picked my way toward our—my—apartment. Squirrels ran fearlessly across my path. I imagined Blue in doggie heaven, chasing squirrels, eating Reese's peanut butter cups without dying from it, looking down on me from a cloud like he used to look down from the window of our apartment when I came home at night, his huge paws hanging out the windowsill like oven mitts. The leaves on the trees lining the campus walkway shimmered a fresh apple-green, as if they'd just burst out of their buds. I could smell cut grass, the first mowing of the summer.

It was the prettiest day I could remember since coming to business school.

I stopped by the student center for one last check of my campus mail folder. The only thing inside the bin was a tattered manila envelope, the official kind the university used for sending, and resending, interoffice mail. It was empty. I turned it over.

On the back, a note was scribbled in black ballpoint,

along with a stick figure of a little boy like a kindergartner would draw for his mom. Above the note Conor had written my maiden name, instead of the name I'd taken when we'd married.

Good-bye Retard—
I wish you all the best.
Sorry we didn't make it together.
I'll always think of you.

Conor

I cried there in the darkened b-school hallway, alone. Those five lines made for the shortest, saddest good-bye ever. How could he think a few banal phrases could capture the end of our relationship? His note made my love for him and all we'd been through sound trite, easily dismissed on a scrap of paper. My tears splashed on the orange manila envelope.

We'd come here together, embittered but still a makeshift family, less than two years before. How could it be that I planned to depart alone, Blue dead, Conor a cipher I feared passing on the street? After a few weeks of visiting friends and bumming at Rehobeth Beach with Sylvia, I would move out of the apartment we'd lived in as a married couple. I'd start a new job, a new life, hundreds of miles from Conor, with an unlisted phone number and a post office box instead of a published address, on the same day I turned twenty-seven. As alone as I'd ever been.

I kept walking on the campus pathway until I got to the dean's crowded cocktail party, silly-drunk classmates spilling out of the flagstone courtyard. I could see the footbridge where five months before I'd screamed at Conor until I thought my screams would tear me apart. Surrounded by Cherie and dozens of other friends, I sipped a club soda and scanned the crowd of my fellow M.B.A.s, all of us poised to scatter in different directions to seek whatever the future held.

Across the sea of graduates, I glimpsed the back of Conor's blond head above a knot of people talking together. My heart seized.

He didn't see me. He was wearing the same navy-blue Brooks Brothers sport coat he wore on that magical spring day only four years before, when we picnicked at the museum and later made love for the first time. I clenched my jaw and looked down at the butterfly ring on my wedding finger. Tried to breathe.

I had to look at him one more time. It would probably be the last time I saw my husband, my supposed soul mate, the man who almost killed me.

He held a drink in his hand. There was a blond woman standing at his side, a woman I did not recognize from our class. As I watched, he rested his hand possessively on her slim waist and she leaned in toward him. Conor moved his head closer and his lips brushed her smooth golden hair in a caress that paralyzed the muscles in my face.

It was impossible to break my gaze. I could tell by the

way his head moved that Conor was laughing. I could practically hear his strong, confident laugh ring out across the courtyard, just as it had that night at P.J. Clarke's in New York when I'd started to fall in love with him.

Finally, I looked away. I took off my glasses, so that he'd get lost in the blur of classmates in the crowd.

Good-bye, Conor.

I never saw him again.

Epilogue

CONOR STANDS TOO CLOSE TO ME IN A SQUARE, shadowy room. His face glows like a candle in the dark. Thick wheat-colored hair, freckles across his nose. People always said we seemed more like brother and sister than husband and wife. His eyes search mine.

Conor doesn't care that I have three young children whom I love in exactly the way I used to adore him: without demanding anything but love in return. I can feel Conor's certainty that what he wants trumps the devastation his actions will wreak upon my marriage, my kids, my life. I don't resist when he starts kissing me.

I wake with a start, sickened, lying next to my husband in our warm bed.

It takes a minute to realize I am safe, behind locked doors in an old house in one of the most crowded cities in the United States. Sheltered by our blue down quilt, my head deep in a pillow that covers a menagerie of Beanie Babies, earplugs, and cough drops. My husband's breath comes in rhythmic whooshes like waves on a beach. I've been safe for years.

Trying to shake off the nightmare, I slip from the warm bed and tiptoe into my daughters' room, the polished wood floor cold beneath my bare feet. Next door in the darkness our boy sleeps on the bottom bunk, sprawled sidewise, clutching the basketball he holds all night in lieu of a stuffed animal. One of the girls stirs in her narrow bed. Even when she was an infant, a profusion of strawberry blond ringlets surrounded her tiny, heart-shaped face. Her red hair was a surprising and welcome resurgence of my charismatic, auburn-headed grandmother Frankie, dead from alcoholism almost twenty-five years now.

I slide into the rocker between the twin beds and softly glide back and forth, listening to my daughters breathing, my husband snoring. To distract myself, I review message points for a television interview I have to give the next day about stay-at-home moms who return to full-time work after years raising children. The neighbor's automatic sprinkler comes to life, whirring like a dentist's drill in the yard out back.

Two floors below me, in our dusty boiler room, there is a small cardboard box that's been duct-taped shut for more than fifteen years. The box holds fragments of my life with Conor, once-precious objects I can't consign to one hundred years of biodegradation amid the East Coast's cigarette butts, old lawnmowers, and dirty diapers. Our wedding album, bound with creamy, sweet-smelling leather. An envelope with several black-and-white pictures of five-year-old

Conor and his grandparents that I found after I no longer had an address to send them to. Still in Frankie's silver frame but with only a few shards of glass left is the wedding photo he broke over my head the last time he beat me. On top of the stack lies my folded wedding veil, the lace probably yellow and brittle by now. I kept Conor's résumé from our first date. Another piece of paper is there, too—the permanent family court restraining order against him dated four years later.

For a long time after I left Conor, I struggled with how I fit our society's stereotype of an abused woman. Exactly why and how had I lost myself to a man who I was intelligent enough to see was destroying me? I kept silent during cocktail party debates about why women—Mary Winkler, Nicole Simpson, Farrah Fawcett, Laci Peterson, or whoever was in the news that week—stayed in violent relationships. I walked away after the inevitable pronouncement that women who let themselves be abused are weak, uneducated, self-destructive, powerless.

I fit none of those stereotypes. I never met a "battered woman" who did.

I paid for loving Conor. For years I lived with an unlisted phone number and took my mail at a post office box. I sold the Vermont house at a 40 percent loss. It took me almost a decade to settle both our business school debts.

I imagine I will always flinch when a man, any man, raises his voice, whether it's in a boardroom or my backyard.

I've had to tell everyone I dated about Conor. I've had to

tell every employer, too, so their security desk would know to turn Conor away if he ever came looking for me. And although I don't have to, nearly every time I speak publicly I briefly mention that I was once married to an abusive man—because I never know who is listening, who my words might help.

I don't imagine I will unpack that cardboard box very often. But I can't deny that our story is part of me, my life, who I am. It's taken me years to understand the particular, dangerous chink in my self-esteem that let Conor slip in. But in one profound way I was lucky: While still in my twenties, I learned to spot—and stay away from—abusive men.

Some women don't learn from their mistakes. Most people don't get second chances in life. I was able to marry again, to raise children with a stable, loving man, and to pursue a career that has given me financial freedom and professional rewards beyond my childhood dreams.

Conor is gone. He may appear in my dreams every few years, but he'll never have power over me again. I don't regret loving him. But I'm happy to bury our past in a corner of my basement, next to the furnace, where it belongs.

Acknowledgments

This book was difficult to write. Sharing this story is either one of the stupidest or bravest things I've ever done. But I wrote it for women, like me, who are in violent relationships and don't know how to leave, and for their families and friends, who also suffer. And for those who have left but are too scared or ashamed to tell their stories. You are not alone.

I owe thanks to many people who believed in me when I did not believe in myself: Scott Adam, Helen Allen, Kristin Auclair, Skippy Redmon Banker, Linda Baquet, Mary Anne Baumgold, Larry Benders, Cheryl Yancey Biron, Martin and Sennait Blackman, Missy Everson Blum, Brooke Boardman, Mel Bornstein, David and Katherine Bradley, Beth Brophy, Jennifer Brown, Vivian Brown, the Caiola family, Ellie Callison, Julie Chavez, Susan Cheever, Gay Cioffi, Sarah Crichton, Patricia and Burt Davidson, John and April Delaney, Hermine Dreyfuss, Michele Dreyfuss, Dawn Drzal, Sarah Patton Duncan, Charlie Esposito, Brooke Evans, Page Evans, Donna Farnandez, Will Fuller, Heath Kern Gibson, Sarah Gordon, Don Graham, Michael Gray, Anne Hunter Greene, Rolf Grimsted, Brett Groom, Julie Gunderson, Dan and

Betsy Habib, Bobby and Mary Haft, Cathi Hanauer, Bunkie and Anne Harmon, George Harmon, Grant Harmon, Miriam Harmon, Janet Heezen, Jack Henry, Steve Hills, Monica Holloway, Jamie Hull, Kurt Inderbitzen, Martha Inman, Bo Jones, Willie Joyner, Therese Kauchak, Leonard King, Janet Kinzler, Julia and Barry Knight, Benn and Linda Konner, Anil Kothari, the Kressy family, Lew Kunkel, Carol Kurilla, Elisabeth LaMotte, George Lardner, Ethan and Karen Leder, Micki Leder, Gene and Mary Legg, Leslie Lehr, Nancy Lewin, Jody Levinson, Caroline Little, Sara London, Ann McDaniel, Leslie McGuirk, Adam Mansky, Ruth Marcus, Aaron Martin, Carolina Martinez, Susan Mathes, Chris Mathna, Sabrina Maxine, Terri Minsky, Stephanie Modder, Julia Harmon Morgan, Perri Jae Morgan, Tim Morgan, Robbie Myers, John Nicholas, Bill Nielsen, Jeremy Norton, Kelly O'Brien, Susan and Tim O'Leary, Dale and Melissa Overmyer, Tallie Parrish and family, Paula Penn-Nabrit, Jodi Delhi Peterson, Nancy Kline Piore, Carmen Pitarch, Neil Polo, Brian and Gwen Potiker, Elin Rachel, Ivan Ramirez, Marissa Rauch, Katherine Russell Rich, Bradford Hamilton Richardson, Midge Turk Richardson, Catherine Rose, Ann Sarnoff, Ania Sender, Susan and Roger Smith, Sarah and David Steinberg, Erna Steiner, Joseph and Marilyn Steiner, Marjo Talbott, the Taney family, Jake and Carrington Tarr, Jeri Curry Thorne, Jim Thornton, Sarah Tomkins, Ken and Karen Troccoli, Ampy Vasquez, Jackie B. Walker, Kate Wallis, Elsa Walsh, Pat Walsh, Judith Warner, Anne Terman Wedner, Katherine Weymouth, Laurie Wingate, Sarah Woolworth and the Culture Club crew, Natalie Zett, my friends at Longacre Farm, the Westside Club, *The Washington post,* Johnson & Johnson, Leo Burnett, D.C. Heat, Little Folks, Harvard University, the Radcliffe Institute, Down Dog Yoga, and the Maret School. I am lucky and proud to know you all.

Special thanks to my agent, Alice Fried Martell, and the team at St. Martin's Press led by Jennifer Weis, for believing in this book from the beginning. Thanks also to Bruce Vinokour at CAA, and his talented partner, Stephanie Vinokour, for having faith in my story.

Most of all, I owe thanks to my husband, Perry Winter Steiner, and my children, Max, Morgan, and Tallie, who have made my dreams of a happy family come true at last.

IF YOU OR SOMEONE YOU KNOW MAY BE SUFFER-
ing from family violence, help is available. If you are in immediate danger, call 911. Relationship violence is a crime.
You deserve immediate protection from the police in your
community if you are being abused.

For advice and support, call or visit the following free,
anonymous helplines:

- National Domestic Violence Hotline: 1-800-799-SAFE
  (7233), TTY 1-800-787-3224, www.ndvh.org
- National Sexual Assault Hotline: 1-800-656-HOPE
  (4673), www.rainn.org
- Family Violence Prevention Fund: 1-888-RX-ABUSE,
  www.endabuse.org
- National Teen Dating Abuse Helpline: 1-866-331-
  9474, TTY 1-866-331-8453, www.loveisrespect.org
- Childhelp National Child Abuse Hotline: 1-800-4-A-
  CHILD, www.childhelp.org
- Gay, Lesbian, Bisexual, Transgender National Help Center: 1-888-843-4564, www.glbtnationalhelpcenter.org
- National Center for Victims of Crime/Stalking Re-
  source Center: 1-800-394-2255, TTY 1-800-211-7996,
  www.ncvc.org
- National Center on Elder Abuse: 1-800-677-1116,
  www.ncea.aoa.gov
- Resource Center on Domestic Violence, Child Protection and Custody: 1-800-527-3223, www.ncjfcj.org
- National Network to End Domestic Violence: www
  .nnedv.org

५।७९